Henretta, James A.
"Salutary neglect"; colonial administration under the Duke of Newcastle

DATE DUE

"Salutary Neglect"

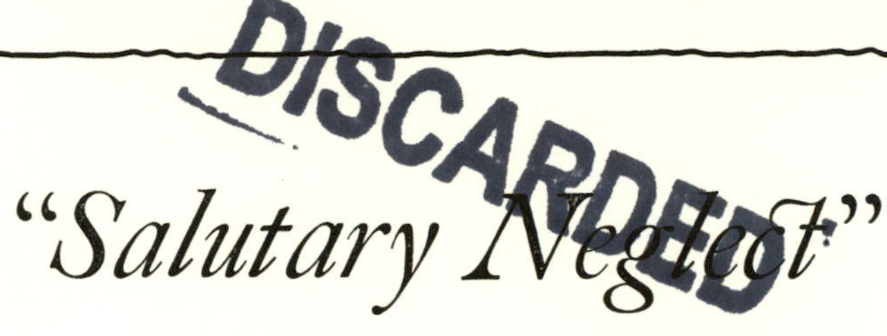

"Salutary Neglect"

COLONIAL ADMINISTRATION UNDER THE DUKE OF NEWCASTLE

by

James A. Henretta

PRINCETON UNIVERSITY PRESS

PRINCETON, NEW JERSEY

1972

Library of Congress Catalog card number: 70-166377

ISBN 0-691-05196-8

This book has been composed in Linotype Caslon Old Face

Printed in the United States of America

by Princeton University Press, Princeton, New Jersey

To

ANNA THOMAS HENRETTA

and

GERTRUDE THOMAS

Preface

THIS book began as an investigation of the role played by the Duke of Newcastle in the disposition of colonial patronage during his long tenure as Secretary of State. It soon became apparent, however, that a strictly "biographical" approach would be incapable of portraying the complexity of the patronage system and, more broadly, the character of the administrative process within the English government. The framework of the study was therefore extended to encompass other individuals and agencies with a role in the determination of colonial policy and patronage. Merchants, bankers, and West Indian planters find a place in this story; so also do the leading ministers of the Walpole and Pelham eras, the various members of the Board of Trade, and the several individuals who sat on the Privy Council committee for plantation affairs. In the end, this study has become less an individual biography than a group portrait, less a discussion of "Anglo-American" patronage and politics than an analysis, from a colonial perspective, of the developing political and administrative system of the mother country during the first half of the eighteenth century.

This has not been an easy or a straightforward task. American problems did not often bulk large in the minds of English ministers and Members of Parliament. Supplicant colonials frequently complained of the "little knowledge of (or indeed Inclination to know) American affairs, among most of those concerned in the Administration."[1]

[1] William Franklin to Elizabeth Graeme, December 9, 1757, in Leonard W. Labaree, ed., *The Papers of Benjamin Franklin*, New Haven, 1959-, VII, 290.

This ignorance and lack of interest notwithstanding, those patronage decisions which were made, those lines of policy which were chalked out, were directly related to the distribution of power and prestige in London and to the beliefs and prejudices of the leading ministers and bureaucrats. "There are historians who dismiss eighteenth-century patronage as little more than private charity," J. H. Plumb has observed, but "this is absurd, and arises from considering the pecuniary rewards of place only. Place was power; patronage was power; and power is what men in politics are after."[2]

Both casual requests for an American position and concerted colonial efforts to alter a traditional policy thus take on a new importance when viewed against the backdrop of domestic political controversy. The initial reception, handling, and eventual disposition of these initiatives makes it possible to trace shifts in power and interest among government ministers from year to year and from decade to decade; to outline, with precise if sometimes faint strokes, the structure of the decision-making process within the administration; and, finally, to suggest the crucial factors underlying the formation of colonial policy during the period of "salutary neglect."

What follows, then, is not a comprehensive account of the Anglo-American relationship, nor even a complete examination of all aspects of English colonial administration, but rather an analytical framework which elucidates the often tenuous connection between domestic politics and imperial programs and patronage during the first half of the eighteenth century. The colonial side of this story must be told in another place. Events which took place in the new world are introduced into the narrative only in so

[2] *The Growth of Political Stability in England, 1675-1725*, London, 1967, 189.

far as they impinged upon or reflected developments in London. Similarly, American officials enter into the story only as they influenced or were affected by events in the mother country. The emphasis throughout is on the conduct of colonial administration by those in England and on the ways in which certain American problems, such as the commercial and territorial conflicts with Spain and with France, altered the course of English political history.

One final word is in order. The following account emphasizes the *changes* which occurred in the structure and content of colonial administration during this period. This organization should not obscure the fact that none of these alterations was of fundamental importance; nothing in this period compares to the great watershed of 1688-89 when a relatively strong and coherent colonial policy collapsed in the aftermath of the glorious revolution, or that of 1756-63 when a new and vigorous imperial program was adumbrated amidst the exigencies of war. This fact is of great interest in itself. Possible explanations of the era of "salutary neglect" appear in nearly every chapter, and these are brought together in a tentative synthesis at the end. At this point it is necessary only to recognize that this period was one of relative stability; that bodies such as the Board of Trade, while not the static institutions or Hegelian entities of the traditional accounts, changed more by degree than by kind; and that the major problem is not to explain the alterations which did occur but rather to determine why more far-reaching changes did not take place.

In transcribing from manuscript and printed sources, original spellings have been retained; punctuation has been altered only when absolutely necessary for clarity. All superscript letters have been brought down to the line. All dates are in the Old Style, until the adoption of the

Gregorian calendar in 1752. In all cases, however, January 1 has been taken as the beginning of the new year. Thus, March 15, 1723/4 O.S. is written as March 15, 1724.

The research for this study was supported by a dissertation fellowship from the Woodrow Wilson Foundation. The expense of preparing the final manuscript for publication was defrayed in part by a grant from the Committee on Research in the Humanities and Social Sciences of Princeton University. Investigation of manuscript materials was greatly facilitated by the staffs of the University Library, Cambridge, and the British Museum. Permission to quote from the Walpole and Newcastle papers was kindly given by the Marquess of Cholmondoley and by the Trustees of the British Museum.

At an early stage in my graduate career Bernard Bailyn converted me to the study of colonial history by the force of his example and the perceptiveness of his thought. Subsequently he suggested the topic of this book and supervised its development as a doctoral dissertation. The revised manuscript was read with great care by W. Frank Craven, who made a number of valuable suggestions. My thanks go also to Lewis Wurgaft and R. H. Johnson for the encouragement and intellectual stimulation they have offered over the years.

Contents

Contents

"Salutary Neglect"

List of Abbreviations

Add. MSS	Additional Manuscripts, British Museum
AHR	*American Historical Review*
C.O.	Colonial Office Papers, Public Record Office
CHS	Connecticut Historical Society
D.A.B.	*Dictionary of American Biography*
D.N.B.	*Dictionary of National Biography*
EHR	*English Historical Review*
H.M.C.	Historical Manuscripts Commission
JBS	*Journal of British Studies*
JMH	*Journal of Modern History*
MHS	Massachusetts Historical Society
NJHS	New Jersey Historical Society
NYHS	New York Historical Society
PMHB	*Pennsylvania Magazine of History and Biography*
P.C.	Privy Council Papers, Public Record Office
P.R.O.	Public Record Office
S.P.	State Papers, Domestic Series, Public Record Office
VHS	Virginia Historical Society
W.C.	Walpole Correspondence, Cambridge University Library
W.P.	Walpole Papers, Cambridge University Library
WMQ	*William and Mary Quarterly*

CHAPTER 1

The Structure and Politics of Colonial Administration 1721-1730

IN APRIL, 1724, Thomas Pelham-Holles, the Duke of Newcastle, became Secretary of State for the southern department of the English government. The appointment of a thirty-year-old man of dubious abilities to such a position of power and prestige elicited considerable surprise and adverse comment at the time. What followed was even more unusual. For most men the secretaryship was the reward of a lifetime of political endeavor; for Newcastle it was only a long apprenticeship for even higher offices of state. The Duke administered the southern office for twenty-four years. In a ministerial reshuffle of 1748, he moved to the more prestigious northern department. Then, on the death of his younger brother, Henry Pelham, in 1754, Newcastle became the First Lord of the Treasury and the leading minister in the government. From this time until his death in 1767 the Duke was one of the most important men in English public life.

Newcastle's long tenure as Secretary of State placed the management of American affairs in his hands for nearly a quarter of a century. This was an exceptional period of service. In the years between 1696 and 1724 there had been thirteen southern secretaries; in the twenty years following the Duke's departure in 1748 there were to be nine more.[1]

[1] The southern secretary managed colonial affairs and conducted diplomatic negotiations with the states of southern Europe; his

A generation of colonial Englishmen was to grow to maturity while this remarkably durable politician served as chief colonial administrator. That the connection between the plantations and the mother country was less firm at the end of his career than at the beginning demands explanation: twenty-four years was more than enough time to achieve both political dominance over the colonial bureaucracy at home and administrative control over the officials and settlers in America.

In many respects the domestic and imperial situation was conducive to such an initiative. The extension of bureaucratic supervision over all areas of national life was the postulate upon which the mercantile system was founded. And, in an administrative organization based on personal patronage, Newcastle's control of the power of appointment gave him the ability, over a long period of time, to determine the composition of the expanding imperial bureaucracy.[2] Constructive effort during this era of peace and of relative political stability might drastically have altered the history of the years that followed.

That few significant changes were forthcoming during this quarter of a century was the result of a number of factors. There was a positive antipathy to political and administrative reform in England during the first half of

---

colleague in the northern department dealt with the countries of northern Europe. The latter post was the more important after 1714 because it included Hanover. Although the two secretaries of state shared the responsibility for domestic affairs, the southern secretary had more patronage at his disposal through his connection with the church and with the colonies. See Mark A. Thomson, *English Secretaries of State, 1688-1832*, London, 1932.

[2] Herman Finer, "State Activity before Adam Smith," *Public Administration*, x (April, 1932), 168-69; Daniel A. Baugh, *British Naval Administration in the Age of Walpole*, Princeton, 1965, 123.

the eighteenth century. Moreover, the power of a single official to effect even a marginal change in the system of colonial administration which had evolved since the restoration of the Stuarts in 1660 was severely circumscribed by bureaucratic inertia and traditional policies. Finally, the character and abilities of the new Secretary of State did not inspire much confidence. Two years after the Duke's appointment, the imperial ambassador to the Court of St. James's reported to the Habsburg Emperor that "it is known to everybody that Newcastle is nothing but a figure of Secretary of State, being obliged to conform himself in everything to Lord Townshend, who is *proprié autor et anima negotiorum.*"[3]

I

Newcastle's subordinate position within the ministry headed by Lord Townshend and his brother-in-law, Robert Walpole, was the result of both his tender age and his political background. The eldest son of Sir Thomas Pelham, Sussex landholder, Member of Parliament, and sometime junior Lord of the Treasury, Pelham-Holles was the first member of his family to aspire to national political power. This was not surprising, for the Duke's title, as well as the bulk of his fortune, came from his maternal ancestors. From his mother's brother, John, Duke of Newcastle, and Lord Privy Seal from 1705 until 1711, Pelham-Holles inherited estates in ten counties with a yearly rent role of nearly £15,000, a strong political interest in Nottinghamshire, and complete control of two pocket boroughs in Yorkshire. When combined with the legacy from his own father, this princely inheritance provided the young aristocrat with

[3] Quoted in Basil Williams, *Carteret and Newcastle: A Contrast in Contemporaries*, Cambridge, Eng., 1943, 61.

an annual income of £20,000 and some influence over the election of ten members of Parliament.[4]

The timing of these considerable bequests was as important as their size. Born in July, 1693, Pelham-Holles was still a very young man when his uncle died in 1711, and his father passed away a year later. Denied the personal guidance of the men whose ambitions he shared and whose political and financial resources placed him in a position to realize them, the young heir was slow to develop their balanced judgment and political acumen. "I am going out of your dependence," the essayist Richard Steele wrote to Pelham-Holles in 1713,

> and will tell you with the freedom of an indifferent man that it is impossible for anyone who thinks, or has any public spirit, not to tremble at seeing his country in the present circumstances in the hands of so daring a genius as yours.[5]

The impulsiveness and immaturity which Steele perceived in his patron were in fact the distinguishing characteristics of Pelham-Holles' behavior during the first years of his political life. In August, 1714, the young aristocrat obtained his majority and assumed his seat in the House of Lords as the Earl of Clare. Once in Parliament, he entered into a close relationship with the Whig politicians who were maneuvering to secure the peaceful accession of

[4] Newcastle's political power at this stage in his career is exaggerated by Stebelton H. Nulle, *Thomas Pelham-Holles, Duke of Newcastle: His Early Political Career, 1693-1724*, Philadelphia, 1931, chaps. 1-3. A detailed analysis of the Duke's income is presented herein, below, chap. 4, note 38.

[5] Quoted in Nulle, *Pelham-Holles*, 18. Both Steele and Newcastle were members of the Kit-Kat Club, the influential Whig political organization, and the Duke had brought Steele into Parliament for his Yorkshire constituency of Boroughbridge.

George I. Clare contributed substantially to this endeavor, spending thousands of pounds in the Hanoverian cause. This vast expenditure won considerable prominence at Court for the fledgling politician; by August, 1715, the new King had named him Duke of Newcastle-on-Tyne. However impressive this success, it was purchased at a very high price. In the following year Newcastle encountered the first of a long series of financial crises which were to punctuate his career at regular intervals and to influence profoundly his personal life and his political activities.

The initial collapse of Newcastle's credit was resolved by marriage and by a long-cherished position in the ministry. Indeed, the two were intimately related. The Duke's marriage to Harriet Godolphin in 1717 brought with it a dowry of £20,000, an appointment as Lord Chamberlain at a salary of £1,200 per annum, and a seat on the Privy Council. This substantial political advancement was the work of his wife's grandfather, the aging Duke of Marlborough, who intervened on Newcastle's behalf with Lord Sunderland, his son-in-law and the Lord Privy Seal.[6] At one stroke Newcastle had secured temporary financial security, a position of considerable status, and what turned out to be a long and happy marriage. There was only one drawback to these fortunate developments. When his younger brother Henry Pelham followed Lord Townshend and Robert Walpole into opposition following a schism among the Whigs in 1717, Newcastle found himself bound by the strong ties of marriage and money to the weak ministry headed by Sunderland and Stanhope.

Consigned by his financial extravagance and his inner craving for the trappings of office to service in a declining administration, Newcastle sought to make the best of his new position. As Lord Chamberlain from 1717 to 1724,

[6] Nulle, *Pelham-Holles*, 84-89, 95-96, 99.

the Duke mobilized support for the ministry through the careful distribution of patronage. The appointment of two of his relatives, Thomas Pelham and Thomas Fane, the sixth Earl of Westmoreland, to the Board of Trade during these years represented some return on his massive financial investment in the Hanoverian cause.[7] But most of the nominations made by the young aristocrat were not rewards to personal supporters but direct bribes to win votes for the government interest in Parliament. At this early stage in his career Newcastle did not have an independent political interest. His power in borough elections derived primarily from his national position and from the ministerial patronage at his command. Only in later years would this relationship be reversed and then only to a limited extent.

The circumscribed character of Newcastle's political influence was well appreciated by Stanhope and Sunderland. A "List of Members" who were dedicated supporters of the administration in the House of Commons clearly indicated the Duke's subordinate role. Only 4 of a total of 126 "placemen" or "men of business" owed their election to the budding politician.[8] Some of the other members whose elections were managed by the Lord Chamberlain

[7] I. K. Steele, *Politics of Colonial Policy: The Board of Trade in Colonial Administration, 1696-1720*, Oxford, 1968, 150-52.

[8] Stowe MSS 247, foll. 193-200. Stanhope was credited with the partial or complete control of the elections of 9 of these 126 administration supporters, Cadogan with 11, Sunderland with 13, and the Craggs family with 25. Newcastle to Craggs, August 6, 1720, Stowe MSS 247, foll. 164-67 gives an exaggerated view of the Duke's importance. In 1762, after nearly 40 years in a major office, Newcastle was credited by his opponents with only 13 seats in his "Independent Interest." At the same time the Duke controlled 100 M.P.'s through Crown patronage. See the Jenkinson Papers, Add. MSS 38334, foll. 269-72.

might vote with the ministry on most occasions, but they did not constitute the backbone of the administration forces in the parliament. The Duke's help was valuable in forming a government majority in the Commons, but it was by no means indispensable.

Indeed, Newcastle's promotion to Secretary of State in 1724 proceeded as much from financial weakness as political strength and was part of a larger transformation in the composition of the ministry. In 1720 Townshend and Walpole rejoined the government as Lord President of the Privy Council and Paymaster of the Forces. Then, during the political crisis produced by the failure of the South Sea Company, the brothers-in-law sought to achieve a dominant position within the administration. By the spring of 1721 Townshend had become Secretary of State for the northern department, and Walpole had succeeded the disgraced Sutherland as First Lord of the Treasury. This initial consolidation of power was followed, in January, 1723, by an attempt to undermine the position of Lord Carteret, the Secretary of State for the southern department and the last member of the Sunderland faction still holding major office. Within six months the new leaders of the ministry had won the appointment of Horace Walpole as Ambassador to Paris, the most important capital in the southern department. "Putting so near a relation of ours over Schaub's head at a court where the whole scene of affairs centers in Carteret's province," Townshend confided to his brother-in-law, "is publication to the world of the superiority of our credit."[9] The confidence of the northern secretary was not misplaced. By early 1724 the King had been brought to acquiesce in the ouster of Carteret and his dispatch to Ireland as Lord Lieutenant. There

[9] Quoted in Charles B. Realey, *The Early Opposition to Sir Robert Walpole, 1720-1727*, Lawrence, 1931, 130.

Walpole hoped his longtime rival would fall into further disgrace in the controversy engendered by the flagrant manipulation of Irish currency by public officials in England.[10]

In fixing upon Newcastle as Carteret's successor, Walpole and Townshend were not swayed primarily by the Duke's electoral influence. It was not that considerable; in any event, it was already at the disposal of the ministry because of Newcastle's relationship with Henry Pelham and, more important, because of the Duke's continued dependence upon his government salary. For the second time in his short political career Newcastle was on the verge of bankruptcy and was seeking additional support from the government. In conjunction with an extravagant life-style and an extensive housebuilding spree, the Duke's electoral expenses in the Whig cause had bitten deeply into his huge income and had encumbered his estates with expensive mortgages. The improvident aristocrat had no choice but to switch his allegiance to the new ministry and to hope for financial salvation through ministerial largesse.[11]

Yet more than charity to a hard-pressed supporter was involved in Newcastle's appointment as Secretary of State for the southern department. Walpole and Townshend were acutely aware of their precarious control over the new ministry and hesitated to bring a man of ability, such as William Pulteney, into the government. Newcastle ap-

[10] Middleton to Broderick, December 12, 1724, Add. MSS 9234, foll. 53-54; J. H. Plumb, *Sir Robert Walpole*, Boston, 1961, II, 50-51, 75-76.

[11] Chichester to Newcastle, June 12, October 12 and 26, 1723, Add. MSS 33064, foll. 218-37; Nulle, *Pelham-Holles*, 86-99; Romney Sedgwick, ed., *Some Materials towards the memoirs of the reign of King George II*, by John, Lord Hervey, London, 1931, 6-7.

peared to be a perfect choice; not only was the Duke young and inexperienced but also his perilous financial position would deter him from any hasty adventures. After the protracted struggle to remove the Sunderland Whigs, the senior ministers were anxious to have a submissive colleague. Initially, this arrangement was satisfactory to Newcastle as well. Shortly before receiving the seals of office, the Duke confided to Horace Walpole that

> nothing but my dependence upon the friendship and great ability of my Lord Townshend at home and the information and advice that I shall receive from you abroad could have induced me to undertake an office which at present must be so difficult to me. . . . I shall in everything act in concert with My Ld. Townshend.[12]

II

Newcastle's acknowledged dependence upon Townshend and the Walpoles severely limited his authority over the management of colonial affairs. Indeed, during his first six years in the southern department Newcastle was able to secure American posts for only two of his friends and supporters. With the assistance of Nathaniel Gould and Hum Morice, two London merchant-bankers, he won the appointment of Alexander Henderson as Attorney-General of Jamaica in 1727. Subsequently, he arranged for the nomination of Alexander Forbes, a loyal supporter of his political interest in Sussex, to the Provost Marshal's office

[12] April 2, 1724, Add. MSS 32738, foll. 178-79. Newcastle's promotion would also bolster the position of the chief ministers with regard to the King, for the Duke was on very good terms with George I and, as Lord Chamberlain, held the most honorific post at Court. See John M. Beattie, *The English Court in the Reign of George I*, Cambridge, 1967, 246, 250.

in the same colony.[13] But this was the extent of his influence over the disposition of important offices. The Duke urged Lieutenant-Governor Dummer to enlist William Woodside as a captain in the militia of Massachusetts Bay; recommended a clerk of the Earl of Lincoln for employment in Barbados; sanctioned a land grant in Pennsylvania for former Governor William Keith; and wrote the Governor of Barbados on behalf of a near relation of a gentleman with "a very great Interest in Monmouthshire."[14] Yet these were minor matters; they represented the appurtenances of authority rather than the real thing. The southern secretary possessed the seals of office and the formal status they accorded. What he lacked was the effective power that constituted the core of the position.

This fact was all appreciated by aspirants to American offices. Most applications for colonial posts were sent to the northern secretary rather than to Newcastle. In November, 1725, for example, the Earl of Warwick apprised Townshend of a complaint being entered against one of the governors in the West Indies. Warwick took the opportunity to remind the minister "of the encouragement your Lordsp was pleased to give me to Expect your Interest and Assistance in obtaining either the Government of Jamaica, Barbados or the Leeward Islands, which should first happen to become vacant."[15] In 1725 and again in 1728, John Lloyd petitioned Townshend for preferment in South Carolina. And when a group of "London mer-

[13] Gould and Morice to Newcastle, October 14, 1727, S.P. 36/4, foll. 100-101; Morice to Newcastle, June 16, 1729, C.O. 137/47, foll. 20-21.

[14] Newcastle to Dummer, July 19, 1725, C.O. 324/34, p. 151; "Memdum," February 18, 1725, C.O. 28/44, fol. 235; Gordon to Newcastle, November 24, 1724, C.O. 5/1088, fol. 167; Newcastle to Howe, September 14, 1732, S.P. 36/28, fol. 129.

[15] November 13, 1725, C.O. 152/40, fol. 57.

chants trading to Bermuda" complained of the "Oppressive Methods" of Governor Hope, they courted the favor of Townshend rather than his junior colleague. Even political cranks appreciated the hierarchy of authority within the ministry. In 1727, "A.D." of Maryland warned the senior secretary of a Roman Catholic plot in that colony.[16]

The few petitions for colonial preferment that were addressed to the southern secretary during this period were mostly for the sake of bureaucratic formality. "I hope I have been recommended in as full a manner as almost can be desir'd, to both his Grace the Duke of Newcastle, & Sir Robert Walpole," Woodes Rogers wrote to Newcastle's secretary with regard to the governorship of the Bahama Islands; "[I] . . . have often had Sr. Robt & my Lord Townshend promise that I would be employ'd. . . ."[17] And when Samuel Vetch petitioned the Duke in 1725 for the government of New England, he was careful to point out that he had "the honour to be particularly known . . . to my Lord president, Lord Townshend and the Chancellor of the Exchequer. . . ."[18] Newcastle might hope to supervise the governor once he was appointed, but it was the brothers-in-law at the head of the ministry who made the initial nominations to these lucrative positions. The pattern of solicitation for American positions reflected in microcosm the relative levels of power and influence in English political life.

Sensitivity to the informal gradations of status and

[16] Lloyd to Stanyan and to Townshend, May 20, 1725, and October 1, 1728, C.O. 5/387, foll. 184 and 334; Petition, May 16, 1727, C.O. 37/26, fol. 183; A.D. to Townshend, April 8, 1727, C.O. 5/721, fol. 123.

[17] Rogers to Delafaye, August 12, 1728, C.O. 23/14, foll. 49-50.

[18] January 22, 1725, C.O. 5/12, foll. 14-15; Vetch to Walpole, July 21, 1729, W.C., no. 1628.

authority within the administration was especially acute among those with a first-hand acquaintance with the colonial bureaucracy. Townshend's initiative in ordering the Board of Trade to prepare its comprehensive report of 1721 had established once and for all the northern secretary's concern with American affairs.[19] As a result, matters of policy as well as of patronage found their way to his desk. In 1724, a group of London shipwrights unsuccessfully petitioned Townshend for legislation to prohibit the construction of ships in New England. Two years later, Martin Bladen of the Board of Trade directed his memorandum on the state of the colonies to the senior secretary rather than to Newcastle, a procedure that was repeated by Sir William Keith in 1728. Indeed, by this time much of the ordinary administrative business of the colonies was being handled by Townshend's office.[20]

This diversion of American business into the northern office was not accidental. Townshend stood to gain from this game of administrative imperialism. As a member of the upper house, Townshend could not easily match the political influence of the First Lord of the Treasury in the Commons. Nor could he expect to counterbalance the patronage at the disposal of the treasury chief with the resources of his own department. Control over the forty-odd American posts formally in Newcastle's gift would significantly increase Townshend's leverage within the min-

[19] John Shy, *Toward Lexington; The Role of the British Army in the Coming of the American Revolution*, Princeton, 1965, 29-30; Popple to Townshend, July 22, 1720, H.M.C., *Eleventh Report*, pt. IV, 296; Charles M. Andrews, *The Colonial Period of American History*, New Haven, 1938, IV, 389.

[20] Townshend to Board of Trade, October 19, 1724, S.P. 44/122, p. 250; Steele, *Politics of Colonial Policy*, 167n.; Townshend to Board of Trade, December 12, 1728, C.O. 323/8, fol. 302; Arnold to Townshend, September 14, 1728, S.P. 36/8, fol. 130.

istry. For the northern secretary, colonial patronage took on an importance out of proportion to its intrinsic value.

The intrusion of other officials into the management of colonial affairs was as often the result of overlapping administrative jurisdictions as of calculated aggrandizement. A case in point was Horace Walpole, the younger brother and close advisor of the chief minister. As Auditor-General of the Plantation Revenues from 1717 to 1757, Walpole had a direct interest in the supervision of colonial finances. By the early 1720's, he had begun to build up a personal following in America. There were deputy auditors to be named in each royal colony, and the appointment of such influential men as James Blair in Virginia and George Clarke in New York brought forth requests for positions outside of the Treasury. In 1724, the younger Walpole intervened to secure a royal warrant directing the payment of the salary of Philip Livingston, the Indian Agent and Clerk of the Town of Albany, out of the Crown revenues in New York. In return for this favor Livingston used his connections in the assembly to secure the appointment of Peter Leheup, Walpole's personal secretary, as one of the agents for the colony in England.[21]

This minor patronage activity did not measure the full extent of the influence of the Auditor-General. For the duties of his office placed Horace Walpole in a position to oversee nearly all public spending in the royal colonies.[22]

[21] R. Carter to Lord Fairfax, June 24, 1729, Add. MSS 30306, foll. 91-92; George Clarke to H. Walpole, November 24, 1725, C.O. 5/1092, foll. 188-91; Lawrence H. Leder, *Robert Livingston, 1654-1728, and the Politics of Colonial New York*, Chapel Hill, 1961, 271-73, 283. This Horace Walpole (1678-1757) should not be confused with the son of Sir Robert, the famous essayist and correspondent. The latter (1717-97) is referred to in this account as Horace Walpole the younger.

[22] See, for example, the memoranda prepared at Walpole's re-

When Newcastle proposed that Paul George be named Lieutenant-Governor of Montserrat and that a stipend be attached to this previously unsalaried post, the Auditor-General entered a strong protest at the treasury. "I find by ye news," Horace wrote to his brother in August, 1724,

> that Paul George is to have a pension out of ye Quit rents as Governor to one of ye Leeward Islands. It is a precedent that will be of very ill consequence, especially if it be granted out of those in Virginia. It will not stop there all ye Quitt rents by degrees will be granted away. . . . I hope you will take care of what you do in this case; I have put a stop to severall such demands at foreseeing ye consequences of them.[23]

What the younger Walpole failed to mention was that he had just engineered a similar raid on the crown revenues for his friend Livingston in New York, and that he had authorized an additional salary for himself from the same funds.[24]

Yet there were important administrative principles at stake in New York and they excused, to some degree, Walpole's inconsistency in the distribution of American revenue and his concerted attempt to build a personal following in the colony. The Auditor-General had been engaged in a long and bitter fight with the Assembly concerning the responsibilities of his deputy, George Clarke. Clarke claimed the right to audit all the accounts of the legislature and to retain a percentage of the funds for his effort. The Assembly had resisted this claim and had placed the audit

---

quest by William Wood on the Jamaica revenue bill of 1724: C.O. 137/52, foll. 71-72 and C.O. 137/54, foll. 122-33.

[23] August 5, 1724, W.C., no. 1157.

[24] Colden to Collinson, May, 1742, Colden Papers, New York Historical Society, *Collections*, New York, 1918-37, LI, 257-63.

of non-Crown revenues solely in the hands of its own treasurer. Upon Walpole's petition the Lords of the Treasury labeled this action "a very Arbitrary and Unwarrantable proceeding, and a Contempt of his Majtys Authority."[25] But it was only by securing the support of Governor Burnet and of Robert Livingston, the Speaker of the Assembly, that Walpole was able to translate this reprimand into salary arrears and the restoration of the audit to his deputy.

From an administrative point of view, the patronage bestowed upon the Livingstons was an acceptable price to pay for the retrieval of this important fiscal office from the hands of the Assembly. It pointed up the possibility of reversing a dangerous trend in all of the colonies. In 1723, the legal counsel of the Board of Trade, Richard West, called attention to the "practice in all the American Colonies for their respective Generall Assemblys to assume to themselves the nomination of all Officers Relateing to the Revenue."[26] To forestall the encroachments of the representative bodies in the colonies, it would not be enough to promulgate new regulations or to recall old precedents; rather, it would be necessary to enter into the factional politics of the colonies and to use the monetary and patronage resources of the home government to beat the assemblies at their own game. Paradoxically, it was Horace Walpole's willingness to raid the royal quit rents which temporarily preserved the prerogatives of the Crown in

[25] Treasury Lords (R. Walpole, R. Edgecumbe, H. Pelham) to Burnet, April 28, 1722, C.O. 5/1085, foll. 149-50; Clarke to H. Walpole, October 10, 1724, C.O. 5/1085, foll. 187-88; Burnet to Newcastle, November 17, 1725, C.O. 5/1085, foll. 213-16; Leder, *Robert Livingston,* 262-65.

[26] Quoted in Jack P. Greene, *The Quest for Power: the Lower Houses of Assembly in the Southern Royal Colonies, 1689-1776,* Chapel Hill, 1963, 245.

New York. Any substantial renovation of colonial administration would require just this blend of personal involvement by a senior minister and acceptance of considerable short-run expense.

This latter requirement contrasted sharply with the cautious fiscal policy outlined by the Auditor-General in his letter of August, 1724. And this conservative statement reflected the long-time sentiments of Sir Robert Walpole as well. In the aftermath of the South Sea Bubble, the First Lord of the Treasury was intent upon keeping government expenses to the minimum, whatever the cost to administrative efficiency. This retrenchment was especially severe with regard to colonial expenditures. On a number of occasions Sir Robert ignored plans designed to strengthen Crown control of the colonial governments because they involved a drain on the exchequer. At the same time, the Treasury chief diverted from America part of the revenue that might have been used to make local administration financially self-sufficient.[27] As far back as 1717 one reform-minded American had attempted to circumvent these discriminatory policies through a scheme which would reduce expenditures by rationalizing the colonial bureaucracy. "I have liked my Proposals the better," Thomas Banister wrote to Walpole,

> Since they have the Honour to concur with your Thoughts When I last waited on you. you said you was for no Projects that call'd for Money abroad when it was so much wanted at home.[28]

[27] Dora Mae Clark, *The Rise of the British Treasury: Colonial Administration in the Enghteenth Century*, New Haven, 1960, chap. 1.

[28] January 24, 1717, W.C., no. 767; Andrews, *Colonial Period*, IV, 340, notes Banister's other activities.

This careful calculation of financial priorities was accentuated in the 1720's. One member of Parliament noted that when a petition was presented to the House of Commons in 1724 seeking relief for the subscribers to the Bahama Island Company,

> the House being pretty full and the inclination seemed to [be to] refer it to a committee [for action]; just as the question was putting, Mr. Walpole came in and spoke two or three words against it, hoping gentlemen would not begin to unravel the misfortunes of the year [17]20 for then there would be no end . . . so he turned the House, so submissive is the majority. . . .[29]

It was not only Parliament which felt the weight of Sir Robert Walpole's authority. Newcastle was also acutely conscious of his massive presence. As First Lord of the Treasury, Walpole controlled the award of provisioning contracts for the independent companies stationed in America and used these lucrative gifts to bolster his political leverage at home. Thomas Missing, the M.P. for Portsmouth and a loyal Walpole supporter, held a Treasury contract for the delivery of food and supplies to the troops in Nova Scotia.

The interest of the chief minister in American affairs was not confined to these "legitimate" extensions of his domestic activities. Walpole had a major voice in the distribution of customs posts in the colonies and he was hesitant to relinquish control of other colonial patronage either to Townshend or to Newcastle. When the Earl of Orkney requested a leave for his deputy governor in Virginia in 1726, he reminded Newcastle that "it was yr very

[29] A. N. Newman, ed., *The Parliamentary Diary of Sir Edward Knatchbull, 1722-1730*, London, 1963, 27-28.

good friend Sir Robert Walpole that recommended him to me. . . ."[30] Four years later, in response to a request from Abraham Meure, the First Lord of the Treasury secured the appointment of William Mathews as Lieutenant-General of the Leeward Islands.[31] An even more serious usurpation of the authority of the southern secretary had taken place in 1726. On the death of Governor Portland of Jamaica, the president of the local Council advanced his own pretensions for the post with "an offer of fifteen hundred pounds p ann Sterl." to the chief minister. "It's usual," John Ayscough explained to Walpole, "for [the] Governor to give the Sallary to Some Person in England for their favour."[32] That this offer was made to the First Lord of the Treasury and not to Newcastle testified once again to the Duke's impotence in the determination of major colonial matters.

The southern secretary was well aware of the various formal and informal obstacles which hindered his freedom of action. In 1728 he advised the Duke of Montagu to approach the Treasury directly for a patent for the island of Tobago. "If I should procure ye King's Warrant . . . ," Newcastle explained, the Attorney-General

[30] May 5, 1726, C.O. 5/1344, foll. 3-4; Plumb, *Walpole*, II, 91-102, describes Walpole's enormous appetite for patronage.

[31] Meure to Walpole, August 20, 1730, W.C., no. 1752.

[32] July 11, 1726, W.C., no. 1344. Charles Cox, the brother of a member of the Jamaican council, had made a similar offer in 1720 (Cox to ?, March 2, 1720, C.O. 137/51, fol. 215), but the post was bestowed upon Portland as compensation for his losses in the South Sea Bubble: Lord Berkeley of Stratton to the Earl of Stafford, November 12, 1720, James J. Cartwright, ed., *The Wentworth Papers, 1705-1739 . . .* , London, 1883, 450. Stanley N. Katz, *Newcastle's New York: Anglo-American Politics, 1732-1753*, Cambridge, Mass., 1968, 140n. mentions Walpole's interest in colonial matters.

> should have a Difficulty in obeying it as not coming thro ye proper Channel. And even if that could be got over & I should carry it on thro' the Signet Office, when it comes to the Privy Seal it must stop there, till upon a Docquet's being presented to the Commissioners of the Treasury, they have under their hand signified their Allowance which they would undoubtedly refuse to do as being a Grant wholly within their Department.[33]

For Newcastle, during his first years as chief colonial administrator, one channel of influence led back to Sir Robert Walpole at the Treasury, and another could be traced back to the senior Secretary of State. "Mr. Tilson having mentioned Some time ago the affair of South Carolina," the Duke wrote to Townshend in August, 1728,

> I must beg you would do nothing on it . . . you know how desirous I am of getting it for Colo Horsey, from whom Colonel Montague is to have an advantage . . . however I do not press to have any thing done in it yet.[34]

Effective power over colonial policy and patronage remained in the hands of the senior ministers who had brought the young aristocrat into the southern department. Paul George, the man for whom the Duke had attempted a raid on the American quit rents in 1724, applied to Townshend two years later for the government of Bermuda.[35] This was not ingratitude but political realism. It was almost as if Carteret had been removed but not

[33] April 6, 1728, S.P. 36/6, fol. 9.

[34] August 6, 1728, Add. MSS 32687, fol. 137.

[35] George to Townshend, February 26, 1726, C.O. 175/1, no. 1; Meure to R. Walpole, August 20, 1730, W.C., no. 1752.

replaced in the ministerial reshuffle. Decisions on American matters were implemented in Newcastle's name and with his consent, but they were not always to his liking and almost never on his initiative.

Gradually Newcastle came to resent his impotence. The immediate target of his discontent was Townshend. The northern secretary was going behind the back of his colleague to manage diplomatic negotiations in the southern province and was interfering in the formulation of military strategy in the West Indies.[36] These jurisdictional antagonisms came out into the open in the late 1720's. "I have been long endeavouring to gett the better of My own Temper in this matter," Newcastle wrote to Townshend, "but I have of late found it impossible for me to do it. . . ." The southern secretary continued:

> I was indeed in hopes when by your Lordships Means I came first into the Office I am now in, that dilligence and Application on My part . . . & having a deference always to the opinions of Those whose Experiences and other Qualities had rendered them more [?] perfectly Masters of the Business I was to be engag'd in . . . would have made the discharge of My Office Easy to My Self, and agreeable to others.
>
> But . . . Experience has for some time convinced Your Lordship and Myself that either too Early a Desire to appear capable of what in reality I was not, or too little attention to sett the few Qualities that I have in the best light, has made My situation not easy to me. . . .[37]

[36] Thomson, *Secretaries of State*, 93-94; Delafaye to Newcastle, August 21, 1725, S.P. 35/57, foll. 257-58; Hart to Townshend, May 9, 1729, W.C., no. 1609.

[37] No date, Add. MSS 32992, foll. 68-70; Plumb, *Walpole*, II, 189, 193, 195.

Newcastle's offer to resign tied in perfectly with Townshend's hope of replacing him with the Earl of Chesterfield. Only Walpole's intervention, backed by the Queen, put an end to this intrigue.[38] With his instinct for the winning side, Newcastle had sided with the First Lord of the Treasury in Walpole's continuing struggle with Townshend for the control of foreign policy. With Townshend's forced departure from the ministry in 1730, the Duke assumed his informal position as chief Secretary of State.

This was no more than Newcastle deserved after six years in major office. Up to this time, minor diplomatic negotiations and routine administrative responsibility were all the Duke had to show for his efforts—except, of course, his annual salary of £5,000 as southern secretary and the additional personal financial credit that his position in the government made possible. Neither the economic security nor the social prestige accruing from the secretaryship was sufficient to satisfy the ambitions of the Duke. His personality was such that he had to be at the center of affairs—making deals, conducting negotiations, dispensing patronage—in a word, exercising power. This pleasure had largely been denied to him up to this point. Only with the resignation of Townshend did Newcastle become southern secretary in fact as well as in name. Only then did he begin to leave his personal imprint on colonial affairs.

III

The successful intervention of the senior ministers in the formulation of colonial policy and the dispensation of American patronage was not simply the result of Newcastle's subordinate position within the government. For the southern secretary had traditionally shared these re-

[38] Williams, *Carteret and Newcastle*, 62-69.

sponsibilities with the Board of Trade, the advisory body on colonial affairs created by William III in 1696. The predominance of Walpole and Townshend in the conduct of American business was as much a result of the decline in the authority of the Board of Trade as of the political weakness of the new minister.

Indeed, the deteriorating administrative position of the Board of Trade was more significant in many respects than the temporary eclipse of the southern secretary. During the first years of its existence the board had used the active support of the King and the impressive personal reputations of its members to capture effective control of colonial policy and patronage.[39] This hegemony lasted until 1702. In that year the newly appointed Secretary of State, the Earl of Nottingham, dispatched a circular letter to the colonial governors instructing them to correspond with him directly as well as with the board. At the same time he bypassed the board in appointing provincial councillors in New York and New Jersey; ignoring the board's remonstrance against this infringement of its specified authority, Sutherland repeated this usurpation when he came into the southern department in 1706.[40]

By that time, however, the scales had been decisively tipped in favor of the Secretary of State. The informal influence of the advisory body had been weakened by the resignation of several influential members and the death of William III in 1702. The powers which the board had quietly inherited from its more powerful predecessor, the

[39] Peter Laslett, "John Locke, The Great Recoinage, and the Origins of the Board of Trade: 1695-1698," *WMQ*, 3rd ser., XIV (July, 1957), 370-402.

[40] Board of Trade to Nottingham, September 3, 1702, C.O. 5/390, foll. 36-37; Board of Trade to Sutherland, August 13, 1707, C.O. 28/38, fol. 6; Steele, *Politics of Colonial Policy*, 29-30, 86-88, 109-10.

Lords of Trade, were gradually assumed by the southern secretaries. Between 1702 and 1704, Nottingham successfully asserted his right to nominate over forty colonial officials. Only the selection of councillors continued to be reserved to the Board of Trade.

This successful attack upon the patronage powers of the board was followed, in 1714, by a reduction of the board's role in the formulation of policy and in the settlement of colonial disputes. Upon the accession of George I, Henry McCulloch explained in his survey of colonial administration written in 1756,

> The Orders formerly issued by several of the Kings of England previous to the Instituting A Council of Trade were renewed . . . impowering the whole Privy Council or any three or more of them to be a Committee for the Affairs of . . . the Plantations. . . .[41]

Up to this time the Board of Trade had functioned almost as a committee of the Privy Council. Now that the superior institution had created a duplicate body from within its own ranks the influence of the board was bound to decrease. Its recommendations would henceforth be subject to detailed review by the Privy Council committee as well as by the southern secretary before being presented to the King in Council. One more level of discussion and debate had been added to the process of colonial decision-making.

Together the southern secretary and the Privy Council had usurped the powers of patronage and policy-making within the competence of the board at the time of its crea-

[41] Essay on Trade in America, 1756," Add. MSS 11514, foll. 42-44. In fact, these orders had been renewed by William III in 1696 (Edward R. Turner, *The Privy Council of England . . . 1603-1784*, Baltimore, 1928, II, 357), but it is significant that McCulloch believed that they were utilized extensively only after 1714.

tion by William III. In 1751, the President of the board erroneously but understandably informed Newcastle that, "The Power of recommending Governors & c. and in general all the other officers of the Crown in America (excepting only Such as are within the Department of the Lords of the Treasury or the Commissioners of the Customs) has always been exercised by the Secretary of State." As the Earl of Halifax continued,

> Those Powers in the Commission . . . of representing to the King upon all matters relating to Trade & Plantations, of recommending what may be proper to be passed in the Assemblies; of hearing Complaints of Oppression and Male-Administration & representing thereupon, have not for many Years been Exercised, the Board having been given to understand that they shou'd represent only on Such Points as shou'd be referred to them by ye Secretary of State or Council.[42]

During the first quarter of the eighteenth century, more and more colonial business was transacted outside of the purview of the administrative agency originally charged with its conduct. The board had lost its high qualifications for membership, its uniqueness as a forum for the discussion of colonial business, and even its monopoly of detailed information on American affairs. "It has been usual heretofore," Deputy-Governor Spotswood of Virginia reminded Bolingbroke, the southern secretary, in July, 1714,

> to trouble those in yr Lo'p's post, only with the more important Transactions of the Government . . . but if y'r Lo'p thinks fit that I should enlarge y'r Trouble,

[42] Halifax to Newcastle, August 25, 1751, Add. MSS 32725, foll. 91-92.

by the same detail of Affairs as I gave to the Lords Commiss'rs of Trade, I shall punctually observe y'r Commands.[43]

Those administrators with a relatively disinterested position and with a fairly objective estimate of the "national interest" were increasingly distant from the locus of power. For more than a generation the Board of Trade became just another pressure group seeking to influence the choice of American officials and the formation of colonial policy. Instead of being the focus of attention, the board now joined merchant groups, colonial agents, and patronage hunters around the periphery of the small circle of politicians who exercised effective authority.[44]

Initially, the Board of Trade fought a strong rearguard action against the encroachments of the secretaries of state. At the same time the advisory body sought to impress its standards upon its political superiors. Late in 1714, for example, the board reminded Secretary Stanhope that "the public Service has frequently suffered by the absence of Councillors from their posts." "For the future," the board urged that "no such Licenses [of absence] be granted till We have been acquainted therewith and shall have made our Report thereupon."[45] In April, 1715, the board re-

[43] July 21, 1714, Virginia Historical Society, *Collections,* new ser., Richmond, Va., 1882, II, 73-74.

[44] From 1696 to 1721, there were 32 resignations from the board, but only 12 in the years from 1722 to 1749. There was therefore an inverse relationship between stability of membership and efficiency of administration for the board was most active before 1721, when it was not composed of long-term "placemen." Steele, *Politics of Colonial Policy,* 110, 133, 171-72, offers a slightly different interpretation, while detailed information on the commissioners of trade is available in Add. MSS 30372, foll. 32-33 and Katz, *Newcastle's New York,* appendix A.

[45] March 17, 1714, C.O. 324/10, p. 65.

newed its efforts. This time it requested Stanhope to inform it of "such Commissions for Lieut Generals or Lieut Governors, as have been already granted, and are now in force, & that for the future We may be apprized of such Nominations before the passing of their respective Commissions. . . ."[46] If such notification was given, the board argued in a letter to Stanhope five months later, "We should be inabled to lay before You from time to time, such matters in relation to ye said Nominations as shou'd occur to Us, & might be for the public Service."[47]

This statement was less the enunciation of an abstract principle than a considered reaction to a current problem. From the London *Gazette* the board had learned of the appointment of George Vaughan as Lieutenant-Governor of New Hampshire. The board promptly expressed its concern that the new official would be unlikely to protect the King's woods because of his financial interest in several sawmills in the province. "To set a Carpenter to preserve Woods," the board warned the Secretary of State, "is like setting a Wolf to keep Sheep. . . ." The board then proceeded to quote former Governor Bellomont of New York as to the standards which should be employed in the future selection of personnel in America:

> First, That there be great care taken in the choice of the Persons employ'd by the King, from the Governor to the meanest Officer; I mean, that they be men of undoubted probity, & well born; Secondly, That they be not Men of the Country, but English Men. Thirdly, That they be Men of some Fortune in England, to be a Tye upon them to behave themselves honorably in their respective Trusts.[48]

[46] April 14, 1715, ibid., p. 67.

[47] August 3, 1715, C.O. 5/931, fol. 92.

[48] Loc. cit.

Within a few weeks of this pronouncement the board found yet another opportunity to formulate an administrative principle for the benefit of the southern secretary. Governor Hunter of New York had appointed Lewis Morris to the chief justiceship of the province as a reward for his support in winning the approval of the Assembly for a five-year revenue act. Noting this development with satisfaction, the advisory body suggested to Stanhope that for the future "such Places as are in the Disposal of the Governors" should be given to those "who shall distinguish themselves in His Majesty's Interest and for the Good of the Government. . . ."[49]

In its rush to develop sound administrative guidelines for the disposition of places in America, the board failed to note that its proposals were not completely consistent. If colonial posts were to be reserved for Englishmen, as Bellomont suggested, then it would be impossible to reward Americans such as Morris for their services and to create a strong "government" party in the local representative assemblies.[50] While the board's principles represented an advance upon the blatantly political use of American positions by the secretaries of state, they contained hidden drawbacks of their own.

This confused adumbration of the requirements of an intelligent patronage policy was only one aspect of the activist role assumed by the Board of Trade which sat during the first years of the Hanoverian period. In rapid succession, the advisory body dispatched comprehensive questionnaires to the several governors, undertook the

[49] August 31, 1715, C.O. 5/1085, foll. 57-58.

[50] Thomas C. Barrow, *Trade and Empire; The British Customs Service in Colonial America, 1660-1775*, Cambridge, Mass., 1967, 52-53, 58-59, and 132, traces the resolution of this dilemma in another branch of the administration.

settlement of the Bahama Islands, secured the compilation and printing of all legislation passed by the American assemblies, dispatched a request to the Treasury for information on colonial revenues, and won the permanent appointment of its own legal advisor.[51] This burst of intellectual energy, a reflection in part of the political impotence felt by many of the members of the board, culminated in 1721 in a major report on the state of the colonial system and on a series of proposals for reform. The board recommended the abolition of proprietary governments, the elimination of sinecures and deputy office-holders, and the nomination of a governor-general over all of the continental colonies.

Many of these suggestions had been advanced previously; yet the report of 1721 was more than a codification of old principles. For the experience of the previous decade had made it quite obvious to the members of the board that the administrative system of 1696, weakened by the encroachments of the southern secretary after 1702 and undermined by the creation of a Privy Council committee in 1714, was not an efficient bureaucratic structure for the management of American affairs. The continued frustration of its policies by competing elements in the administration prompted the board to propose a fundamental alteration in the hierarchy of power. The board suggested that its president be given immediate and direct access to the King "in all matters relating to the Plantations, in such Manner as the first Commissioner of the Treasury and the Admiralty. . . ." Such an arrangement was necessary, the board stated, to enable those with the greatest knowledge of American problems and the firmest sense of the national interest to secure the enactment of required legislation,

[51] See C.O. 324/10, pp. 81, 133, 139, and 145; C.O. 23/12, foll. 84, 112-14, and 119; S.P. 44/120, p. 323; and Steele, *Politics of Colonial Policy*, 152-57.

the prompt dispatch of the requisite orders, and the appointment of the proper officials.[52]

It was to be thirty years before the first steps were taken to implement this proposal. The lapse of a generation was not fortuitous, for the creation of a new administrative hierarchy hinged on the ability of the Board of Trade to amass enough political support to wrest the control of patronage from the hands of the Secretary of State and the formulation of policy from the Privy Council committee for plantation affairs. The appointment of a president of the Board of Trade with cabinet rank would, in effect, create a new administrative department within the government with its own clearly defined lines of power and authority. This, in turn, would make it exceedingly difficult for other ministers to intervene at will in the management of American affairs. The overriding need for this kind of central direction and direct accountability was clearly perceived by Thomas Pownall as late as 1764. "The Board of Trade," Pownall wrote in *The Administration of the Colonies*,

> should either be made what it never was intended to be, a Secretary of State's office for the Plantations, or be confined to what it really is, a committee of reference for examination and report . . . while the affairs of the Colonies are administered solely by the King in Council, really acting as an efficient board for that purpose.[53]

Both of these alternatives had been tried by Pownall's time. Between 1696 and 1702, the Board of Trade had

[52] The board's report is printed in Edmund B. O'Callahan, ed., *Documents relative to the colonial history of the state of New York*, Albany, 1853-1887, v, 593-630.

[53] London, 1764, 25-27.

functioned successfully because of its position as an adjunct of the King in Council. After 1748, and especially after 1752, the board became, under the Earl of Halifax, essentially a secretary of state's office for the colonies. In both cases expertise, responsibility, and authority were concentrated in the same place. It was the increasing fragmentation of administrative control over American affairs in the intervening years which accounted in some measure for the declining standards of service in the plantation office and for the deterioration of the Anglo-American relationship. "It is found by experience," Thomas Povey had noted in the 1670's, "that whatsoever Councel is not enabled as well to execute as advise, must needs produce very imperfect and weake effects."[54]

It was the growing importance of the secretaries of state and other senior ministers which was primarily responsible for this bureaucratic chaos. Politicians concerned primarily with borough elections, parliamentary debates, and diplomatic negotiations, these officials had neither the experience nor the incentive to undertake the duties of colonial administrators. More often than not their views on imperial policy reflected the selfish sentiments of domestic lobbies rather than a detached estimate of the national interest. Moreover, their intimate involvement in the corrupt politics of the House of Commons prompted them to use American offices for their own advantage. From Nottingham onward, few secretaries of state had been able to resist this temptation; fewer still had succeeded in matching the early efforts of the Board of Trade to formulate and implement a coherent colonial policy.

By the time Newcastle entered the southern department

[54] Quoted in Steele, *Politics of Colonial Policy*, 8. For a similar development in Scottish administration see Patrick W. J. Riley, *The English Ministers and Scotland, 1707-1727*, London, 1964, 285.

in 1724, the implementation of a rational patronage policy administered by the Board of Trade would have deprived the senior ministers of the disposition of at least forty American offices, including ten colonial governorships. The salary and perquisites of five of these amounted to more than £1,000 sterling per annum; the most lucrative was worth more than £8,000.[55] All of these major posts were extremely attractive to politically influential Englishmen who were anxious to trade their electoral interest for a government position. Even the less alluring offices—those of naval officer, attorney-general, clerk of the courts—were eagerly sought after, if not by those in the forefront of English political life, then by their friends and associates. And there was the additional advantage that many of these lesser posts, held on the authority of a patent issued by the King, could be managed from home. Despite the protests from the Board of Trade more than one half of the American positions formally under the control of the southern secretary were served by deputy.[56] Political expedience outweighed administrative efficiency in nearly every aspect of policy and patronage.

However eloquently the Board of Trade might argue for changes in the structure and practice of colonial administration, it could not alter the inherent logic of the

[55] "Income of Colo Worsley . . . ," no date, C.O. 28/39, foll. 65-66; Barrow, *Trade and Empire*, 127; Beverly McAnear, *The Income of the Colonial Governors of British North America*, New York, 1967.

[56] These offices were usually granted "for life" as a reward for service to the King or to the ministry. They were therefore a form of private property and were often "rented out" to deputies who performed the actual work. As the patentees received their authority by a direct grant from the Crown, they were not easily controlled by the Board of Trade, the colonial governors, or the local assemblies. See chap. 5, sec. III, below.

situation. Ambitious politicians with debts to pay and friends to satisfy would not easily accept such a loss of influence, and even the most enlightened statesman would be moved to a reform of this magnitude only if a vital national interest was at stake. In the 1720's, with American affairs on the periphery of English political life, there was only a small chance that the public interest would triumph over the private demands of the senior ministers.

IV

The problems posed by the political exploitation of the administrative system were not quite so apparent to Newcastle during his first years in office. He sensed, perhaps, that if he wished to attain a position of authority within the ministry he would have to assert complete control over the affairs of the southern department. But it was not obvious to the Duke, at least at this time, that his attempts to extend his influence might impair the strength of the colonial relationship. For Newcastle, power was its own reward and its own justification. He entered upon the conduct of colonial business with a strong determination to succeed but without a clear definition of success.

Nevertheless, it was apparent immediately that Newcastle's approach to American problems was considerably different from that of Lord Carteret, his immediate predecessor. To contemporaries, Carteret and Newcastle seemed to be contrasting rather than similar figures, the one intelligent, a lover of ease, a gentleman-statesman; the other mediocre, a man of incessant activity, a grasping politician. There was something to these overdrawn portraits both with regard to personal style and political strategy. Although Carteret used the patronage of the southern department between 1720 and 1724, he never attempted to distribute these offices in a systematic way in order to build a strong political base in the English boroughs. Instead, he relied on his abilities as a diplomat and on his friendship with the King. Newcastle pursued a very different course. From the outset of his political career the Duke sought to establish himself firmly in the House of Commons through his control of borough elections. This committed him to a political strategy which involved the wholesale accumulation of patronage posts. To a much greater degree than Carteret, Newcastle was tempted to utilize the administrative resources of America for his own political ends.

Carteret's weakness as a colonial official stemmed from other causes. Unlike Newcastle, he had American interests to defend. Since 1711, Carteret had served as one of the eight proprietors of Carolina and had taken an active part in the management of the undeveloped colony. He personally appointed the governor, approved the legislation enacted by the Assembly, and paid the secretary who supervised the routine administration of the province. For nearly a decade before his appointment as southern secretary, Carteret had been dealing on a first-hand basis with colonial problems, although the depressed condition of Carolina in 1720 was hardly a tribute to his efforts.

Nevertheless, this experience provided Carteret with a good grasp of the American situation and with a fairly clear understanding of the interests of the mother country. On more than one occasion this knowledge prompted him to support the creation of a more efficient administrative system. Twice in 1723, the southern secretary supported the Board of Trade in successful efforts to depose councillors who were absent from the colonies without leave. This action represented a welcome tightening of the standards of colonial service, as the elimination of absentees had long been one of the reforms urged by the board. Carteret also backed the reformist policies of the advisory body in two controversies in New York. In 1721 he intervened on behalf of George Clarke, the Deputy Royal Auditor, in that official's battle with the assembly for the control of the public accounts; and in the following year he restored the perquisites of the Admiralty court in the province to the proper recipients. Carteret was instrumental, likewise, in preserving the King's woods in Nova Scotia, in pressing for a complete overhaul of the revenue system in Jamaica, and in winning the support of the monarch for a major survey of the West Indian colonies by the Board of Trade.[57]

In a number of other cases, however, Carteret's personal interests placed him in opposition to the flexible mercantilist pattern of empire sketched by the board in its report of 1721. In 1715 he had marshaled resistance in Parliament against the bill "for the better Regulation of the Charter and Proprietary Governments."[58] His presence in the secretary's office when the Board of Trade recommended a similar measure in 1721 helped to doom that initiative as well. Carteret was equally unsympathetic to an increase in the powers and competence of the local representative bodies. He and his co-proprietors continually ignored the requests of the Assembly of Carolina and refused to come to the financial assistance of the colony in 1715 in the aftermath of a devastating Indian war. The attitude of the proprietors was completely exploitative, and Carteret was the worst among them. He accepted a Crown-

[57] Warrants, February 25 and May 8, 1723, C.O. 324/34, pp. 221, 234; Carteret to Burnet, May 16, 1721, and April 14, 1722, C.O. 324/34, pp. 56-57, 113; Stanyan to Burchett, April 14, 1722, S.P. 44/147; Carteret to Board of Trade, May 20, 1723 and February 26, 1724, S.P. 44/123, pp. 255 and 302; Carteret to Board of Trade, March 9, 1724, C.O. 323/8, fol. 145.

[58] Jeremiah Dummer dedicated his *Defence of the New England Charters*, London, 1721, to Carteret.

appointed governor in 1721 only to prevent outright resumption of the royal charter. When the other proprietors relinquished their share of the government of the colony to the Crown in 1729, Carteret, then Lord-Lieutenant of Ireland, used his position in the ministry to retain his portion. He remained Palatine and co-proprietor with the King until 1744, thus shifting the cost of administration and defense of the so-called Granville district to the public treasury while safeguarding his income from the quit rents.[59]

If the defense of proprietary interests was the first principle of the colonial policy of the southern secretary, then the support of private English interests in the colonies was the second. Carteret's administration established a series of precedents of secretarial intervention in internal American affairs. In January, 1723, the chief colonial administrator addressed a strong letter to Governor Burnet of New York directing him to inquire into the arrears of pay allegedly due to two officials in New Jersey.[60] This was perhaps a defensible use of the authority of his office; but there were a number of more dubious incidents. On two occasions in 1722 Carteret attempted to extract money from the Assembly of Jamaica for services performed in the island by his friends and associates. One of these cases involved the highly irregular appointment of a lieutenant governor and an instruction directing the receiver-general of the colony to pay the new appointee a salary

[59] Carteret to Newcastle, January 21, 1740, Add. MSS 32693, foll. 37-41; Charles L. Raper, *North Carolina: A Study in English Colonial Government*, New York, 1904, 111-14.

[60] January 16, 1723, C.O. 324/34, p. 216, Neville to Gower, July 19, 1774, Neville Papers, P.R.O. 30/50/63, fol. 78, invokes a colonial precedent established by Carteret in 1744 when he was Secretary of State for the northern department.

of £1,000 sterling per annum.[61] At the same time, the southern secretary stepped into a dispute over a patent office in the island. When the Assembly contested the validity of several of the perquisites of John Coleman, the Clerk of the Crown, Carteret interposed on his behalf. He directed the Governor to see that the rights of patentees were upheld in the colony. Subsequently, Carteret extended this interventionist policy to another West Indian possession. In 1723, he supported the complaint of Wavell Smith of the Leeward Islands against the action of Governor Hart in taking control of the nominations to several minor offices. Simultaneously, he supported Hart in the Governor's battle with the Assembly over the disposition of other local positions.[62]

Here was the third principle of Carteret's colonial "policy." Where proprietary or patent rights were not in question, the supremacy of the home government was to be maintained. Local prerogatives were to be sacrificed whenever they conflicted with imperial considerations, and the authority of the English administrative system was to be extended as much as possible over the lives of the colonists. On these matters Carteret adopted an uncompromising attitude early in his career and remained steadfast in his views throughout his political life. As President of the Privy Council in 1759, Carteret, then Lord Granville, bluntly informed Benjamin Franklin that

> Your People in the Colonies refuse Obedience to the King's *Instructions*, and treat them with great Slight,

[61] Stanyan to Hamilton, July 31, 1722, S.P. 44/123, p. 130; "Instruction," May 21, 1722, C.O. 324/34, p. 120.

[62] Carteret to Portland, July 17, 1722, C.O. 324/34, pp. 162-63; W. Smith to Carteret, October 4, 1723, C.O. 7/1, no. 26; Frederick G. Spurdle, *Early West Indian Government . . .*, Palmerston North, New Zealand, no date, 185-87, 197-99.

as *not binding*, and *not Law*, in the Colonies; wheras . . . those Instructions are not like little Pocket Instructions given to an Ambassador or Envoy, in which much may be left to Discretion; they are first drawn up by grave and wise Men learned in the Laws and Constitutions of the Nation; they are then brought to the Council Board, where they are solemnly weigh'd and maturely consider'd, and after receiving such Amendments as are found proper and necessary, they are agreed upon and establish'd. The Council is *over all* the Colonies. . . . The King in Council is THE LEGISLATOR of the Colonies; and when his Majesty's Instructions come there, they are the LAW OF THE LAND: *they are* . . . the Law of the Land, and as such *ought to be* OBEYED.[63]

On the subject of colonial rights and duties, Carteret and the Board of Trade were in close agreement. They were at the opposite ends of the spectrum, however, when it came to the matter of the continuance of patent offices and proprietary governments in America. It was the southern secretary's intimate financial connection with Carolina and also with the Bahama Islands which hampered his effectiveness as a colonial administrator. For Carteret, proprietary interests and private rights overrode mercantile principles.

Newcastle had considerably more scope for maneuver than his predecessor. He entered the southern department in 1724 with little or no knowledge of American conditions and with no prior commitments. The short-term effect was to bring about a hiatus in the flow of administrative decisions. It was October, 1724, nearly six months after his appointment, before Newcastle fixed a day for

[63] Franklin to Norris, March 19, 1759, Labaree, *Franklin Papers*, VIII, 291-97.

the consideration of West Indian affairs.[64] This temporary loss of continuity and expertise was more than compensated for, however, by the Duke's candid approach to colonial problems, his determination to acquit himself well in his new position, and his willingness to accept expert advice. Indeed, the initial effect of the change in southern secretaries was to increase the administrative leverage of the Board of Trade. When the board learned in August, 1726, that the Duke had obtained an order from the King naming Othniel Haggot to the Council in Barbados, it promptly reminded him that "it has always been esteem'd the Right of this Board to propose the filling of such Vacancies . . . even when the Crown has been disposed so to do. . . ." A few months after receiving this gentle reprimand Newcastle took care to follow the prescribed procedure in an identical case. At his request the board recommended George Lillington to the King for the first vacancy in the Barbados Council.[65] Subsequently the board had no difficulty in maintaining the position of primacy in the nomination of councillors which it had struggled to preserve at the turn of the century.

This was a victory of some magnitude. The right of nomination to the councils in each of the royal provinces in America gave the board a considerable measure of influence. The southern secretary or the Privy Council held the power to dismiss the colonial chief executive; but the board could express its feelings and affect the conduct of business through its recommendations of councillors. The

[64] Lillian Penson, *The Colonial Agents of the West Indies*, London, 1924, 225.

[65] Board to Newcastle, August 31 and December 15, 1726, C.O. 5/4, fol. 103 and C.O. 28/39, fol. 164; Newcastle to Board, December 15, 1726, S.P. 44/125, p. 39; Wheelock to Burrington, August 4, 1730, C.O. 5/308, fol. 18.

board's decisions, moreover, provided a constant indication of the standing of the governor in England. "As the Lords Commers for Trade and Plantations to oblige some friends . . . distinguish Persons, without any information of their Characters from hence . . . ," Governor Portland of Jamaica complained in 1724, "the only influence one can have here, is gone and lost."[66]

The board's successful defense of its right of nomination provided some indication of the balance of power within the administration during Newcastle's first years in office. There was little evidence that the Duke had embarked upon a serious campaign of aggrandizement. Indeed, at this juncture it was more likely that the Board of Trade would attempt to take advantage of Newcastle's inexperience to improve its own position. In 1729, Martin Bladen suggested to the southern secretary that a member of the Board of Trade should be present at all meetings of the Privy Council called to discuss colonial matters. And in the following year, the board itself used the opportunity presented by a request from the House of Lords for a report on the government establishment to voice its dissatisfaction with its minor role in the management of American affairs:

> We take leave to observe, that the Receipts and Payments of Money, either for the Governors or any of His Majesty's Officers in the Plantations, not passing through this Office, we cannot give Your Lordships so particular a State of their respective Establishments as we could wish. . . .[67]

[66] Portland to Newcastle, December 25, 1725, C.O. 137/52, foll. 155-56.

[67] April 7, 1730, C.O. 324/11, pp. 167-235; [Martin Bladen], "For the Settling of Carolina," C.O. 5/4, foll. 159-63.

Whatever the extent of the board's discontent, Newcastle was not to blame. The southern secretary questioned the board's report on the proposed settlement of the island of Tobago, but accepted the recommendations once the advisory body outlined its reasoning.[68] Similarly he endorsed the decision of the board on the long-standing dispute between Wavell Smith and Governor Hart in the Leeward Islands. In 1726, after a lengthy discussion, the board reported its opinion on the right of appointment to the disputed offices. It was, the members of the board claimed, such a complex matter that they looked upon it as "a Controverted Point, which they cannot take upon them[selves] to determine. . . ."[69] Their report suggested that the question be settled in a court of law. Newcastle readily concurred in this decision despite the fact that it removed the controversy from his control. Given his views on patent rights in the colonies and his prior intervention on Smith's behalf, it was unlikely that Carteret would have allowed the problem to be resolved in this way.

The disposition of this case by the new southern secretary was indicative of his equivocal attitude toward patent offices during his first years in office. He did not intervene actively on behalf of any patentee, but neither did he heed the recommendation of the Board of Trade that the patent system be abolished. Gradually, political and personal pressure from those with a financial stake in America pushed the Duke into a position moderately favorable to their interests. On the death in 1729 of William Congreve, the playwright who had been made Secretary of Jamaica for his political services to a past

[68] Newcastle to Board of Trade, March 15, 1728, S.P. 44/125, pp. 206-10.

[69] Newcastle to Hart, November 30, 1726, C.O. 324/35, p. 290.

ministry, Newcastle asked Governor Hunter to assist the deputy of the new secretary. Four years later the southern secretary directed Governor Howe of Barbados to support the incumbent Clerk of the Court of Exchequer against a possible lawsuit from a rival for the post. The Duke advised the Governor to do all in his power to uphold the validity of the patent place and so avoid any "vexatious proceedings" at law.[70] By 1733, Newcastle was not quite as willing as at the beginning of his tenure to relinquish control of the situation and to allow legal proceedings to decide the matter.

If the Duke's actions represented a shift toward the protection of private property, it was strictly a limited one. The note to Hunter on behalf of John Anthony Balaquier, the new Secretary of Jamaica and an official in the southern department, was little more than a perfunctory gesture for a subordinate. The more positive support given to Charles Huggins in Barbados represented only a decision in favor of one of two competing individuals. Up to this point Newcastle had not been called upon to decide a controversy in which there was a conflict between private and public interests.

The southern secretary was confronted with precisely this dilemma in Barbados in 1734. Several patent officers with deputies in the colony protested against the Assembly's action in reducing the fees that could be legally charged and in abolishing certain perquisites authorized only by custom. With the schedule of fees reduced to the level of actual administrative costs, the deputies were finding it difficult to pay the "rent" of their offices to the English patentees. The Duke was therefore approached on their behalf by Colonel John Selwyn, a close associate of

[70] Newcastle to Hunter, February 10, 1729, C.O. 137/53, fol. 116; Newcastle to Howe, May 22, 1733, C.O. 324/36, p. 424.

the King. Writing to Newcastle in July, the Colonel referred to a letter of twenty years before from Secretary Bolingbroke to Governor Lowther of Barbados. "Your Grace will see," Selwyn noted,

> how Yr. Predecessor exerted in favour of the Patentees of that time, & [I] don't doubt but you will be equally concern'd for Yr friends at present . . . who thought they had a good right to such Fees. . . .[71]

This petition placed the southern secretary in a delicate position. It was not merely a question of choosing between rival policies or even simply of reaffirming historical precedent. For any decision meant preferring one set of friends and supporters over another. The movement for the revision of the schedule of fees had been initiated by Governor Howe. It was on his arrival in 1733 that the Council of the island had revived this perennial issue of Barbadan politics; it was Howe, moreover, who had suggested Assembly action when the Council reported that many fees were not established by law.[72] What tied Newcastle's hands was the fact that the Governor had received his post from the Duke in return for his political support in the Nottinghamshire elections. For the southern secretary to repudiate this legislation would be to undermine the position of his own appointee and to oppose the combined will of Council and Assembly.

To accept this regulatory act would be equally difficult. Selwyn would be alienated, so also would the patentees, many of whom were influential in English public life.

[71] Selwyn to Newcastle, July 25, 1734, Add. MSS 33689, fol. 322; Bolingbroke to Lowther, October 19, 1713, C.O. 324/33, pp. 15-16; John H. Jesse, *George Selwyn and His Contemporaries*, London, 1882, I, 1-4, 25.

[72] "Case of Several Patent Officers . . . ," Add. MSS 33689, foll. 326-27.

Three years earlier Thomas and Francis Reynolds, who held the patent for the post of Provost-Marshal, had combined with Collector of the Customs Henry Lascelles to secure the recall of Governor Worsley because of his attempts to curb the excesses of their deputies.[73] Finally, there was the question of the imperial relationship itself. The southern secretary might find himself in the position of having to defend the right of a colonial assembly to regulate patent offices granted under the great seal. Were the colonists to be allowed to thwart the will of the King and his ministers in the provision of lucrative sinecures for English placemen? Questions of high principle were hopelessly intertwined with matters of low politics. In the background but virtually obscured from view was the question of the just and efficient management of the colonial administrative system.

Newcastle's response to this predicament provided a good indication of the vast gulf separating him from Carteret. By the 1730's, the Duke had become too proficient a politician to declare himself on one side or the other by a clear statement of policy. He did not attempt to decide the issue on intellectual or emotional grounds at all. Rather he played for time and position. Initially he sought to diffuse responsibility as widely as possible. In April, 1735, Newcastle secured an order from the Privy Council committee for plantation affairs directing Howe to transmit a list of fees in order that an inquiry might be made by the Board of Trade.[74] This policy of delay yielded

[73] See C.O. 28/45, foll. 87, 165-68. Also Worsley to Newcastle, August 14, 1726, October 16 and December 4, 1727, C.O. 28/44, foll. 377-84, 428-30, 440-45. Worsley's tie to Carteret was one factor in bringing about his recall in 1731: Worsley to Newcastle, October 23, 1727, C.O. 28/44, foll. 434-35.

[74] Newcastle to Howe, April 30, 1735, C.O. 324/36, p. 501; Howe to Newcastle, February 4, 1734, C.O. 28/45, foll. 311-12.

one immediate gain to the southern secretary. Howe's death early in 1735 meant that if the final decision went against the colony, the Duke would not have compromised the position of his own appointee. By keeping his options open, Newcastle had avoided at least one possible embarrassment. Indeed, he managed in the end to circumvent the controversy entirely as the issue died a natural death in committee.[75] High fees and the patent offices remained, but the southern secretary had escaped damaging personal involvement.

Whatever one might think about the intrinsic merit of Newcastle's position, there can be no doubt that he managed a difficult and complicated problem with the finesse of a master politician. The Duke was really not concerned with the substantive aspects of the question at all. He was more intent throughout with the various actors on the scene. The content of the drama interested him only at second remove; it was important only in so far as it affected the various characters, as it checked the power of one or enhanced the position of another. This was not the world of Carteret, the self-conscious statesman with a set of definite principles and prejudices. Nor was it the mental universe of a bureaucrat with a clearly articulated program and a set of regulations for every situation. Rather, it was the flexible, fluctuating, and chaotic cosmos of the politician; the man whose success depends on the

[75] Dotten to Newcastle, April 17 and June 12, 1736, C.O. 28/45, foll. 359-60, 371-87. For earlier complaints about the patent system: Portland to Newcastle, December 30, 1724, C.O. 137/52, foll. 95-102 and Pitt to Newcastle, October 30, 1728, C.O. 37/29, fol. 16. Philip Haffenden, "Colonial Appointments and Patronage under the Duke of Newcastle, 1724-1739," *EHR*, LXXVII (July, 1963), 427-28 attempts to defend the Duke's record with regard to patent offices but his argument is not convincing. See below, chap. 5, note 100.

degree to which issues are obscured and not clarified. To confront a problem directly was to be compelled to decide it. And this could only alienate more people than it pleased. Such a result did not bother Carteret, for he was only concerned with rallying those who were already sympathetic to his views. For Newcastle the tactical situation was very different. His basic aim—more an impulse—was to secure the backing of as many people as possible; the lack of a definite policy was the price to be paid. For the Duke's purposes it was better to slip around an issue, to delay it in committees, to smother it with discussion, and finally to let it decide itself. With Carteret's dismissal as southern secretary in 1724, the clear dark lines of colonial policy and politics were to become a maze of indistinguishable gray in the hands of his successor. If Carteret neglected mercantile principles because of his personal financial interests, Newcastle ignored them because they interfered with his political style.

V

During the years of Newcastle's apprenticeship, Townshend and Walpole used the perquisites of the southern department to maintain the ministry in power, for even the demotion of Carteret did not place the brothers-in-law in a completely secure position. The imminence of a general election and the death of George I raised once again, in 1727, the possibility of a new administration formed from the ranks of the opposition. "Our future Prospect was so delightfull," Lord Boyle wrote to a friend in Virginia,

> that we even despised Ourselves. Each Man had fixed upon a Place of Profit and Honour and was to be awarded according to his great Deserts. Bribery and Corruption were to be destroyed. . . . Foreigners were

> to be banished, and even Scotch-men confined to their own Country. These were the Schemes, these were the Chimeras of our noble true-born Britons. . . . Sir Robert Walpole was to be demolished; the Duke of Newcastle's Head taken off. . . .[76]

It was believed in some quarters that Walpole would lose his place as chief minister to Sir Spencer Compton, "a plodding, heavy fellow, with great application, but no talents," according to Walpole's friend Hervey.[77] There was also a presumption, a correspondent in London informed the Earl of Marchmont, that "my Lord Carteret will be made Secretary of State, in place of Duke of Newcastle, and the latter Lord Lieutenant of Ireland."[78]

In the event, Compton did not move quickly enough to insure his own ascendancy. The intervention of the Queen and the promise of a generous civil list persuaded the King to retain Walpole as his chief minister. Compton was bought off with the lucrative paymastership of the forces and elevation to the peerage as Lord Wilmington.

This allocation of offices by George II was confirmed in the general election of 1727. The control of Parliament combined with the support of the King placed Walpole in a position of complete dominance. "A whole race of Chetwynds, Sir Robert Walpole's declared ill-wishers, were turned out in a lump," Hervey noted in his diary, "and, what was reckoned the strongest demonstration of his power, Lord Berkeley [was] removed from the head of the Admiralty, and Lord Torrington appointed to

[76] Boyle to William Byrd II, September, 1737, E. C. Boyle, ed., *The Orrery Papers*, London, 1903, I, 53-57.

[77] Sedgwick, *Hervey's Memoirs*, I, 30-31; Newcastle to Townshend, June 15, 1727, Add. MSS 32687, fol. 212.

[78] George H. Rose, ed., *Marchmont Correspondence*, London, 1831, II, 413-14; Sedgwick, *Hervey's Memoirs*, III, 446-48.

succeed."[79] With the firm support of King and country Walpole had embarked on a campaign to drive all of the former adherents of Sunderland and Stanhope out of the government. The necessity for the new King to renew the formal authority of all those serving under the aegis of the crown insured that this domestic purge would extend to America. Nor was this blow long in coming. By the end of 1728, five American governments had changed hands.

One of these was Bermuda, where John Hope had served as Governor since 1721. An appointee of Carteret, Hope had maintained a close correspondence with his patron. "This place is no worse than what I expected," he assured the southern secretary in 1723.[80] The Governor's troubles, however, increased in direct proportion to those of his superior. From the beginning of his administration Hope had been engaged in a financial struggle with the Assembly. The undeveloped state of the island meant limited taxable resources and difficulty in funding governmental services. These problems were exacerbated by the demotion of Carteret and by the growing hostility between the Governor and the local merchants. A number of complaints were entered at the Board of Trade, and in August, 1724, Hope wrote directly to Newcastle in an attempt to clear himself of these charges. Noting that it was his "misfortune" not to know the Duke personally, Hope informed the new secretary that he intended to dispatch a personal representative to "clear up my behavior from the malicious aspersions thrown upon me."[81]

[79] Sedgwick, *Hervey's Memoirs*, I, 38-39; Realey, *Early Opposition to Walpole*, 215-25; Plumb, *Walpole*, II, 162-72.

[80] Hope to Carteret, June 25, 1723, C.O. 37/26, foll. 124-26.

[81] Hope to Newcastle, August 19 and 22, 1724, and February 1, 1725, C.O. 37/28, nos. 21, 22, and 26; Hope to Ballequier and

Governor Hope's fears were not groundless: there was a definite possibility that he might be removed. As always, the rate of incoming requests for preferment provided the most sensitive barometer of political vulnerability. Lady Portland heard a rumor in April, 1726, "yt ye Governor of Bermudas was recalled" and asked Newcastle to recommend the eldest son of Lord Berkeley of Stratton, "an unfortunate nephew of mine."[82] The following year Thomas Smith, a merchant to Bermuda and an old associate of Newcastle's uncle and benefactor, petitioned the Duke for the post.[83] Neither of these appeals had much chance of success. A connection with the Pelhams was of little consequence when the southern secretary had so little power. And the solicitation of Lady Portland was even more inappropriate under the circumstances. Her husband had been named to the government of Jamaica in 1721 because of his connection with Stanhope and Sunderland. With this faction out of power, what had once been an asset was now a liability. On the death of Lord Portland in 1726, Walpole and Townshend nominated one of their own associates, former Governor Robert Hunter of New York, as the new chief executive of the island.

It was the acknowledgment by Hunter of the shift in the balance of power within the ministry which insured his success in the struggle for American patronage. A similar perception shaped the political strategy of John Pitt, who replaced Hope in Bermuda when the beleaguered Governor returned to England in 1727 to defend his ad-

---

to Board of Trade, November 23 and 25, 1722, C.O. 37/26, foll. 88-89 and 104-105.

[82] Lady Portland to Newcastle, April 8, 1726, Add. MSS 32687, fol. 190; Berkeley to Stafford, Cartwright, ed., *The Wentworth Papers*, 450.

[83] Smith to Newcastle, September 13, 1727, C.O. 37/28, no. 38.

ministration before the Board of Trade. The new chief executive was a relation of Thomas Pitt, the wealthy East India merchant who controlled the boroughs of Old Sarum and Oakhampton. The elder Pitt had married a daughter to James Stanhope and had supported Sunderland in Parliament. On the latter's death in 1722, Thomas Pitt had considered going into opposition but was dissuaded by the appointment of another of his relatives, George Pitt, to a Treasury post. The death of the elder Pitt in 1726 elicited this new effort by the ministry to retain the loyalty of the family. John, Member of Parliament for Old Sarum since George Pitt had joined the Treasury, accepted the government of Bermuda and, in return, placed the family boroughs at the disposal of the Walpole ministry.[84]

The man behind these maneuvers was Lord Godolphin, himself a one-time Sunderland supporter and Newcastle's father-in-law. With close connections to both factions of the Whig party, Godolphin was the ideal mediator between the Walpole administration and the hesitant Pitts. "My Lord Goodolphin," Pitt stated some years later, was the onely man who procur'd mee this Government. . . .[85] Both parties gained from the bargain. The Pitts had succeeded in retaining their access to ministerial largesse while Walpole had pushed a client of Carteret out

[84] Realey, *Early Opposition to Walpole*, chap. 4. There were three occasions between 1715 and 1740 when Old Sarum was not represented by a member of the Pitt family. In 1716, Thomas Pitt gave up his seat upon appointment to the government of Jamaica; in 1728, two of Pitt's relatives were given governorships; and in 1734, there was another lucrative appointment, this time on the domestic establishment.

[85] Pitt to Charles Cholmunly, October 11, 1729, C.O. 37/29, foll. 31-32; Pitt to Delafaye, April 30, 1729, C.O. 37/29, foll. 21-22.

of office and had seduced a friend of Sunderland with a lucrative position. It was only a matter of time before the entire complexion of the colonial bureaucracy would be changed.

A second American appointment involving the Pitt family contributed to this end. Walpole's preparations for the general election of 1727 resulted in the replacement of John Hart by the Earl of Londonderry as Governor of the Leeward Islands. Hart had served as Governor of Maryland before Carteret nominated him for the West Indian post in 1724, perhaps as a favor to the Calverts, the proprietors of the colony and longtime allies in the battle against reforming bureaucrats of the Board of Trade. Hart, however, was not completely satisfied with his new post. The salary was inadequate, he told Carteret, especially as "no Governour of the Leeward Islands has lived to return to Great Britain for Thirty Three Years past, Mr. Douglas excepted."[86] It was the Governor's concern for his health which prompted him to return to England just as the ministry was preparing for the election and just as Walpole needed a place for Londonderry, the impecunious second son of Thomas Pitt, in order to create a vacancy for a candidate of his own at Old Sarum. Hart was expendable because his patron had fallen from power. Even his close friendship with Martin Bladen, the most influential member of the Board of Trade, was not sufficient to preserve his position.[87] As usual, the prime consideration was not the

[86] December 3, 1723, C.O. 7/1, no. 27; Michael G. Hall, "Some Letters of Benedict Leonard Calvert," *WMQ*, 3rd ser., XVIII (July, 1960), 363n. Carteret had worked closely with Lord Guilford, the legal guardian of the 5th Lord Baltimore, in opposing the Resumption Bill of 1715. See Steele, *Politics of Colonial Policy*, 159-60.

[87] Bladen to Walpole, June 10, 1729, W.C., no. 1619; Hart memorial, no date, C.O. 152/40. Hart eventually received monetary compensation.

performance of the Governor as a colonial administrator but rather the exigencies of domestic politics.

This basic fact was illustrated again in October, 1728, with the appointment of Woodes Rogers as Governor of the Bahama Islands. Rogers replaced George Phenny, yet another Carteret nominee. There was a good deal more than factional politics at stake here, however; considerations of policy as well as patronage were closely bound up with the alteration of governors. The complexity of the Bahamian situation stemmed from the colony's origins as a proprietary venture. As in the case of Carolina, the political influence of the proprietors in England had stifled all attempts to bring the islands under royal control. Carteret was one of the owners; Lord Berkeley, President of the Board of Trade in 1714 and 1715, was another.[88] Indeed, one frustrated reformer had written to Walpole at that time to urge Treasury action without a report from the Board of Trade:

> My Lord Berkeley being a Proprietor of those Islands and at the Lead of the premention'd Commission, it will no ways answer the Present Design which is to bring them under a Royal Protection. . . .[89]

Just as the resumption of Carolina had to wait upon the decline of Carteret, so the fate of the Bahamas depended on Berkeley's removal from the Board of Trade.

Within three years of Berkeley's resignation in 1715, Captain Woodes Rogers successfully petitioned the ministry for permission to make a permanent settlement in the Bahamas. With the assistance of the royal navy Rogers quickly ousted the pirates who had used the deserted islands as a base of operations. At this point Carteret re-

[88] Steele, *Politics of Colonial Policy*, 150.

[89] Philip Horneck to Walpole, no date, W.C., no. 3272.

lieved the naval captain of his position and placed Phenny in his stead. The southern secretary proceeded to keep the development of the island under close personal supervision. In 1723 he secured the appointment of a chief justice and a chaplain. His co-proprietor was equally active. From his new post as First Lord of the Admiralty, Berkeley alerted the ministry to the dangers of increased Spanish naval activity in the area. The culmination of this concern came in 1724, when the proprietors petitioned the King for a new charter. Under the terms of the proposed document the settlement of the islands was to be encouraged and the salaries of five major officials were to be assumed by the Crown.[90]

This calculated attempt to finance a proprietary settlement with public funds lapsed with the ministerial reshuffle of 1724. Three years later, on the eve of Berkeley's dismissal from the Admiralty, Rogers sought to retrieve his old position. Phenny's administration had produced the usual complaints from a dissident faction in the islands, the power of the proprietary clique was on the wane, and, most important, the former naval officer had secured the support of Charles Wager. Wager was an admiral of the fleet and a close political associate of Lord Townshend and Sir Robert Walpole. In August, 1728, Wager urged quick action upon the ministry. "Some determination should be come to, in that affair," the Admiral told Undersecretary of State Charles Delafaye, "that poor Rogers may be out of his pain."[91] Within seventy-two

[90] Carteret to Phenny, May 3, 1723, C.O. 324/34, p. 232; Andrews, *Colonial Period*, IV, 398; Newcastle to Berkeley, July 26, 1725, S.P. 35/37, foll. 91-92; Memorandum, April, 1724, C.O. 23/12, foll. 147-48.

[91] Wager to Delafaye, August 10, 1728, C.O. 23/14, fol. 45; Rogers to Walpole, May 19, 1726, and June 13, 1727, W.C., nos. 1331 and 1435.

hours of this appeal there was a positive response from the government, as Townshend forwarded the papers condemning Phenny's conduct as Governor to the Board of Trade for a report.[92] This was followed in the middle of October with the reappointment of Rogers to the government from which he had been removed seven years before. Wager's intervention had played a key role in this development, but the Admiral's initiative had come in a favorable political climate and had the support of the senior ministers. The new Governor wrote to an English friend in 1730, "I beg you'll be pleas'd to make my Duty acceptable to my Lord Townshend and humble Service to his Excellency Horatio Walpole . . . to own for their great favours & Obligations."[93]

Three threads ran through this and the other appointments made in 1727 and 1728: Newcastle's complete lack of influence in these patronage decisions, the political allegiance of the men displaced, and the decreasing influence of the proprietary faction in the management of American affairs. Within a period of eighteen months, a definite policy of removing the protegés of the Sunderland-Stanhope Whigs from colonial governorships was conceived and implemented. This plan had its genesis in the desire of Townshend and Walpole to strengthen their political coalition for the forthcoming election. The fortuitous death of Portland in 1726 and Hart's illness in the following year presented the brothers-in-law with an opportunity of introducing their supporters into the govern-

[92] Townshend to Board of Trade, August 13, 1728, S.P. 44/125, p. 298.

[93] Rogers to ?, October 11, 1730, C.O. 23/14, foll. 135-36. Rogers promptly hired Wager's secretary as his agent in England. See, in general, Michael Craton, *A History of the Bahamas*, London, 1968, 100-21.

ments of Jamaica and the Leeward Islands.[94] The death of George I and Walpole's victory in the factional struggle which followed removed all need for subtlety and caution. The abrupt dismissals of Hope and Phenny left little doubt as to the direction in which patronage policy was moving. The leading ministers were determined to reduce Carteret and Berkeley to a position of political impotence through a systematic purge of their supporters in the administration.

This strategy was well-appreciated by those Whigs with a non-ministerial allegiance. In 1731, William Byrd of Virginia wrote to Lord Boyle, the son-in-law of the governor of the colony, to suggest that Boyle persuade the aging Earl of Orkney "to make over his Government of Virginia to you in his Life-time . . . least if he should dye in possession of it, it might drop into other hands and be lost." Byrd's analysis was an astute one. Henry Worsley, another Carteret appointee, had just been removed as Governor of Barbados to make way for a political associate of Walpole.[95] And when Orkney died in 1737, the Virginia post was bestowed on Lord Albemarle, a close personal friend of the Duke of Newcastle.

The shifts in the balance of power within the government in 1724 and 1727 meant that the old friends of Stanhope and Sunderland could prosper only if they were willing, like the Pitts, to switch their fealty to Walpole. If they continued their allegiance to Carteret and Berkeley, they could expect no favors from the ministry. As Henry Pelham put it some twenty years later when he had succeeded Sir Robert as chief minister, "we are none

[94] Hunter to Walpole, July 20, 1727, W.C., no. 1449.

[95] Byrd hoped to become deputy governor: Boyle, ed., *Orrery Papers*, I, 88-90; Newcastle to Worsley, May 14, 1731, C.O. 324/36, p. 270.

of us in places for life, the best thing we can do is therefore to serve our friends whilst we are able."[96] The younger Pelham had the advantage of good teachers. In less than two years Townshend and Walpole had placed the majority of the governments in the West Indies in the hands of their adherents.

This initiative on the part of the brothers-in-law had one result which they had not intended and of which they were probably not aware. After the events of 1727 there was a real possibility of a major reform in the colonial system for the first time since the last decade of the seventeenth century. Between 1696 and 1701, the royal servants who dominated the new Board of Trade had campaigned actively for the resumption by the Crown of the proprietary and charter colonies in America. With the failure in 1701 of its bill for "Reunion with the Crown," the advisory body lost its initial crusading zeal, though it did proceed to introduce similar measures into Parliament in 1702 and 1706.[97] By the end of the reign of Queen Anne, the proprietors had amassed enough support among both Whig and Tory Members of Parliament to safeguard their political and economic privileges in the colonies. Indeed, with Lord Berkeley, himself a part-owner of the Bahama Islands, at the head of the Board of Trade, the proprietary interest had seized the initiative. The board did not use its influence at the Treasury in 1713 when William Penn tentatively offered to sell his colony to the Crown.[98] Two years later, the advisory body did not protest when the ministry returned Maryland to the Calverts; nor did it advocate resumption of Carolina when that colony was

[96] Pelham to Trevor, August 12/23, 1746, Trevor MSS, H.M.C., *Fourteenth Report*, pt. IX, 149.

[97] Steele, *Politics of Colonial Policy*, 71-81.

[98] Ibid., 159-60; Hall, "Calvert Letters," 358-70.

ravaged by Indian attacks in the same year.[99] And when a general resumption bill did grow out of a petition from the settlers in Carolina, Lord Guilford, President of the Board of Trade in 1712 and 1713, joined Carteret in opposing it. At a crucial moment in its history the board had been infiltrated and rendered politically impotent by its old enemies.[100]

As in the past, the resumption legislation of 1715 failed for lack of parliamentary support. The proprietors were able to win the interest of some Whigs because of the proposed bill's threat to property rights and because of widespread fears as to the extension of the fiscal and patronage powers of the Crown. They were also able to influence Tory elements in the legislature by drawing attention to the implications of parliamentary abrogation of royal charters.[101] The resulting political phalanx, composed of members of normally disparate factions, easily resisted the assaults of the reforming bureaucrats on the Board of Trade and their few supporters in Parliament.

It was this proprietary alliance which had disintegrated during the 1720's. As Walpole removed first Carteret and then Berkeley from major office, the spectrum of alternative colonial policies lengthened considerably. The rights of private and corporate property in America would no longer be prized quite so highly by those in positions of high authority. The Board of Trade, increasingly staffed

[99] Clark, *Rise of the Treasury*, 55; Andrews, *Colonial Period*, IV, 395-96.

[100] This interpretation goes beyond that offered by Steele, *Politics of Colonial Policy*, 150 and 160, but his evidence would seem to confirm it.

[101] This argument follows that of Steele, *Politics of Colonial Policy*, 60-61, 72-79 and of Alison Gilbert Olsen, "William Penn, Parliament, and Proprietary Government," *WMQ*, 3rd ser., XVIII (April, 1961), 176-95.

by associates of Walpole and Newcastle, was now presented with an opportunity to implement some of the proposals outlined in the abortive report of 1721. Moreover, with Newcastle rather than Carteret at the head of the southern department, there was some possibility that the advice of the advisory body would be heeded and acted upon. There were still substantial problems of financial stringency, parliamentary ignorance, and administrative inertia to be overcome. But for the first time in more than a generation the political climate and the structure of authority within the ministry were propitious for such an initiative.

CHAPTER 2

The Movement for Reform

THE single serious and sustained attempt to alter the character of the colonial administrative system during the first half of the eighteenth century took place in the half-dozen years between the accession of George II in 1727 and the passage of the Molasses Act in 1733. The timing of this movement was determined by a variety of bureaucratic and imperial considerations, but the central factor was the hegemony of Sir Robert Walpole in English political life. The period just previous to the failure of the Excise Bill marked the apogee of Walpole's power. The implications of this predominance for American affairs were considerable. For this was the one time during the Walpole era in which colonial problems were neither ignored because of domestic political strife nor subordinated to foreign policy or military strategy. The time had come when the English political nation could begin to fashion a new imperial relationship.

One of the prerequisites for a strengthening of the old administrative system was the concentration of authority over American affairs in the hands of a single official or body. In the late 1720's there was an abundance of candidates. Under the direction of the Earl of Westmoreland the Board of Trade had revived the movement to resume the charter and proprietary colonies to the control of the Crown. At the same time the new southern secretary and the Privy Council committee on plantation affairs took the lead in attempting to enforce stricter financial control of the possessions in the western hemisphere. Underlying both of these initiatives was the increasingly active role played by Parliament in the consideration and determination of colonial policy.

Indeed, it was the possibility of extensive parliamentary intervention in American affairs which determined the character of this reform movement and differentiated it from its predecessors. Previously reformers had looked for inspiration to the Stuarts and their program of royal control of the colonial empire; now enterprising administrators began to glance in the direction of Parliament as they pondered the feasibility of change. The model was no longer the Dominion of New England. Rather, a transition had begun which would eventually lead to the spectacle of George III championing the supremacy of the home legislature over his American subjects. Not surprisingly, events in Massachusetts Bay mirrored the changing reality of the colonial relationship. In 1726 George I granted an "Explanatory Charter" to the colony. Less than three years later the ministry was threatening parliamentary abrogation of all charter rights and privileges because of the refusal of the Assembly to grant a permanent salary to the royal governor.

I

Immediately upon entering the southern department in 1724 Newcastle ordered the Board of Trade to make a report on the Massachusetts Bay controversy before taking up any other business.[1] Since 1722 Governor Shute had been in England presenting his case for charter revision and a fixed salary to the Board of Trade and the various members of the Privy Council. All the while the Governor had to fend off countercharges leveled by the agents of the Assembly. Shute made little progress initially,

[1] Newcastle to Board of Trade, April 25, and October 29, 1724, S.P. 44/123, p. 330 and S.P. 44/124, p. 71.

perhaps because of the informal assistance given the Massachusetts agents by Secretary of State Carteret.[2] It was only after the Carolina proprietor was transferred to Ireland that the Governor succeeded in any part of his task. In July, 1725, the Privy Council finally approved an explanatory charter for Massachusetts Bay. This document clarified a number of obscure points in the original charter granted by William III and, in general, upheld the position assumed by the Governor in his battle with the Assembly. The Privy Council sustained Shute's claim of full authority over military affairs and also his power to regulate the adjournment proceedings and the meeting place of the general court. The lords of the council also felt that the Governor had made good his charge that the assembly had encroached upon the prerogatives of the chief executive and of the Crown. The new charter was intended to bring this illegal aggrandizement to an end.[3]

If Shute could rejoice that the House of Representatives had received its due, he could not say the same for himself. Up to this point no action had been taken on his claim for a fixed salary and for the arrears which had accumulated during his long absence from America. The Governor proceeded therefore to petition the King to enjoin the colony to establish a permanent salary for its governor to be paid out of the provincial exchequer.[4] Before

[2] Carteret to Attorney-General, February 22, 1724, S.P. 44/123, p. 290; Henry Russell Spencer, *Constitutional Conflict in Provincial Massachusetts . . .*, Columbus, Ohio, 1905, 79; but see also Carteret to Board of Trade, March 11, 1724, S.P. 44/123, p. 304.

[3] Orders in Council, June 1 and July 20, 1725, C.O. 5/869, foll. 206-10; Dummer to Newcastle, January 8, 1726, C.O. 5/898, fol. 165.

[4] March 4, 1725, C.O. 5/869, fol. 220; Memorial, no date, W.P., vol. 84, no. 50/1.

the resulting controversy was over the Assembly of Massachusetts Bay, which had only grudgingly accepted the restrictive charter of 1726, refused flatly to comply with instructions issued by the King in Council.

That the issue ever reached such a high degree of definition was remarkable in itself. The first response of the Board of Trade to Shute's appeal amounted to an abject capitulation to the colonial legislature. Reporting to the committee of council on March 30, 1726, the board recommended that the Governor be paid from England "till such time as the People of New England can be brought to a better Temper of Mind and induced to make a Suitable fixed and perpetual Provision for His Majesty's Governors of that Province."[5] The advisory body seemed more disillusioned than cheered by its recent success in writing an explanatory charter. It could offer no method of insuring the financial freedom of the Governor without a drain on the English exchequer.

This proposal of the Board of Trade was not likely to appeal to the Treasury. In 1714, Lord High Treasurer Godolphin had directed the advisory body to report "how the Affairs of her Majesty's Several Plantations may be put into Such a Method as to be able by ways and means among themselves to Support the whole charge of their Government. . . ."[6] This clearly defined policy had been faithfully pursued by Godolphin's successors. Sir Robert Walpole was no exception; if anything, his administration of the nation's financial resources had been more rigorous than that of his predecessors. In his first years at the Treasury Board Walpole had refused to complete the purchase of Pennsylvania, partly because of the cost in-

[5] March 30, 1726, C.O. 5/915, pp. 450-52.

[6] Board of Trade to W. Lowndes, February 4, 1714, C.O. 324/10, p. 39.

volved; and in 1721 he vetoed the creation of a new post of comptroller of the woods in New England on the same grounds.[7] It was not surprising, therefore, that as soon as the board's recommendation came to the attention of the chief minister and his associates it was decisively rejected. On June 21, 1726, the Privy Council committee on plantation affairs returned the report to the board and enjoined it to find the most effectual means of inducing the legislatures of New Hampshire and Massachusetts Bay to provide a fixed salary for their governors.[8]

This directive brought into the open the different conceptions of imperial responsibility held by the various agencies concerned with the formulation of colonial policy. The traditional position of the Treasury was one of strict financial accountability. The colonies should pay the cost of imperial administration; they should also provide a surplus out of their revenue for the use of the home government. The emphasis in the Treasury was on the colonies as potential assets on the ledger of national income; the revenue to the Crown accruing from the American account would be used to offset domestic liabilities.

The Board of Trade took a somewhat different position. From its perspective, the creation of an effective administrative system occupied the highest priority and far outweighed the expense involved. In the board's view the additional expenditure on colonial administration would

[7] Clark, *Rise of the Treasury*, 55. Shute had won the support of Lord Barrington, his brother-in-law and a junior Lord of the Treasury, for his own appointment to the new post of comptroller in order to bolster his salary. The plan was approved by several ministers and perhaps even by the King before being vetoed by Walpole: Shute to Walpole, no date, W.C., no. 1156; Craggs to Barrington, August 16, 1720, W.C., no. 806; Board of Trade to Treasury, May 10, 1722, C.O. 324/10, p. 500.

[8] Board of Trade Report, July 28, 1726, C.O. 5/915, pp. 458-61.

be minuscule compared to the benefits received from American trade. The advisory body felt it was far better to forgo the ideal of a self-financing colonial system if the plantations could be more efficiently and more closely governed by officials paid from England. This view fitted in perfectly with the board's interpretation of mercantilist principles. The colonies were dependent and inferior parts of the empire. As such they should receive the benefits of military defense, economic preference, and just government; and, in return, they should be prepared to submit to the enlightened dictates of the home authorities. For the members of the Board of Trade the firm political control of the colonies had a much higher priority than the doctrines of fiscal responsibility propounded by the bureaucrats at the Treasury.

During the first three decades of the eighteenth century the leading ministers of the English government had incorporated certain aspects of these two programs of financial accountability and administrative control into an ill-defined imperial policy which was based in the first instance on the realities of domestic and of international politics. The various sections of the bureaucracy could hope for ministerial support only if their measures coincided with wider national objectives, received support from a powerful interest group outside the government, or did not endanger domestic political stability.

This haphazard and amorphous approach to colonial problems, a conspicuous feature of imperial administration since 1689, blended perfectly with the political style and goals of Sir Robert Walpole. While he was building a stable parliamentary majority through the lavish use of patronage, Walpole sought to avoid contentious issues which would split the country on ideological grounds or engender the determined opposition of established interest groups. This cautious politics of compromise and accommodation served to protect the colonists from restrictive parliamentary legislation and from the full imposition of the bureaucratic and financial control proposed by the royal bureaucracy. As long as imperial trade worked to increase domestic commercial prosperity, Walpole was content to let the settlers in America govern themselves.

By the late 1720's, however, there were definite signs that this period of ministerial indifference was coming to an end. The increasing affluence of the nation after a decade and a half of peace encouraged the chief minister to implement some of the mercantilist policies outlined by the Board of Trade. In 1728, Walpole agreed to underwrite the cost of bringing the Carolinas under royal control, a clear reversal of the Pennsylvania precedent of 1713.[9] He also sanctioned the use of Crown revenue from the quit rents in North Carolina for the local civil list and the diversion of income from other royal duties for the payment of a limited number of colonial officials.[10] Subsequently, it was his insistence that the governor of the newly-subsidized colony of Georgia be directly accountable to the ministry which was an important factor in deterring the trustees of the colony from ever appointing a chief executive.[11] Previously the policy of the Treasury had been to give the colonists control over their own administration by placing financial responsibility in their hands. Now the ministry was beginning to use economic weapons to persuade the assemblies and the proprietors to do as it wished.

[9] Clark, *Rise of the Treasury*, 50.

[10] Ibid., 66; Greene, *Quest for Power*, 142.

[11] Trevor R. Reese, *Colonial Georgia; A Study in British Imperial Policy in the Eighteenth Century*, Athens, Ga., 1963, 19.

In addition to these financial inducements for the improvement of colonial administration and the development of central control, Walpole supported other policies which were consistent with a liberal mercantilist system. Subsidies designed to promote the production of naval stores continued to be paid by the Treasury, and the colonies were given special exporting privileges in lumber and other products. In the mid-1730's, the chief minister backed the strong defense of the Board of Trade of these preferential policies against the attack of vested interests in England.[12] In this instance, as indeed in the case of the parliamentary subsidy granted to the new colony of Georgia, Walpole was influenced partly by considerations of military advantage and diplomatic strategy. American naval stores would decrease English dependence on the traditional sources of supply in the Baltic countries, just as the new frontier settlement would counteract increased Spanish activity in Florida.

Nevertheless, the ministry was still unwilling to accept unconditional responsibility for the military defense of the American dependencies. The Treasury underwrote the cost of the various independent companies stationed in the colonies, but when Jamaica sought assistance against a possible Spanish attack in 1729 Newcastle reminded Governor Hunter of the government's traditional position that "His Majesty's Plantations abroad are . . . to provide themselves with such Necessarys for their Defense."[13] This

[12] Clark, *Rise of the Treasury*, 48-49; Board of Trade Report, January 23, 1734, Add. MSS 33028, foll. 246-47. Plumb, *Walpole*, II, 235-36, 241, and 268, notes Walpole's dislike of many English commercial groups.

[13] June 17, 1729, C.O. 137/53, foll. 162-63. War preparations had just raised the land tax to four shillings in the pound; Wal-

ambivalent policy continued in the following decade when the ministry dispatched regular troops to suppress a slave revolt in Jamaica only to withdraw them when the local Assembly refused to defray the cost.[14]

The lines were even less clearly drawn with regard to Treasury subsidies for day-to-day colonial administration. The danger of French or Spanish expansion might justify the quashing of a slave uprising in the valuable sugar islands or the assumption of the Carolinas and the founding of Georgia, but it was not obvious that the political and administrative encroachments of the American legislatures constituted a threat of the same kind or magnitude. The ambiguity of the internal colonial situation was an important deterrent to a consistent ministerial policy. So also was the lack of an immediate threat to the continuance of English rule. When such a danger existed, the ministry had not been slow to act. In the aftermath of Leisler's revolt in New York in 1689, an event which seemed to represent a definite threat to the colonial system, the home government had stepped in to defray the cost of the legal system of the colony. For over twenty-five years the salary of the attorney-general of New York was defrayed by the quit rents of the Crown.[15]

---

pole reduced this to one shilling in 1730 to relieve the burden on the landed gentry, the group with which he identified most. See Plumb, *Walpole*, II, 186-87, 239.

[14] Abstract of letters on Jamaica, 1731-34, C.O. 137/55, foll. 25-40; Privy Council Report, June 10, 1735, C.O. 5/36, foll. 36-40. Shy, *Toward Lexington*, 29-31, offers an overview of military policy during this period.

[15] The Treasury cut off Richard Bradley's salary in 1724, leaving him at the mercy of the Assembly; political influence rather than "national policy" won the restoration of Treasury support in 1733. Bradley to Montgomery, November 9, 1728, C.O. 5/1086, foll.

With the establishment of internal peace in the colonies, the ministry lost its interest in the provision of efficient administration. It was this unwillingness to expend English resources in America which had prompted the Privy Council committee for plantation affairs to reject the Board of Trade's proposal that home government defray the cost of Governor Shute's salary. On July 28, 1726, the advisory body affirmed that it was "just and reasonable" that the colonists support their own governor. The board now maintained that it was imperative for the preservation of the authority of the Crown that Shute be sent back to New England with a royal letter commanding the payment of the salary. Even then, the commissioners of trade warned, "it is doubtful whether the People of New England will pay a ready obedience to his Majty's Order." In that eventuality the advisory body could only echo the suggestion of the governor that the matter be laid before Parliament.[16]

It was precisely this bold course of action which was endorsed by the ministry. On March 28, 1727, the King in Council accepted a report of the Privy Council committee for plantation affairs which called for the dispatch of a letter under the royal sign manual warning the Assembly of the consequences of further defiance. If the House of Representatives disregarded the personal directive of the King to establish a permanent salary of £1,000 sterling, the committee suggested

1-2; Bishop of Durham to Newcastle, March 11 and June 19, 1725, January 31, 1730, and November 16, 1732, C.O. 5/1092, fol. 170, C.O. 5/1085, fol. 210, S.P. 36/17, fol. 51, and C.O. 5/1086, foll. 56-59; Newcastle to Treasury, February 22, 1732, S.P. 44/128, pp. 1-4; Bradley to Newcastle, October 5, 1733, C.O. 5/1093, fol. 288.

[16] Report, July 28, 1726, C.O. 5/915, pp. 458-61.

> that it may be worth the Consideration of the Legislature, in what manner the Honour and Dignity of your Majesty's Government ought to be supported in these provinces for the future.[17]

With this recommendation the chasm between the broad generalities of mercantilist principles and the specific requirements of administrative practice had been bridged. The Governor, supported initially by economy-minded members of the Privy Council and belatedly by the Board of Trade, had secured the promise of national backing for his salary demands. All that needed to be done now was for Shute to initiate the confrontation between the ministry and the Assembly by the presentation of the King's letter.

II

Before the Governor could return to America he was superseded in his post by William Burnet, the Governor of New York and New Jersey. This was not part of a carefully calculated plan to enforce the newly enunciated administrative policy. Rather, it was another by-product of the accession of George II to the throne in June, 1727. Burnet was removed from his position in New York to make way for Colonel John Montgomery, an old associate of the new King.[18] It was only by use of personal interest himself that the son of the famous Bishop of Salisbury was able to secure a partial reprieve. Cadwallader Colden later recounted the story:

[17] Report, C.O. 5/869, foll. 377-78.

[18] William Smith, *History of New York . . . With a Continuation . . .* , Albany, 1814, 272; "The Colden Letters on Smith's History, 1759-1760," NYHS, *Collections*, I, 217; Plumb, *Walpole*, II, 169-70.

> Mr. Burnet's friends at court obtained an audience of the Queen in hopes by her influence to divert the King from removing Mr. Burnet. The queen answered . . . that the King was very sensible of Mr. Burnet's merit . . . that the people of New England were a troublesom people and therefor the King thought it necessary to appoint a Gentleman of Mr. Burnet's abilities governor of that colony of Massachusetts Bay.[19]

This was mere rationalization. The removal of Shute at this junction was no less than the destruction of policy by patronage. As the Board of Trade had declared over a year before, "it is highly necessary for His Majty's Service that Colo. Shute . . . should be sent back again in the Quality of Govr to that Province, that the People of New England may see that His Majty will support His faithful Servants in the Discharge of their Duty."[20] In the event, the King's service had been jeopardized by the action of the monarch himself.

By this time, however, the salary issue was clearly joined. Moreover, the precarious financial position of the new Governor insured that the momentum of reform would be maintained. With Burnet as with Shute, self-interest coincided with the national interest. When the Governor's instructions were being prepared by the Board of Trade, Burnet's brother petitioned the ministry for a fixed stipend of £2,000 sterling, double the amount requested by Shute. Further, Thomas Burnet suggested that "an Independent Company be sent thither under him

[19] NYHS, *Collections*, I, 218-19. Burnet had been Comptroller of the Customs, an English patent post worth £1,200 per annum, until 1720, when he exchanged posts with Governor Robert Hunter. See ibid., I, 205.

[20] Report, July 28, 1726, C.O. 5/915, pp. 458-61.

as Captain to take possession of the Fort, which will be the only means to bring these people to have a respect for the Government. . . ."[21] Forty years were to elapse before English regulars were dispatched to Massachusetts Bay to coerce the colonists into obedience. In 1728, Burnet was given an additional instruction in lieu of a military force. Still, armed with this royal mandate and backed by the force of ministerial opinion, Burnet was set to mount a strong attack against the independence of the New England colony.

The new Governor was no more successful than his predecessors. In September, 1728, he reported to Newcastle that he had met with the Assembly on July 24 "and have been sitting with them ever since . . . ," but all to no avail. In October, Burnet adjourned the general court to Salem to deprive the hostile townspeople of Boston of business and to prevent them from turning the opinions of the country representatives against the salary grant. At the same time the Governor urged Newcastle to send "decisive commands" by the first vessel leaving England in the spring. Personal experience with the stubborn colonists had shattered Burnet's hopes of an "easy" administration; he now believed parliamentary action was necessary to achieve an acceptable solution.[22]

The possibility of such radical action depended upon the sentiments of those in London. The Board of Trade had long recommended such intervention but had been unable to win the active political support of the senior members of the ministry. As Martin Bladen remarked: "the Justice, the Reason, and the Utility of a Proposition, are not al-

[21] "Memo," no date, C.O. 5/1092, fol. 339. Internal evidence suggests that Thomas Burnet was the author.

[22] Burnet to Newcastle, September 13 and October 26, 1728, C.O. 5/898, foll. 230-33.

ways sufficient to carry it through."[23] Now, however, there was the possibility that the pleas of the advisory body would be heeded by the chief ministers.

The key figure was the new Secretary of State. Since his appointment in 1724, Newcastle had devoted considerable time and energy to colonial problems.[24] In addition to supervising the administrative routine of the southern department, the Duke took a close interest in developments in America. When the Jamaica Assembly passed a new twenty-one-year revenue measure in 1728, Newcastle wrote personally to Governor Hunter to congratulate him on this success.[25] Two years earlier, the southern secretary had reproached Governor Hart of the Leeward Islands for requiring his lieutenant-governor to reside at the capital, to the neglect of his plantation. "You are certainly the best Judge . . . that an Officer under you should reside in one Island rather than another . . . ," Newcastle advised Hart in July, 1726,

> but as you reside your self at present at St. Christophers, it does not seem necessary, that Col. Matthew should be there at the same time. . . .[26]

[23] Jack P. Greene, "Martin Bladen's Blueprint for a Colonial Union," *WMQ*, 3rd ser., XVII (October, 1960), 523.

[24] Newcastle's letter books for the period 1726-32 (S.P. 44/125-27) are full of references to American and West Indian affairs. The book for the years 1724-26 (S.P. 44/124) contains less colonial material, but still more than those of his predecessors in the southern department (S.P. 44/97-123). Haffenden, "Colonial Appointments," 420n., mentions the Duke's regular attendance at the Privy Council committee for plantation affairs.

[25] Newcastle to Hunter (draft), December, 1728, C.O. 137/53, foll. 94-96; Newcastle to Board of Trade, July 1, 1724, S.P. 44/124, p. 30.

[26] C.O. 324/35, p. 249.

An even more careful and significant scrutiny of the conduct of a subordinate had been made by the southern secretary in 1725. In a long letter to Governor Burnet of New York, the Duke apprised him of royal approval for two controversial appointments and then proceeded to extend a word of caution. "I must in a very earnest manner recommend it to you," Newcastle declared,

> to be carefull in the choice of Persons, in whose favour you apply, that they be well qualified for the Employments for which you design them, and Gentlemen, who by their personal Interest in the Country where they reside may contribute to the Support of His Majty's Authority. . . .[27]

It was, therefore, not without reason that the Board of Trade was optimistic of ministerial support in its campaign against the assembly of Massachusetts Bay. Newcastle's first years in office gave no indication that he intended to let the empire run itself. And this impression seemed to be confirmed by recent events. In October, 1727, the southern secretary drew the attention of the Board of Trade to a complaint lodged against the Assembly of Barbados by Governor Worsley. The irregular practices of the Assembly, the Duke noted, "he represents to be in a like manner with what was lately practised by the House of Representatives in New England & as tending to encroach upon His Majty's Prerogative." Newcastle requested a quick report from the advisory body "that there may be no time lost in sending proper Instructions to the Governor."[28] In the following year the southern secretary again pointed to the inter-colonial ramifications of the con-

[27] June 3, 1725, C.O. 324/35, pp. 145-50.

[28] Newcastle to Board of Trade, October 24, 1727, S.P. 44/125, pp. 178-79.

troversy in Massachusetts Bay while denying permission to Deputy-Governor Gooch to accept a monetary "gift" from the Virginia Assembly in lieu of an increase in salary. "There is so clear and explicite an Article of your Instructions in that behalf . . . ," the southern secretary reminded Gooch, that "His Majty can by no means consent. . . . If it could be dispensed with in your Case, it would be a very ill Precedent for others. . . ."[29]

There was little doubt whom the Duke had in mind. The intransigence of the Assembly of Massachusetts Bay had become his prime colonial concern. Immediately upon receiving Burnet's report of continued failure, Newcastle wrote in his own hand to the Board of Trade to condemn the "irregular and undutiful behaviour of the Assembly." He ordered the advisory body to deliver within a fortnight its opinion of "what may be the most proper Expedient for Supporting His Majty's Authority in that Province."[30]

Enforcement was indeed the crux of the matter. Over the years this problem had defied the ingenuity and sapped the will of the Board of Trade. The colonial bureaucrats were no closer to a solution in 1729 than they had been a generation before or were to be forty years hence. As Alexander Spotswood, the former Deputy-Governor of Virginia, explained to William Byrd at the time:

[29] December, 1728, C.O. 5/1137, foll. 126-27. The concern with precedent was reciprocal. William Byrd II advised the Earl of Orrery on February 3, 1728, that "We never compliment with one Penny more than their established Income. We dare not be generous to those who are Good, for fear of setting a Precedent for those who are bad. Most of the colonies have been imprudent this way." Boyle, *Orrery Papers*, I, 57-59.

[30] January 29, 1729, C.O. 5/870, foll. 152-53. It was very unusual for Newcastle to write in his own hand to administrative officials.

> if the Assembly in New England would stand Bluff, he did not see how they cou'd be forct to raise Money against their Will, for if they shou'd direct it to be done by Act of Parliament, which they have threatened to do, (though it be against the Right of Englishmen to be taxt, but by their Representatives), yet they wou'd find it no easy matter to put such an Act in Execution.[31]

It was a similar perception of the situation which determined the tone of the Board of Trade's response to Newcastle's request. While reiterating its position that full compliance would be guaranteed only by recourse to Parliament, the advisory body suggested that Burnet should not demand a permanent establishment but one limited to his own time in office. This conciliatory proposal was designed to make ministerial policy more palatable to the Assembly while insuring the financial independence of the Governor. As in 1726, the board was attempting to resolve the dispute without forcing an all-out confrontation between the home government and the House of Representatives. Political realism overrode the opinions of those who wished to provoke a final showdown.[32]

The strategy propounded by the majority of the members of the advisory body was accepted by the Privy Council. There were advocates of a coercive policy in the higher body as well as on the Board of Trade. Already these councillors had designated the committee for plantation affairs with the temporary title of the "Committee for

[31] Quoted in Edmund S. and Helen M. Morgan, *The Stamp Act Crisis; Prologue to Revolution*, rev. ed., New York, 1963, 16.

[32] Report, March 27, 1729, C.O. 5/916, pp. 184-89. The board consciously disregarded Burnet's letter advocating immediate submission to Parliament: Burnet to Board of Trade, January 24, 1729, C.O. 5/870, foll. 195-97.

laying before Parliamt the Proceedings of the Assembly. . . ."[33] Still, there was a conspicuous lack of unity within the ministry on this issue; Colden wrote to his old friend Burnet from his vantage point in New York that

> Your Excys Friends are truely under some concern because they Apprehend that you have gone so far that you must go on & that you have no back game to play . . . some who are supposed to know the Temper of the Ministry say that they will be backward in espousing any thing that looks like forceing in the giveing of Money. . . .[34]

At this point those councillors advocating a tough policy still had the upper hand. On April 22, 1729, the committee of the Privy Council proposed that "this whole matter . . . be laid before the Parliament of Great Britain." This recommendation was accepted a month later by the Queen in Council. It was commonly believed in London, a correspondent wrote to Colden, "there will be no fixed determination untill [the] next Ses[sion] of [the] Brit. Parl."[35]

The independent existence of the colony of Massachusetts Bay, partially undermined by the charters of 1692 and 1726, was once again in jeopardy. This was clearly recognized by the agents of the colony in London, Francis Wilks and Jonathan Belcher. In a printed letter to the Speaker of the House of Representatives, the agents re-

[33] April 22, 1729, P.C. 2/90, p. 484; W. L. Grant and J. Munro, eds., *Acts of the Privy Council, Colonial Series*, London, 1910, II, 108-11.

[34] November 29, 1728, NYHS, *Collections*, L, 273-74.

[35] Grant and Munro, *Acts*, II, 108-11; W. Douglass to Colden, July 14, 1729, NYHS, *Collections*, L, 388.

counted the dismal proceedings and the discouraging prospects. Yet, in the end, they counseled defiance rather than despair:

> If we must be finally compelled to a fixt Salary, [the agents argued,] doubtless it must be better that it be done by the Supream Legislature than to do it our Selves: if our Liberties must be lost, much better they should be taken away, than we be in any measure accessory to our own Ruin.[36]

There was a streak of the dissenting temperament in this advice. There was also, perhaps, a shrewd calculation that the ministry would not ask a Whig parliament to force a representative body to grant money without its consent. As Spotswood and Colden had noted, such action would raise constitutional questions of the first magnitude. There was a vital political issue at stake as well. The control by the House of Commons of the financial affairs of the nation was not yet assured. And the similarity between the Commons' battle with the monarch for the control of taxation and the Assembly's struggle with the King's representative was too obvious to be overlooked. Whatever the reasoning, the stand taken by Wilks and Belcher was decisive. Burnet reported to the Board of Trade that the colonists "seem to acquiesce in their Agents opinion, to Stand it out in Parliament."[37]

This decision by the Assembly of Massachusetts Bay played into the hands of the reform-minded members of the Board of Trade. In a long memorandum on colonial affairs composed for Newcastle's guidance in the autumn

[36] London, April 25, 1729, C.O. 5/898, fol. 278.

[37] July 19, 1729, C.O. 5/870, foll. 269-70. The Governor had already requested the dispatch of two independent companies (March 31, 1729, C.O. 5/870, foll. 224-25).

of 1729, Martin Bladen argued forcefully that the New England legislature was determined not to accept the compromise settlement proposed by the ministry. He urged the southern secretary to direct the lords of trade to collect evidence of the past insubordination of the colony in order that a complete case would be ready for transmission to Parliament. Bladen's final judgment, less an analysis of the present impasse than the expression of a long-contemplated verdict, was that "Nothing can Effectually cure these Evils but the Repeal of their Charter, and the providing some other way a Salary for their Governor."[38]

The proposal for a salary paid from the English exchequer had been advanced, probably on Bladen's initiative, by the Board of Trade in 1726 only to be rejected by the committee of the Privy Council for plantation affairs. Now it was coupled with a provision, virtually unthinkable three years before, calling for the end of charter government in Massachusetts Bay. The stakes of the contest had changed. The salary question had become inextricably intertwined with the larger issue of the reconstitution of the colonial empire on rational principles. Within the space of a few years diverse disputes had coalesced into one. It was suddenly obvious that all American problems were related in some way to the strength of royal authority in the colonies. Lord Townshend had commented as early as 1725 that the controversy was one "wherein the prerogative of the Crown & the Interest of this Kingdom are much concerned."[39] With the attention of the ministry fastened on the western hemisphere, a far-reaching reform of the colonial system, once a remote contingency, now seemed a distinct possibility.

[38] "For the Settling of Carolina," September 27, 1729, C.O. 5/4, foll. 159-63.

[39] Townshend to Cracherode, May 4, 1725, S.P. 44/122, p. 283.

Enthusiasm for change was strongest in the lower ranks of the colonial bureaucracy. "The Lords of Trade," Richard Partridge warned the Governor of Rhode Island in 1732, ". . . are glad of any opportunity to lay hold of an advantage against the Charter Governments that if possible they may be resumed to the Crown."[40] During the first two decades of its existence the board had failed repeatedly in its frontal assaults on the charter and proprietary interest. Beginning in the 1720's, a new type of strategy gradually began to evolve. In 1726 Martin Bladen wrote to Lord Townshend of a plan which would accomplish the desired end "without Injustice to the present Proprietors." And in the following year the Earl of Westmoreland, President of the Board of Trade, could claim the support of "all the Kings Ministers & Council" for a scheme to bring all the American plantations under a common type of government reserving "only the Property of the Soile to the Proprietors thereof."[41] No longer would there be a general attack on corporate "rights." Rather, the charter and proprietary colonies would be resumed one by one as their owners encountered financial difficulties or as their assemblies ran afoul of imperial administrators.

By 1729 the Carolinas had already succumbed, and there was a possibility that one or more of the New England governments would follow shortly. When Connecticut sought parliamentary relief following the invalidation of its intestate law by the House of Lords, the Board of

[40] Partridge to Wanton, July 10, 1732, Gertrude S. Kimball, ed., *The Correspondence of the Colonial Governors of Rhode Island, 1723-1775*, Providence, 1903, I, 30-31.

[41] Bladen to Townshend, July 5, 1726, C.O. 5/4, fol. 100; Westmoreland to Newcastle, June 17, 1727, C.O. 5/387, foll. 264-66; Andrews, *Colonial Period*, IV, 391-94.

Trade sought to undermine the independence of the charter government. "You'll find by the Lords of Trade Report," the agent for Connecticut wrote to Governor Talcott in 1731,

> they recommend with equal force that the Colony should have a New Charter, and to be put on the footing the People of Massachusetts Bay now are, as they do the matter in the article petitioned for. Under the circumstances I am at loss how to act . . . if I get a recommendation to Parliament, the one will certainly be tacked to the other. . . .[42]

"We are not willing . . . ," replied the cautious Governor on behalf of the Assembly, "to Hazard the Charter by bringing it into Parliament on such a footing."[43]

Connecticut's northern neighbor had been less circumspect. The outright defiance of the home government by the Assembly of Massachusetts Bay had raised the prospect of parliamentary intervention into its internal affairs and constitutional status. The crucial element now was the willingness of the senior ministers to undertake a legislative campaign. In a "public" letter to Burnet on June 26, 1729, Newcastle declared that the obstinacy of the province had "produced the final determination of laying the whole matter before Parliament."[44] A "private" communication of the same day hinted that this threat was as much bluff as intent. If the Assembly would act promptly, the southern secretary informed the Governor, the Crown would settle for a salary covering only Burnet's time in office.[45] Clearly the ministry preferred a compromise to a

[42] Wilks to Talcott, March 12, 1731, Talcott Papers, CHS, *Collections*, Hartford, 1892, IV, 222-23.

[43] Ibid., IV, 233-35.

[44] C.O. 5/871, foll. 9-10.

[45] C.O. 5/10, foll. 42-43.

fight. Yet if the colony remained adamant, there was every indication that the home administration would lay the matter before Parliament, if only to save face. The conflict had grown to such an extent that only a miracle could save the Assembly from the distasteful alternatives of granting a fixed salary or of endangering the existence of its charter.

The sudden and unexpected death of Governor Burnet on September 7, 1729, must have been viewed as such a deliverance by the God-fearing inhabitants of New England. At one stroke a number of their difficulties disappeared. The resources of the home government had been mobilized initially not for the sake of an abstract principle but as a by-product of the attempt of two aging Englishmen to provide for their personal financial wellbeing. Only their stubborn and costly resistance to the blackmail of the Assembly had pushed the endemic dispute over the threshold level and into the hands of the home government. Then only the zeal of several members of the Board of Trade and the Privy Council committee and the fortuitous conjunction with the purchase of the Carolinas had accounted for the enunciation of a definite policy and the possibility of parliamentary intervention. It was problematic whether this nascent reform movement had developed sufficient momentum to survive the loss of its two leading advocates.

III

The first thought of the ministry on Burnet's death was to attempt to replace him with Colonel Shute. The restoration of Shute to his old government had a number of advantages. It would place an experienced man in this difficult post; more important, it would signify the determination of the ministry to secure a fixed salary for the

Governor of Massachusetts Bay. The difficulty was that Shute declined the appointment. Because of age, or unwillingness to confront the hostile assembly, or a simple aversion to life in America, the former Governor refused to return to his post. Thomas Hutchinson described the sequel:

> Upon the news of Mr. Burnet's death, Mr. Belcher applied with all his powers to obtain the commission for the government. Governor Shute . . . generously gave his interest to Mr. Belcher who, fourteen years before, had given £500 sterling, which was never repaid, to facilitate Col. Shute's appointment. The controversy, which it was supposed a governor must be engaged in, caused few competitors, and the ministry were more concerned to find a proper person. Lord Townshend asked Mr. Wilks, who had much of his confidence, whether he thought Mr. Belcher would be able to influence the people to a compliance with the king's instructions, he replied that he thought no man more likely.[46]

Belcher's appointment confounded nearly everyone. That any ministry would name the agent of a long-troublesome colony to a key post in the administrative system seemed an act of incredible folly. The councillors of the colony were alarmed by the news; so also were a number of royal servants in America. "I am sure from my own Observations here," the Surveyor of the Woods wrote from Boston on learning of Belcher's nomination, "that it will not be for his Majesty's Service to have any

[46] *The History of the Colony and Province of Massachusetts Bay*, ed., Lawrence Shaw Mayo, Cambridge, Mass., 1936, II, 278; Belcher to H. Walpole, January 21, 1740, Belcher Papers, MHS, *Collections*, 6th ser., VI, 264-68.

Native of this Country appointed Governour. . . ."[47] The ministry's hope that Belcher as a native and a Dissenter could secure by entreaty what the son of Bishop Burnet had been unable to win by defiance was justified neither by history nor by logic. Governor Dudley, a New Englander, had failed as miserably as Colonel Shute, a religious independent. And just as Belcher's appointment was being announced, Lieutenant Governor Dummer—himself both a Dissenter and a native of New England—reported that the Assembly had refused him a fixed salary by an overwhelming vote of 54 to 18.[48] This resistance could only be confirmed by the sending out of a royal representative with Belcher's record of past support for colonial rights and privileges. Like the replacement of Shute at a crucial moment, this appointment suggested that the ministry was not in earnest.

Lord Townshend was the key figure in this sudden reversal of policy. When the news of Governor Burnet's death had reached London on October 23, the Privy Council committee on plantation affairs dropped its investigation of the complaints lodged against Burnet by the Assembly and ordered the Board of Trade to demand from the agents an account of the colony's compliance with the additional instruction of 1727.[49] The advisory body reported on November 6, 1729, that despite its willingness not to "insist upon forms, provided the substance might be obtained," the agents had declared that it was "their fixed and positive opinion that the assembly

[47] David Dunbar to Newcastle, February 4, 1730, C.O. 5/898, fol. 325.

[48] David Dunbar to Newcastle, November 4, 1729, C.O. 5/752, foll. 192-93.

[49] C.O. 5/870, foll. 281-82; *Journal of the Commissioners for Trade and Plantations from . . . 1728/9 to December 1734*, London, 1924, 61-68.

would never make their Governor independent of them." The board decided, therefore, to "prepare a Report . . . on the great consequence of this Dispute to ye Trade & Interest of Great Britain, as well as to the Authority of the Crown."[50] It was apparently at this point that the northern secretary intervened to offer the post to Belcher. For on November 11, less than a week after their last meeting with the board, Wilks and Belcher

> acquainted their Lordships, that having reflected upon what passed when they attended the Board the 6th instant, having reconsidered their letters, and apprehending that the death of Mr. Burnet might have abated the animosity of the dispute between him and the Assembly, and have made some alteration in the temper of that province, they were ready to transmit any proposition to the Assembly . . . and would, as far as was compatible with their stations, enforce the success thereof.[51]

This last-minute intercession meant that the report of the advisory body contained not a discussion of the alternative ways in which the colony could be coerced into obedience but rather a proposal for allowing the House of Representatives "one more opportunity of debating ye Weight" of the royal instruction.[52]

It was this recommendation which Townshend piloted through the Privy Council committee on November 12, 1729. This important meeting was attended by two privy councillors who had previously taken no part in the controversy. These were Arthur Onslow, the Speaker of the

[50] Board of Trade *Journal*, November 6, 1729, p. 70; Report to Council, November 12, 1729, C.O. 5/916, pp. 210-17.

[51] Board of Trade *Journal*, November 12, 1729, pp. 71-72.

[52] Loc. cit.

House of Commons, and Joseph Jekyll, the Master of the Rolls. It was well known that Onslow preferred accommodation to parliamentary legislation on all occasions; and the influential Jekyll was the uncle of the Collector of the Customs at Boston.[53] If the Assembly again refused to act, the onus of taking the matter to Parliament would fall upon Jekyll and Onslow as well as on the ministers who had carried the main burden of the long struggle. With this possibility in mind, the Privy Council committee for plantation affairs directed Belcher to return to England for further consultation if the Assembly continued in its obstructive mood.

Townshend's grave error of judgment in replacing Burnet by Belcher became apparent almost immediately. Within four months of his return "home," the Governor petitioned the Board of Trade for permission to accept an annual grant of £3,000 New England currency. The new chief executive argued that this offer went "much further than any thing they have heretofore done . . . and What I believe they will never recede from."[54] The House of Representatives had not met the demands of the home government with regard to the duration of the grant, but it had brought the salary to the required level. For Belcher this was more than satisfactory. If his salary was not guaranteed, he still possessed the dignity and authority of a royal governor. What for Shute and Burnet was an expedient financial appointment in a distant land, for Belcher was the pinnacle of success. His problem was

[53] P.C. 2/91, pp. 71-72; J. Steven Watson, "Arthur Onslow and Party Politics," in H. R. Trevor-Roper, ed., *Essays in British History presented to Sir Keith Feiling*, London, 1964, 143-45; Barrow, *Trade and Empire*, 78-79; Belcher to Onslow, October 29, 1731, MHS, *Collections*, 6th ser., VI, 20-21.

[54] Belcher to Board, December 10, 1730, C.O. 5/872, foll. 17-18.

not to win a permanent salary but to preserve his position at the apex of the colonial hierarchy by convincing the ministry of the futility of a policy which might jeopardize his administration.

The Governor's personal interest was diametrically opposite to that of the home government. Belcher's request was quickly and unequivocally refused. Upon receiving a second petition to the same effect, the board declared itself completely "at a Loss, to imagine how Mr. Belcher . . . could think that this might be taken as a Settlemt during his Governmt."[55] Faced with this insubordination, the Board of Trade asked the ministry to direct the Governor to return home for consultation. Three days later, on July 9, 1731, Belcher's son applied directly to Newcastle for permission to accept the Assembly's offer.[56] The Governor had decided to go over the heads of the Board of Trade. As Belcher explained later to Richard Partridge, he had no alternative for the commissioners "opposed it to the last (especially Coll Bladen), which seems to me unjust & unreasonable."[57]

Deprived of the support of the Governor, the Board of Trade could not prevail against the hesitancy of the ministry to take the matter to Parliament. When the Privy Council committee for plantation affairs met on August 4, 1731, it ordered the advisory body to reconsider the matter and gave a strong hint as to the type of report it would prefer. A week later the committee accepted the recom-

[55] Report, June 10, 1731, C.O. 5/961, pp. 415-18; Belcher to Newcastle, April 7, 1731, C.O. 5/898, foll. 332-33.

[56] J. Belcher, Jr. to Newcastle, July 9 and 29, 1731, C.O. 5/898, foll. 390-91, 396-97; Board of Trade to Belcher, July 6, 1731, C.O. 5/916, pp. 419-20; Belcher to Partridge, November 1, 1731, MHS, *Collections*, 6th ser., VI, 37-41.

[57] Belcher to Partridge, MHS, *Collections*, 6th ser., VI, 81-86.

mendation of the board that Belcher be permitted to accept the annual salary offered by the Assembly.[58] Although it was only in 1735 that this allowance was made permanent, the long battle between the royal administrators and the colonial legislature had come to an end. The Assembly had swept the field.

The passage of time obscured the loss of face suffered by the ministry but not the disastrous effects of this capitulation to the intransigence of a colonial legislature. "The People here," John Hammerton reported from South Carolina, "all believe themselves men of greater capasitys than all the Council & Senate of England."[59] From New York, Governor Cosby expressed his concern at the effect of the "extrordinary behaviour of ye boston people," while in Massachusetts Bay itself the Judge of the Admiralty warned that the colonists "now seem Encouraged even to Wrest the Admiralty Court Entirely out of the Kings Hand. . . ."[60] Governor Johnson of South Carolina reported that he had failed "to Induce the Assembly to Settle a fixt Sallary upon me, and his Majestys Officers." Such legislation "being dispenced with now in New England," he told the Board of Trade, "has I believe Influenced the Province."[61] These deleterious results were not confined to the short run. "This Government feels to this

[58] Report, August 4, 1731, C.O. 5/873, fol. 64; Vernon to Popple, July 27, 1731, C.O. 5/873, fol. 48; Courand to Belcher, August 26, 1731, C.O. 324/36, p. 282; Grant and Munro, *Acts*, II, 261-62.

[59] Hammerton to Delafaye, November 16, 1732, C.O. 5/388, fol. 52.

[60] Cosby to Newcastle, January 24, 1733, C.O. 5/1093, foll. 263-64; Byfield to Board of Trade, February 22, 1731, C.O. 5/874, foll. 60-67.

[61] Quoted in Greene, *Quest for Power*, 136.

Day," Governor Bernard claimed in 1767, "the ill effects of Gov'r Shutes not being sent back with an Increase of Salary and Authority."[62]

It was unlikely that a victory for Shute or Burnet would have resolved once and for all the distribution of political power in Massachusetts Bay. Certainly it would not have prevented the increase of "faction" in the other American governments; this was the product of the nature of the colonial relationship itself and not of a discrete event in the history of one colony. Yet this episode was of profound significance both for the domestic political development of the colonies and for the nascent reform movement in England. Since the overthrow of the Dominion of New England in 1689, the Assembly of Massachusetts Bay had moved from victory to victory in its continuing struggle with the home government. The devout Puritans might call it Divine Providence, the irresistible Will of God; Martin Bladen and the other imperial reformers, the working-out of a sustained and concerted scheme for independence. But all they really meant, in either case, was that one success or failure seemed to foreshadow another, because it was always easier to imagine things going on in the same way than to imagine a change. The events of 1727-1731 confirmed the impression of colonial invincibility and made it all the easier for the New Englanders —and all those seeking power for the American assemblies—to believe that history was moving in their direction.

The result might have been very different. A successful imposition of royal authority in Massachusetts Bay by parliamentary action in 1730 would have constituted an initial check on the growing power of the colonial legisla-

[62] Quoted in J. F. Burns, *Controversies between Royal Governors and their Assemblies* . . . , Boston, 1923, 72.

tures: the prestige of the Board of Trade would have been bolstered; the advantage gained by the ouster of the proprietary clique consolidated; and the prospects for a gradual transformation of the colonial system directed by Newcastle and supported by Parliament greatly increased. Most important, a victory for the colonial bureaucracy in 1731 might have reversed the conception of change in the minds of colonists and royal officials alike. The explanatory charter of 1726 might have been seen as a precursor of things to come rather than a fruitless aberration. In 1767, Governor Bernard might have interpreted these years as a decisive turning-point in the administration of the colonies.

In retrospect, Townshend's appointment of Belcher emerges as the single most important cause of the ministry's failure to implement its announced policy. This nomination amounted to a fundamental alteration in the situation, for it shifted the balance of power in England against the campaign for reform. Previously, Shute and Burnet had used their interest with those prominent in English politics to promote the coercive policies of the Board of Trade; thereafter, Belcher petitioned the leading ministers from Boston in an attempt to reverse the declared policy of the administration.[63] In London, the Governor's son and brother-in-law devoted their energies to the same task. "I see you have interest with Lord Islay and Harington and had us'd it in my favour," Belcher wrote approvingly to Partridge in 1731,

> and that you had engaged Sr. Joseph Jekyll (thro' Mr. Sandford) and that you carry'd Jonathan with you to Mr. H. Walpole, and were Kindly recd &

[63] Belcher to Onslow, October 29, 1731, MHS, *Collections*, 6th ser., VI, 20-21; Belcher to Wilmington, May 7, 1734, ibid., VII, 59-60.

talkt over the affair of the salary to my advantage. . . .[64]

Nor did this exhaust the list of the Governor's machinations. By offering the naval office of New Hampshire to the son of the Bishop of Lincoln, Belcher hoped to win the support of the clergyman for his cause.[65] Similarly, his attempt to secure the Collectorship of the Customs at Boston for William Fairfax was an effort to neutralize the bitter opposition of Martin Bladen, a kinsman of Fairfax.[66] These maneuvers were a far cry from the attempts of the Burnets to persuade the home government to send royal troops to Massachusetts Bay or to seek parliamentary legislation to coerce the Assembly into submission.

Neither of these repressive outcomes would have been assured had a less corruptible governor been dispatched to New England in 1730. And yet there was every possibility that the ministry would have been forced to some such action if the dispute had continued much longer. In May, 1730, Francis Wilks had warned the Assembly of the impossibility of resisting the demand for a fixed salary. "The Success of it," he told the Speaker of the House of Representatives, "is made so much the Concern of the principal Ministers, as to render in vain all Endeavours that Way."[67] Here was one of the few times during the first half of the eighteenth century when ministerial intervention into the internal financial and constitutional af-

[64] November 1, 1731, ibid., VI, 37-41.

[65] Belcher to J. Belcher, Jr., November 11, 1731, ibid., VI, 49-53; Belcher to Board of Trade, June 21, 1731, C.O. 5/873, foll. 58-59; Partridge to Popple, March 3, 1732, C.O. 5/874, fol. 45.

[66] Belcher to Bladen, November 23, 1731, MHS, *Collections*, 6th ser., VI, 55-56.

[67] May 21, 1730, C.O. 5/871, fol. 249 (printed in the *Boston Gazette*, no. 567, October 12-19, 1730).

fairs of an American colony was a practical political possibility.

That such action was not forthcoming was not simply the result of Belcher's subversion. Even if the new Governor had persevered in the struggle begun by Shute and continued by Burnet, the ministry might never have brought this sensitive issue before Parliament. Walpole was hesitant to expose his government to the attacks of the opposition, and this particular problem had constitutional as well as political implications. Belcher himself had perceived this fact, and this insight may very well have decided his personal strategy. As he wrote to Richard Partridge upon deciding not to return to England to report the Assembly's continued intransigence:

> I must walk very circumspectly lest the King's ministers shou'd imagine I am not zealous enough for the honour of the Crown, and lest the House of Commons shou'd think I bear too hard upon the privileges of the people. I'll endeavour to steer as nicely as I can between both.[68]

Walpole and Newcastle were attempting to chart a similar course. They wished to increase the power of the home government over the colonies in America, but they would do so only if the domestic ramifications of this policy were favorable. The voluntary surrender of their charter by the proprietors of Carolina and the institution of royal government there was accepted without controversy in Parliament.[69] The forcible abrogation of the charter of Massachusetts Bay or, alternatively, legislation

[68] November 1, 1731, MHS, *Collections*, 6th ser., VI, 37-41.

[69] The House of Commons readily accepted the assumption cost of £25,000, but there were protests because the Governor's salary was to be paid from Crown revenues: Newman, *Parliamentary Diary*, 145-47.

directing the Assembly to establish a fixed salary were much more dubious propositions. As in the past, Whigs might oppose such action because of the strengthening of the prerogative of the Crown, while Tories would be repelled by the assertion of parliamentary supremacy. Here was a pandora's box which only the most courageous or the most foolhardy ministry would dare to open.

Walpole's administration was neither. When Newcastle's determination to uphold the prerogative of the King in America produced an all-out confrontation with the intransigent Assembly of Massachusetts Bay, the senior ministers intervened to restrain their youthful colleague.[70] The highest political priority for Townshend and Walpole was domestic stability; they would initiate drastic measures only if they were absolutely necessary.[71] Once Newcastle's initial enthusiasm for reform was dampened by the political realism of the senior ministers, the plans of Westmoreland and Bladen went unheeded. Except in matters directly and obviously affecting the trade and manufactures of Great Britain, the Board of Trade and its supporters in Parliament did not have enough political power to carry through its policies.

[70] Townshend's intervention may have been motivated by animus toward Newcastle and Walpole who had just won royal approval for the Treaty of Seville, signed November 9, 1729. Townshend advocated an aggressive policy toward Spain and rumors of his resignation followed the adoption of this conciliatory agreement. See Hervey to S. Fox, November 18, 1729, *Lord Hervey and His Friends, 1726-38*, Earl of Ilchester, ed., London, 1950, 38, and Plumb, *Walpole*, II, 198.

[71] Barrow, *Trade and Empire*, 115, describes extensive changes made by Walpole in the customs service in Scotland and England, but Plumb (*Walpole*, II, 71; *Growth of Political Stability*, 181) argues that these were not so much "reforms" of a corrupt system as "purges" designed to place the spoils in more politically reliable hands.

IV

The reassessment of the nature of the colonial system and its reconstitution on rational principles was thus delayed first by the generation of war with France at the turn of the eighteenth century and the resultant financial stringency; then by the reactionary influence of the proprietary faction; and finally by the pusillanimity of the Walpole ministry. The 1730's constituted, nevertheless, a new and distinct phase in the history of English imperial administration. For the first time, Parliament took an active role in the management of the empire. In the five years following the assumption of the Carolinas in 1729, there was parliamentary action subsidizing the establishment of Georgia, regulating the sugar trade between the West Indies and the northern continental colonies, and prohibiting the manufacture of hats in America. In addition, an abortive proposal was introduced into the legislature which would have permitted the King in Council to disallow all laws adopted in the colonies which were detrimental to the English national interest.[72] In the decade preceding the renewal of war with Spain and France, the home government took the first steps in conceiving and implementing a theory of empire suitable for a mature colonial system.

The initial impulse for much of this legislation frequently came from organizations and interest groups outside the executive branch of the government. It was on the

[72] Andrews, *Colonial Period*, IV, 406. There was also legislation designed to preserve American forests for the use of the royal navy. See Robert G. Albion, *Forests and Sea Power; The Timber Problem of the Royal Navy, 1652-1862*, Cambridge, Mass., 1926, 250-51 and Joseph J. Malone, *Pine Trees and Politics; The Naval Stores and Forest Policy in Colonial New England, 1691-1775*, London, 1964, 98-99.

petition of merchants trading to America that the House of Lords called for a comprehensive survey of commercial regulations passed by the colonial legislatures which discriminated against English traders.[73] And it was the agitation of a faction within the lower house of home legislature which led to the settlement of Georgia. The bureaucracy of the colonial office functioned more as a clearing house for petitions than as a purposeful governing organization. Whatever the mercantilist rationale of the empire, the administrative system operated on the assumptions of a *laissez-faire* system.

This did not mean that colonial administrators were completely impotent. Faced with ministerial indifference to their plans of reform, subordinate officials quickly learned to wed their own schemes to those of powerful interest groups. The most active and successful of these minor bureaucrats was Colonel Martin Bladen, a commissioner of trade from 1717 until his death in 1746. Bladen assumed the burden of the defense of the abortive Sugar Bills of 1731 and 1732; and it was the Colonel who seized upon the strategy of converting the measure from a prohibition on the importation of sugar and rum from the French West Indies into a money bill laying a duty on this trade. This stratagem enabled the West Indian interest to push the act through the House of Lords in 1733 after two successive failures.[74] Bladen's initiative in this case stemmed both from his personal financial interest in the islands and from his concern as an adminis-

[73] Andrews, *Colonial Period*, IV, 404.

[74] Leo Francis Stock, ed., *Proceedings and Debates of the British Parliaments respecting North America*, Washington, 1924- , IV, 142-43, 182-86; Mabel Wolff, *The Colonial Agency of Pennsylvania, 1712-1757*, Philadelphia, 1933, 61.

trator with political conditions in the North American colonies.[75] When he was confronted by Sir John Bernard with the argument that the proposed bill would cut off all trade between the northern colonies and the French islands and thus bring about the ruin of the continental plantations,

> Colonel Bladen replied [an observer at the House of Commons debate noted] that the duties proposed would not prove an absolute prohibition, but he owned that he meant them as something that should come very near it, for in the way the northern colonies are, they raise the French islands at the expense of ours, and raise themselves also to[o] high, even to an independency. . . .[76]

At bottom, Bladen's advocacy of the Molasses Act of 1733 was only the culmination of a long series of maneuvers designed to humble the colonists of Massachusetts Bay. In 1729, he had sought the same end through the establishment of a new settlement in Nova Scotia. In addition to providing a buffer against French encroachments, Bladen had argued in a memorandum to Newcastle, the new colony would "drain great Numbers of Inhabitants from New England, where they are daily aiming at an independency & very much Interfere with the Trade of their Mother Kingdom."[77] The failure of the ministry to ask Parliament for legislation to force the Assembly to grant a permanent salary to the Governor

[75] Stock, *Proceedings*, v, 175; Bladen to Townshend, August 20, 1724, S.P. 35/51, fol. 62; Greene, "Martin Bladen's Blueprint," 517.

[76] Quoted in Stock, *Proceedings*, iv, 182.

[77] "For the Settling of Carolina," September 27, 1729, C.O. 5/4, foll. 159-63; Malone, *Pine Trees and Politics*, 95-96, 101.

only caused the Colonel to alter his strategy. The year following the passage of the coercive Molasses Act, Bladen met with Sir Charles Wager and two other members of the Admiralty board, Sir George Saunders and Sir Jacob Ashworth, to discuss the destruction of the King's woods in Massachusetts Bay and the lawless behavior of the people there. The outcome of this conference was a recommendation to the Board of Trade to direct its counsel at law to prepare legislation for "the next Session of Parliament to cure so pernicious an Evil."[78] The preservation of an adequate supply of masts for the royal navy was so clearly in the national interest that the arguments of the reformers were assured of a sympathetic hearing in Parliament. Bladen and his fellow administrators were determined to take advantage of any issue which would permit them to seek legislative support for colonial reform.

Bladen's persistent concern with the problems of imperial administration forced him to articulate a conception of empire suitable to the needs of the changing colonial system. The cornerstone of Bladen's intellectual edifice was the old acts of trade and navigation. "It is evident that this Bill is built upon the Same Principles with the Navigation Acts . . . ," the Colonel wrote to Newcastle in defense of the Sugar Bill of 1739,

> It is calculated to enlarge our Trade, and Settlements and to encrease our Navigation without breaking with any one of the great Principles, upon which our Navigation Laws are built.[79]

[78] Bladen to Popple, November 20, 1734, C.O. 5/876, foll. 79-80.

[79] Bladen to Newcastle, May 30, 1739, S.P. 36/47, foll. 245-46 and enclosure, foll. 247-55. Actually this measure contradicted the letter of the traditional legislation since it permitted the export

The difficulty arose in translating mercantilist principles into administrative precepts. Here Bladen's objective was to prescribe the degree of autonomy required to produce prosperity for mother country and colonies alike. At one extreme was the establishment of a military government. This was immediately rejected by the Commissioner of Trade. Bladen was too knowledgeable, and too much of a Whig, to think that settlers in America would be content without some of the privileges of Englishmen. Thus he advised Lord Harrington in 1739 with regard to a proposed settlement at Darien that

> there should be some mixture of Civil Magistracy in it even from its first Infancy; otherways it will never answer the great End proposed, which are the Benefits resulting from Trade with ye Spaniards as well as the Natives. . . . The want of such a Provision in Nova Scotia, has been one principle Cause why we have no Civil Inhabitants in that Province.[80]

The other end of the spectrum of available administrative solutions was equally uncongenial to the Commissioner of Trade. Charter governments were too independent. Their charters shielded them from the impartial implementation of parliamentary legislation. It was the supremacy of the latter, rather than the resort to military

---

of sugar directly to Europe and since it was conceived primarily in the interest of the powerful West Indian planters rather than that of the nation as a whole. See Richard B. Sheridan, "The Molasses Act and the Market Strategy of the British Sugar Planters," *Journal of Economic History*, XVII (1957), 62-83.

[80] June 18, 1739, Add. MSS 32694, foll. 24-30. In 1722, Undersecretary of State Charles Delafaye had advised Governor Nicholson of South Carolina that "In the Plantations, the Government should be as Easy and Mild as Possible to invite people to settle under it." Quoted in Greene, *Quest for Power*, 17.

force, upon which Bladen relied to ensure a properly managed empire once the bothersome proprietary and corporate governments had been swept away. He contemplated no ideological conflict with the colonial assemblies. They were strictly subordinate bodies which must be regulated in the national interest. Here the Colonel agreed with the former Deputy Governor Keith of Pennsylvania. "We are to consider them," Keith wrote in 1728,

> as so many Corporations at a distance invested with an ability to make temporary By Laws for themselves agreeable to their respective Scituations and Climates, but no ways interfereing with the legal Prerogatives of the Crown, or the true Legislative Power of the Mother State.[81]

This view was shared by the senior ministers of the government. Walpole and Newcastle differed from Bladen primarily in the lengths they were willing to go to insure that administrative practice approximated constitutional theory. The members of the Privy Council relied on the good will of the representative bodies in America to reenact the legislation passed by Parliament and to secure the enforcement of royal instructions. As long as the two sets of representative institutions remained in

[81] Quoted in Winfred T. Root, *The Relations of Pennsylvania with the British Government, 1696-1765*, New York, 1912, 38n., where it is attributed to Bladen. That Bladen agreed with this section of Keith's "A Short Discourse on the Present State of the Colonies in America . . ." can be inferred from his comments on this work in C.O. 5/4, foll. 164-78. The Colonel took issue with several interpretations and suggestions advanced by the former Governor but made no comment with regard to this passage. Bladen himself took a similar constitutional position in his plan of 1739. See Greene, "Martin Bladen's Blueprint," 525-26.

step, there was no need to raise delicate ideological questions. It was Bladen's contention throughout the 1720's and the 1730's that the two systems were severely out of line and that the balance would have to be redressed by drastic ministerial action.

The far-reaching implications of Bladen's position came to light in 1732, when Parliament considered a bill to prevent the exportation of hats out of the colonies and to control the entrance of new apprentices into the American hat industry. This measure was sponsored by the domestic producers of hatware because of their fear of colonial competition. It also commanded a more general respect because it coincided with widely accepted mercantilist principles: the colonies were expected to produce only those manufactures which the home country was unable to supply. In May, 1731, and again in January and May, 1732, the House of Commons had addressed the King to request information regarding "the laws made, manufactures set up and trade carried on" in America that "might in any way be disadvantageous to the prosperity, laws and general interests of the kingdom."[82] Consequently, there was little opposition to the Hat Bill in Parliament, and the bill passed quickly through its first two readings. At this point Bladen intervened to seek to amend the measure. The Earl of Egmont, an opposition Whig, noted in his diary:

> Went to the House, where among other things the hat bill had a third reading. Colonel Bladon of the Board of Trade, opposed it as ineffectual to prevent the making of hats to be exported from our colonies, which is the intent of the bill. He therefore was for

[82] Andrews, *Colonial Period*, IV, 402; Clerk of Parliament to Board of Trade, April 24, 1731, C.O. 5/872, fol. 87.

> adding a clause which in the committee we rejected, namely, that if any person should be acquitted there of an accusation that he had trangressed the act, that person should undergo a second trial in England. He said the juries in the colonies would not find a countryman of their own guilty, and that the colonies are running into all sorts of manufactures, which must be stopped.[83]

A similar measure enacted by Parliament in the 1770's was branded by the colonists as unjust and intolerable. Thirty years earlier this suggestion was unacceptable to those in England as well. Sir John Bernard thought it was "too great a hardship on English subjects and contrary to Magna Charta to try a man twice for the same thing."[84] The majority of the Commons agreed with the chief spokesman for the opposition, as Bladen probably knew it would. The Colonel had sat on the committee which had drafted the Hat Bill and was well aware of the sentiments of his colleagues. His unusual attempt to amend the bill on its third reading pointed up the fact that he expected to suffer a "positive" defeat. The appearance in the debate of a proposal for double jeopardy might deter infringement of the new act; it would certainly begin to set the terms of a subsequent discussion if a stronger measure were required. In his own cunning way Bladen was attempting to steer his contemporaries toward a theory of empire which elevated the principle of central control over that of colonial autonomy and which subordinated the individual rights of the colonists to the national interest.

[83] R. A. Roberts, ed., *Diary of Viscount Percival, afterwards First Earl of Egmont*, London, 1920-33, I, 256.

[84] April 13, 1732, ibid., I, 256.

This first tentative effort to come to grips with the realities of a mature colonial system revealed for a fleeting moment what a later initiative was to expose in graphic detail. This was the fact that the empire as it existed during the first half of the eighteenth century was founded on two potentially contradictory principles. The first of these established the "right" of Englishmen in the plantations to be governed by representative institutions. More generally, it guaranteed the same rights or privileges to the subjects of the King resident in America as to those living in the home country. This tacit understanding was threatened, if not completely undermined, by the implications of the second principle defining the constitutional position of those in the New World. The acts of trade and navigation were based not on the premise of equality between mother country and colony but rather on the assumption of inequality and subordination. As administrative bodies the plantations were clearly inferior, although the individuals who constituted the subordinate units were equal in legal status to those resident in England. Bladen's amendment to the Hat Bill exposed this paradox by bringing these two principles into conflict. Would the "rights" of colonial Englishmen be sacrificed to the acts of trade? Or would the representative bodies in America be permitted to determine the extent of colonial responsibility whatever the cost to the home country?

The two solutions which would reconcile these divergent principles, the direct representation of the colonists in the home legislature or the acknowledgement of the American assemblies as coordinate institutions, surpassed the imaginations of the men of the 1730's just as they were to escape the minds of the statesmen of the 1770's. They were, nevertheless, the only viable intellectual responses. If government emanated from the people, and if those in America had the same rights and privileges as Englishmen in the metropolitan community, then ultimately there was no philosophical justification for the colonial system. The inferiority of colonial institutions was possible only if sovereign authority proceeded from "divine right" or another supernatural source. In a government based on quasi-republican principles it was logically impossible to have an equality of individual rights and an inferiority of economic and political status. The Assembly of Massachusetts Bay proclaimed in 1732, as a postscript to the long struggle over the governor's salary, that

> The Taxing of the People, and putting Money in the Treasury, is what more peculiarly belongs to the House of Representatives, as their Constituents pay it, and therefore what prevents and hinders them in what they are the most peculiar and proper Judges of seems not only to bear upon their Rights by Charter; but also as *Englishmen* and rational Creatures.[85]

The ideological tenets of 1689 were incompatible with those of 1660; the attempted historical graft of representative institutions and fundamental rights to the body of mercantilist thought incorporated in the acts of trade and navigation had never really taken.

In Bladen's view the national interest, once embodied in the royal prerogative and now increasingly in parliamentary enactment, overrode the rights of individuals and, implicitly, the privileges of the colonial assemblies. The Commissioner of Trade had advanced constitutional views; to most of the Whig beneficiaries of the revolution of 1689, sovereignty was not indivisible and absolute.

[85] Quoted in Albert B. Southwick, "The Molasses Act—Source of Precedents," *WMQ*, 3rd ser., VIII (July, 1951), 402-403. Italics in the original.

Rather, Englishmen had certain rights and corporate bodies certain privileges which the sovereign, be it King or Parliament, could not violate. It was this view which was predominant in the higher ranks of the Walpole ministry. The position of Philip Yorke, Newcastle's intimate political adviser, was typical. The right of the Crown to tax the island of Jamaica, the future Lord Hardwicke had declared in 1724 in his capacity as Attorney-General,

> will depend upon the question whether Jamaica is now to be considered merely as a colony of English subjects or as a conquered country. If as a colony of English subjects, we apprehend they cannot be taxed but by the Parliament of Great Britain or by and with the consent of some representative body of the people of the Island, properly assembled by the authority of the Crown. But if it can now be considered as a conquered country, in that case we conceive they may be taxed by the authority of the Crown.[86]

For Hardwicke and his fellow ministers—and even more especially for the Whig opposition—Crown and Parliament were as much antagonistic as complementary institutions. Only if a proper "balance" could be maintained in the constitution of the country would the rights of the subject be protected.

The ultimate failure of the reform movement of 1727-1733, then, was not simply the result of indifference in the higher ranks of the administration. Nor was it merely the product of a conscious policy of "salutary neglect," although this along with administrative inefficiency, financial stringency, and political incompetence also played a

[86] Quoted in Philip C. Yorke, *The Life and Correspondence of Philip Yorke, Earl of Hardwicke, Lord High Chancellor of Great Britain*, Cambridge, Eng., 1913, I, 89.

role. For there was an important constitutional hurdle to be overcome before a far-reaching reform of the colonial system by parliamentary enactment could begin. And the politicians of the Walpole era had neither the inclination nor the energy to surmount this obstacle. In 1734, Parliament refused to consider legislation proposed by the committee of the whole house which would have compelled all of the American colonies, irrespective of their charter privileges, to submit laws within twelve months of their enactment. By refusing even to alter slightly the colonial charters in the interest of efficient administration, the members of Parliament signified their unwillingness to challenge the royal prerogative.[87] Control over most colonial matters remained primarily in the hands of a weak executive; for reasons of its own, Parliament would not act to strengthen the Crown in enforcing its colonial policy.

The local assemblies exploited the situation created by this fragmentation of power and authority in England by encroaching with impunity upon the traditional prerogatives of the Crown. By the third decade of the eighteenth century many of the American representative bodies had achieved a degree of strength and of confidence which allowed them to deal with royal officials on a basis of near-equality. Parliamentary intervention into colonial affairs had not produced a reform of the internal financial and political structure of the American governments, but only legislation designed to benefit the selfish interests of British merchants, absentee planters from the West Indies, and domestic manufacturers.[88] Only thirty years later,

[87] Andrews, *Colonial Period*, IV, 404-407.

[88] The fragmentary nature of this legislation and the fact that it was designed primarily to aid domestic interests rather than to institute a system of tight imperial control explains the paucity of co-

in the 1760's, when American affairs were no longer on the periphery of English political life and when the constitutional struggle between Parliament and King had been transcended by the formula of the "King-in-Parliament," only then would such reform begin.

---

lonial complaints. The protests which were raised, however, prefigured those of the 1760's and 1770's. See Southwick, "Molasses Act," *passim.*

CHAPTER 3

The Beginning of the Newcastle Era

THE inept handling of the salary question in New England and the potentially disastrous policy outlined in the Molasses Act of 1733 testified to the lack of understanding of colonial conditions possessed by most officials in London. The single salutary result of these controversies was a slight broadening of the perspective of those in the ministry. Cadwallader Colden wrote to Micajah Perry after the passage of the Molasses Act:

> The dispute I hope has brought this advantage that the Plantation affairs are now better understood than formerly they were by the Generality of ev'n those concern'd in the Govern^t of the Nation.[1]

The New York official was unduly optimistic. For a considerable time in the future American affairs would be conducted much as they had been in the past. Policies would be conceived and implemented with only the barest knowledge of conditions in the new world; patronage would be dispensed with little understanding of the character of the applicants and even less comprehension of the disposition of political power in the colonies or the significance of factional machinations there.

The difference, in the 1730's, lay in the context in which the old activities took place. With the continuing dominance of Sir Robert Walpole, the political system of Eng-

[1] No date, NYHS, *Collections*, LI, 30-31.

land had entered into a period of relative stability. The frequent alteration of an entire ministry, a common enough occurrence before 1714, was now unheard of. Even the intra-party struggles among the ministerial Whigs had largely abated by the third decade of the century. The reason was clear: by 1730 nearly everyone in a position of power and prestige was, in some sense, a Walpolian.

This was as much the case in the colonies as in the mother country. Virtually all American offices were in the hands of friends of the First Lord of the Treasury and his ministerial colleagues. As long as the Walpole party continued in power in England, there would be no pressure for a large-scale change in administrative personnel. Death and sickness would take their toll; manifest incompetence would add a few more casualties. But there would be no dramatic purges as in the past for the simple reason that there were no longer any issues which were universally recognized as disqualifying an incumbent from continuation in office.

The character of the applicants had changed as well. In the aftermath of the Treaty of Utrecht, colonial governorships had been used on a liberal scale to satisfy the ambitions and to supplement the finances of prematurely retired military men. Shute in New England, Pitt in Bermuda, Hunter in Jamaica, and Hart and George in the Leeward Islands were among those former army officers who continued to serve the Crown as colonial administrators. They were joined after the South Sea Bubble by those sent to America to heal their wounded fortunes. The Duke of Portland in Jamaica, William Burnet in New York, and Attorney-General Richard Bradley in the same province were some of those collecting compensation for their losses. By the third decade of the eighteenth century, these pressures on the patronage market were dying away.

The war was twenty years in the past, and the ministry no longer felt obliged to expiate its speculative sins.

With a dearth of clearly definable issues and obviously deserving applicants, Anglo-American politics was bound to become more personal and private. The spectrum of debate had narrowed. Petty machinations replaced questions of party allegiance and rewards for "national" service as the core of colonial political activity in England. It became increasingly important to have "interest" in London because such influence meant less than before. Like any other commodity, its value decreased as it became widely shared. As long as a colonial bureaucrat was not protected by "civil service" status, it was imperative for him to have as many important friends as possible. Without adequate support at home an official was exposed to the attacks of his political enemies and unable to reward his loyal supporters.[2]

The situation was not much different for the leading ministers who were the objects of these persistent solicitations. It was impossible to satisfy all of the claimants for office, and in a ministry composed of friends, it was not immediately obvious which applicant should be favored. Lord Hervey described an archetypal case in 1735:

> Sir William Yonge was made Secretary-at-War, which left a vacancy in the Treasury. Lord Hervey pressed Sir Robert Walpole extremely to put his friend Mr. Winnington into the vacancy, which would have made one in the Admiralty, where Mr. Campbell, another of his friends, would of course

[2] Katz, *Newcastle's New York*, 5; Stephen Saunders Webb, "The Strange Career of Francis Nicholson," *WMQ*, 3rd ser., XXIII (October 1966) 513n., asserts that 110 of the 180 governors or lieutenant-governors who served in the colonies between 1660 and 1730 were former army officers.

> have come in. The Duke of Newcastle and Mr. Pelham solicited the Treasury for Mr. Clutterbuck, and Sir Robert Walpole, not caring to decide between the two, put in neither . . . he took his son-in-law Lord Cholmondeley into the Treasury . . . to avoid a decision between their claims.[3]

The scarcity of available places made it inevitable that a struggle for patronage would develop among rival factions within the Walpole ministry. This battle would be more restrained than the fight among the bitterly antagonistic Whig leaders in the preceding decade, but the outcome would be no less important to those concerned. By the 1730's, Newcastle had embarked upon a campaign to secure the complete control of American patronage and to extend his influence in the determination of all ministerial business. In so doing he contributed to the internal disintegration of an administration increasingly under severe external attack.

I

The number of colonial places that could be harnessed to the pursuit of domestic political hegemony was greater than ever before. When Newcastle entered the southern department in 1724, there were forty-one places formally at his disposal in America. Six years later the number had risen to sixty. The bulk of the increase resulted from the Crown's acquisition of the proprietary province of Carolina. With the revocation of the old royal charter, the power of nominating officials passed from the proprietors to the southern secretary.

The disposition of these new offices did not pass auto-

[3] Sedgwick, *Hervey Memoirs*, II, 451-52. Plumb, *Walpole*, II, 296-97, 327, notes the persistent scarcity of patronage.

matically or easily into Newcastle's hands. As part of their agreement with the Crown for the surrender of the provinces, the proprietors secured a guarantee that all employments granted before January 1, 1728, were to be retained by their appointees.[4] In accord with this understanding Thomas Lowndes and Hugh Watson received a royal patent for the places of Provost Marshal, Clerk of the Crown, and Clerk of the Peace. Lowndes was related to the former Secretary to the Treasury, William Lowndes, while Watson was a barrister of the Middle Temple. Like the patent they enjoyed under the proprietors, the new document stipulated that their appointment was to be for life. For Lowndes and Watson, at least, the transformation in the status of the Carolinas was irrelevant; their income of £200 per annum from the American sinecure continued unabated.[5]

The governorship, the most valuable and influential post in the colony, was not included in the agreement between the Crown and the proprietors. This office had been taken out of the hands of Carteret and his associates in 1720. In that year the ministry sent out the veteran colonial administrator Francis Nicholson to restore order in the colony and to undo the results of a decade of proprietary mismanagement. Nicholson replaced Robert Johnson, himself on the verge of being relieved of his post because of his disagreement with the policies of his employers. When the imposition of permanent royal control became a distinct possibility in 1727, Johnson sought to regain his post. With the strong backing of the Council and Assembly of the province, the former Governor wrote

[4] "Extract of the Act for the Surrender of Carolina," no date, Add. MSS 33030, foll. 351-52.

[5] "List of Places in the Gift of the Crown in So Carolina," no date, C.O. 5/388, fol. 247.

to Newcastle to seek reappointment and to forestall the return of proprietary influence.[6]

There was some substance to the fears of the colonists that the erstwhile owners would attempt to perpetuate their control over the political life of the colony. Since 1722, the proprietors had been petitioning the Crown for the replacement of Nicholson by Colonel Horsey. Horsey was a casualty of the Utrecht settlement and of the peace which haunted the ambitions of military men for a generation afterward. The Colonel had little choice but to seek his fortune in another capacity, resigning from the Foot and Horse Guards in 1722 in order to settle in South Carolina.[7] Horsey's hopes were thwarted by the unwillingness of the home government to appoint a governor so closely linked to the proprietary interest.[8] Even the presence of Carteret in the southern department was not sufficient to secure his appointment.

With the ouster of the proprietary clique from the inner ranks of the ministry, the Colonel was forced to find new sources of support for his candidacy. Beginning in 1727, he exploited his connection with the proprietors by serving as their "Principall Agent" in the negotiations with the Board of Trade for the surrender of the province. This activity gave him the opportunity to win the backing of the Earl of Westmoreland, the President of the Board of Trade. At the same time, the Colonel won the support of the new southern secretary by means of a private financial transaction. Newcastle wrote to Townshend in August, 1727, with regard to the post, "you know

[6] Johnson to Newcastle, November 7, 1727, C.O. 5/387, fol. 269; Nicholson to Middleton, October 8, 1726, C.O. 5/387, fol. 215.

[7] Memorial, July 20, 1727, S.P. 36/2, foll. 59-60.

[8] John Cotton to Walpole, January 17, 1726, W.C., no. 1272.

how desirous I am of getting it for Colo. Horsey, from whom Colonel Montagu is to have an Advantage."[9] Horsey's solicitation of the reform-minded Westmoreland and of Newcastle had not dulled the enthusiasm of the proprietors toward his candidacy. Late in 1727, five of the owners petitioned the Privy Council not to appoint Johnson; and early the next year they urged Newcastle to select Horsey. If Johnson was nominated, the proprietors threatened to withdraw all support to the colony when it came under royal control.[10]

The combined influence of the proprietors, of Newcastle, and of Westmoreland was not sufficient to secure Horsey's appointment. Their advocacy of the Colonel was offset by the intervention of Archibald Hutcheson with Sir Robert Walpole. Hutcheson, an independent Whig and a one-time member of the Board of Trade, had secured part ownership of the Carolinas by taking over the share of Sir John Tyrell.[11] This, however, was not the main source of his influence. Hutcheson, like Governor Montgomery of New York, had followed the Prince of Wales into opposition in 1719 and consequently found himself in a strong position upon the accession of George II.[12] His

[9] Newcastle to Townshend, August 6, 1727, Add. MSS 32687, fol. 137; Horsey to Newcastle, July 15, 1727, S.P. 36/2, fol. 42; Proprietors to Westmoreland, March 4, 1728, H.M.C., *Eleventh Report*, pt. IV, 256-57.

[10] Proprietors to Newcastle, April 3, 1728, C.O. 5/383, fol. 275.

[11] Horsey to Newcastle, May 14, 1729, C.O. 5/383, fol. 142; Steele, *Politics of Colonial Policy*, 150-51. In 1722, Hutcheson, then in opposition, defeated John Pulteney, Newcastle's candidate, in the election poll at Hastings. See A. Hutcheson, *A Collection of Advertisements, Letters, and Papers . . .*, London, 1722, and Nulle, *Thomas Pelham-Holles*, 49-53.

[12] Hutcheson, *A Collection*, *passim*; Hammerton to Walpole, February, 1730, W.C., no. 2757.

presence undercut Horsey's assiduous cultivation of the lesser officials in the government. In December, 1729, Townshend informed the Board of Trade of the appointment of Hutcheson's candidate, Robert Johnson.

The southern secretary was equally unsuccessful in his quest for other posts in South Carolina. As the influential banker Nathaniel Gould wrote to Charles Delafaye in November:

> I am informed the Governor of South Carolina was named last Saturday, & that as His Grace of Newcastle is out of Town the vacant offices there will be filled up by My Lord Townshend, His Grace made Me Sort of [a] Promise of a Smal Post for Mr. John Montgomery a Particular Friend of Mine. . . .[13]

It was only Townshend's abrupt departure from office early in 1730 that gave Newcastle any hope of controlling the patronage of his own department.

Even then the Duke did not have a completely free hand. The case of the secretaryship of South Carolina, a patent post worth £200 per annum, was a case in point. Under proprietary rule the office had been filled by Charles Hart, an associate of Lord Carteret. When Hart returned to England in 1725, he recommended John Hammerton as his successor. In addition to Hart's support, purchased for a tidy sum, Hammerton had connections with both Newcastle and Walpole.[14] But even this was not sufficient to offset the interest of Archibald Hutcheson, who demanded that some provision be made for his

[13] November 24, 1729, C.O. 5/387, fol. 342.

[14] Hart to Carteret, March 16, 1721, C.O. 5/385, foll. 78-79; Hart to Newcastle, May 6, 1725, W.C., no. 1206; Hammerton to Newcastle, no dates, C.O. 5/383, foll. 32 and 38; Hammerton to Walpole, no date, C.O. 5/383, fol. 40.

nominee, Edward Bertie. On Walpole's mediation the proceeds of the post were split between the two candidates.[15]

It was Hutcheson and not Newcastle who was the dominant figure in the initial creation of the royal establishment in South Carolina. In June, 1730, Hutcheson followed up his earlier successes by urging the southern secretary to continue Chief Justice Robert Wright in office. Wright was a relative of Sir John Tyrell, whose share in the province has been purchased by Hutcheson. This appointment was undoubtedly satisfactory to Newcastle as well, for the Duke had brought Tyrell into Parliament for one of his Yorkshire boroughs in return for political assistance in Nottinghamshire.[16]

Indeed, this favor to Tyrell, accomplished at Hutcheson's request, was the only major office in South Carolina which the southern secretary managed in his own interest. The influence of an important associate or a domestic political interest was visible in nearly every other appointment. Newcastle's friend Nathaniel Gould had to be disappointed, for the post of Attorney-General was promised to Lord Cathcart. This last major appointment went to the Scot James Abercrombie; his countryman Montgomery would have to wait for the division of spoils in North Carolina.[17]

Even the minor places in the province were spoken for by those with influential connections. The military command at Fort Johnson near Charleston was bestowed upon Captain Sunderland, a relative of the former Whig leader.

[15] Affidavit, August 10, 1751, C.O. 324/38, p. 303; Hammerton to Newcastle, June 25, 1744, Add. MSS 32703, foll. 158-59.

[16] Hutcheson to Delafaye, June 16, 1730, C.O. 5/388, fol. 25.

[17] "South Carolina Employments," no date, C.O. 5/388, fol. 432; Gould to Delafaye, July 25, 1730, S.P. 36/19, fol. 216.

The young army man had the backing of his father's old associates in England and also of Governor Johnson, who hoped to use Sunderland's interest to secure a second independent company for the province.[18] Another military place was given to a relation of Lord Monson, a friend of the Pelhams and a future President of the Board of Trade. The only one of the initial appointees to the royal establishment who relied solely on his connection with the southern secretary was Theophilus Gregory, the new Master in Chancery. And his post was worth a mere £20 for annum.[19]

The disposition of places in the neighboring province of North Carolina developed on roughly similar lines. Despite the undeveloped state of the economy and the absence of a commercial center comparable to Charleston, none of the five posts at stake lacked its share of solicitors. As in South Carolina, the jockeying for position had begun before the province came formally under the control of the Crown. In June, 1729, the Judge of the Admiralty wrote approvingly to Newcastle of the land policy of the incumbent Governor, Sir Richard Everard. "Sir Richard," Judge Porter informed the southern secretary,

> has acted with the greatest regard to his Majesty's Interest, and by that means has reathor [sic] chose to loose the many fees which accrew to him by signing Pattents, then to run ye hazard of doing what might be prejudicial or disliked by his Majesty, tho his Commission is at present from under ye Lord Proprietors.

[18] Lord Strathnover to Delafaye, May 8, 1730, C.O. 5/382, fol. 161; Johnson to General Ross, June 24, 1730, C.O. 5/383, fol. 167; Petition, no date, C.O. 5/383, fol. 158.

[19] "List of Places," no date, C.O. 5/388, fol. 247; M. Decker to Newcastle, February 5, 1732, S.P. 36/26, fol. 71.

This cautious procedure was adopted, Porter hinted to Newcastle, "in hopes [it] will meet with your Graces favorable opinion and countenance. . . ."[20]

On hearing that he was likely to be superseded by George Burrington despite his exemplary and costly conduct, Everard suddenly reversed his land policy. By November, 1729, Porter was writing to Burrington to report the Governor was "breaking through by signing Patents."[21] The concern of the Admiralty official was not completely disinterested. The following month, Porter wrote to Newcastle to suggest his own appointment as Receiver-General to examine the state of the lands in the province. Whatever Porter's motives, his charge was fully justified. A subsequent investigation showed that in less than twelve months the Governor had signed 393 patents for 290,000 acres of land. If this munificence was not on the scale of some of the earlier grants made by the governors of New York, it was sufficient to throw the land system of the colony into chaos for a generation. In May, 1730, the Board of Trade declared all grants of land made since the assumption of the province by the Crown as null and void, "Sir Richd Everard having no authority, that we know of, for granting the same. . . ."[22]

It was not these disclosures of misconduct in office which resulted in the Governor's displacement. Newcastle had decided to replace Everard with Burrington before Porter's initial charges reached England. Like Robert Johnson in South Carolina, Burrington had held the governorship under the proprietors and had been dismissed by them for

[20] June 15, 1729, C.O. 5/306, fol. 30.

[21] November 30, 1729, C.O. 5/308, fol. 12.

[22] Board of Trade to Newcastle, May 1, 1730, C.O. 5/306, fol. 41; Newcastle to Board, April 28, 1730, C.O. 5/293, fol. 7; "Patents Granted," July 1, 1731, C.O. 5/308, foll. 128-36.

siding with the disgruntled settlers. Here the similarities ended. Johnson was reappointed to his government over the Duke's wishes while Burrington owed his selection entirely to Newcastle's influence. After six years in office, the southern secretary had finally nominated his first colonial governor.

This was Newcastle's most important success in the disposition of patronage in North Carolina. The post of attorney-general was already promised to John Montgomery as a result of his disappointment in South Carolina. Two of the three remaining offices in the northern colony were spoken for by others with a voice in the management of colonial affairs. "I waited upon the Lords Commissioners of Trade," Burrington reported to the Duke's secretary in August, 1730,

> and shew'd them [my] old list of Councillors without any names against Chief Justice, and Secretary, Coll: Bladen filled them up with his own hand before Mr. Pelham and Mr. Brudenwell; I hope his Grace the Duke of Newcastle (my noble Patron) will not be offended.[23]

There was little chance of this. Brudenell was a close friend of Newcastle's political associate in Sussex, the Duke of Richmond; while Thomas Pelham was a relation of the southern secretary and sat in Parliament for Newcastle's borough of Lewes.[24]

These appointments indicated, nevertheless, the power of Martin Bladen of the Board of Trade. Nathaniel Rice, the new Secretary of North Carolina, was a close relation of the Commissioner. And it was Bladen who took the initiative in proposing William Smith for the post of Chief

[23] Burrington to Delafaye, August 8, 1730, C.O. 5/308, fol. 22.

[24] Jean Wake, *The Brudenells of Deane*, London, 1954, 287-90.

Justice. Smith was a friend of Mr. Verney, one of the King's council at law, and John Scrope, the new Secretary to the Treasury.[25] This appointment in particular illustrated the web of personal relationships linking the various departments of the administrative machine and the influence exerted by the lower ranks of the bureaucracy on the determination of policy and patronage.

Personal friendship accounted as well for the nomination of Daniel Germain as Provost Marshal. Germain was a client of the Earl of Essex, a close acquaintance of the Pelham family. Although he was a correspondent of Bolingbroke, Leveson-Gower, William Pulteney, and other members of the opposition, Essex had been appointed by Newcastle to the embassy at Turin. The appointment of Germain to an American post was merely another indication of the personal regard for Essex of the Pelham brothers.[26]

As their leverage within the ministry increased, Newcastle and Henry Pelham could begin to oblige their friends with the fruits of office. The presence of a Pelham on the Board of Trade was a sure indication of growing influence of the family. As yet these gains were limited and uncertain. They could be consolidated only if the leading members of the family could remain in office and continue to have access to governmental patronage. In time, a personal following could be established within the ranks of the administration.[27] In the early 1730's, how-

[25] "North Carolina Employments," no date, C.O. 5/306, fol. 368.

[26] Loc. cit.; "Private letters received by the Earl of Essex," Add. MSS 27732-35, *passim*.

[27] Both Johnson and Burrington received explicit instructions, apparently from Newcastle, to transmit detailed information on the posts in their colonies at the disposition of the southern secretary. See Burrington to Newcastle, April 7, 1730, C.O. 5/308, fol. 30; "List," no date, C.O. 5/308, fol. 247.

ever, it was more important to placate influential friends and potential supporters. Some investment in security was required before the profits of office could safely be diverted for personal use. The first dividends, the offices on the Carolina establishment, had been plowed back into the business.

II

The first major occasion on which Newcastle exploited the patronage of his office on his family's behalf came in 1731, with the appointment of William Cosby as Governor of New York and New Jersey. Cosby came from a prominent Anglo-Irish family and had risen to the rank of colonel in the English army. His chances for a further promotion were increased by his marriage to Grace Montagu, sister of the second Earl of Halifax and a cousin of Newcastle. These connections won Cosby the governorship of Minorca in the Mediterranean, but the Colonel had greater ambitions than a distant military command. His financial need was apparently greater as well, for his administration was clouded by charges of extortion.[28] Once again Cosby had recourse to his influential relatives. The sudden death of Lord Forbes, governor of the Leeward Islands since 1729, provided an opening in America. By June, 1731, Newcastle had secured the post for his relative.

Cosby was reluctant to assume his new command. No doubt he remembered the fate of Forbes and his predecessor, the Earl of Londonderry, in the deadly disease environment of the West Indies. The military man was still in England when the death of Governor Montgom-

[28] See the entry for Cosby in the *D.A.B.* and Alexander to Colden, February 21, 1732, NYHS, *Collections*, LI, 48-51.

ery of New York presented him with the possibility of a more lucrative and more healthful position. With Newcastle's assistance, Cosby received a patent from the King as Governor of New York and New Jersey in March, 1732.[29]

This favor bestowed upon an impecunious relative was not the only indication of the growing influence of the southern secretary in the disposition of colonial patronage. This success had been preceded by Burrington's nomination to the chief executive's post in North Carolina. Within a year it was followed by an even more significant appointment. This was the designation of Robert Burnet as Secretary of New Jersey in June, 1733. Burnet was a key man in Newcastle's political organization in Sussex. His nomination represented the creation of a direct link between the Duke's responsibilities as a colonial administrator and his activities as a borough politician. Burnet collected the rents of the Pelham estates in the county and sought to influence the votes of the family's tenants. In addition, he supervised the electioneering activities designed to win the financially independent voters in the region. Finally, he served as a mediator between the Pelhams and the lesser gentry of the county.[30] These activities were expensive as well as time-consuming. It was the growing cost of Burnet's invaluable work which prompted the southern secretary to secure him a patent post in America. The duties of the office in New Jersey

[29] Newcastle to Board of Trade, April 20, 1731 and January 12, 1732, S.P. 44/137, pp. 244 and 309; Kimball, *Rhode Island Correspondence*, I, 403n.

[30] See the extensive correspondence in Add. MSS 32688-89 and Basil Williams, "The Duke of Newcastle and the Election of 1734," *EHR*, XII (1897), 448-88.

could be performed by a deputy and the "rent" used to defray the expenses of the election agent.[31] With this assistance from abroad the strength and vigor of the Pelhams' political organization in their "home" county could be maintained.

Success in Sussex was crucial to Newcastle's future political career. For at this juncture the Duke was involved directly only in the political affairs of the three counties of Sussex, Yorkshire, and Nottingham. This was more the result of historical accident that conscious choice. Newcastle's father, Sir Thomas Pelham, had bequeathed him lands in Sussex extending over most of the southeastern part of the county. From his mother's brother, John, Duke of Newcastle, he had inherited a Nottingham estate with a yearly rent role of £6,000 and a dominant voice in the elections of the Yorkshire constituencies of Aldborough and Boroughbridge. The Duke's greatest electoral strength was in these two Yorkshire boroughs. Yet even here the southern secretary did not exercise absolute control. One of the four seats was habitually held by a member of a local family, the Wilkensens. A member of the family advised Newcastle in 1734 that "It will now [be] against ye bent & Humour of ye People, to chuse two yt are neither of them Neighbours to em."[32]

The situation in the other counties was even more un-

[31] This was a new use of this post. From 1703 to 1715, J. Basse served in person under a patent from the King; James Smith then held the post until 1733, but without a royal patent. Smith employed a deputy and probably owed his appointment to the Governor.

[32] Wilkensen to Newcastle, April 7, 1734, Add. MSS 33689, foll. 184-85; "Accompts of the Duke of Newcastle's Properties, 1725-1735," Add. MSS 33320, 208 folios; "Abstract of Voters at Aldborough belonging to the Duke of Newcastle," Add. MSS 33061, foll. 204-05, dated 1766.

certain. In Nottinghamshire, the Duke's influence hinged mainly on his position as a large landowner, while in Sussex his primacy rested as much on government patronage as on personal estate. "The Treasury," Newcastle observed to Rockingham in 1765,

> . . . from the year 1714, 'till I came in to the Treasury myself in 1754, have been so good, as to allow me to have the recommendation to all the employments in the Customs, etc, which should become vacant in the counties of Sussex, and Nottingham. In Nottingham, there are few, or none; in Sussex, a great many.[33]

In addition, Newcastle could rely on the long connection of the Pelham family with Sussex. His father had sat in Parliament for East Grinstead, Lewes, and the county; and in the eighteenth century three branches of the family were firmly established there and were sending M.P.'s to Westminster.[34]

Yet even at its strongest, this powerful phalanx of landed interest, personal prestige, and domestic patronage was not impregnable. More important, it did not encompass the majority of the boroughs even in these two counties. In the Sussex elections of 1715, 1722, and 1727, Newcastle had influence only in the county and in three of the thirteen boroughs and Cinque Ports. Only in the

[33] Quoted in Margaret Cramp, "The Parliamentary Representation of Five Sussex Boroughs . . . 1754-1768," unpub. M.A. thesis, Manchester Univ., 1953, 68-69.

[34] Newcastle kept houses at Haland and Bishopstone. The family of Henry Pelham, Newcastle's paternal uncle, settled first at Lewes and later at Stanmer. The family of Sir Nicholas Pelham, the half-brother of the Duke's paternal grandfather, lived at Catsfield and Crowhurst.

town of Lewes did the Duke exercise complete control and return both candidates on his own interest.[35]

The preservation of even this limited influence in Sussex had become the overriding objective of the family on the eve of the general election of 1734. It was widely believed, among the members both of the opposition and of the government, that the adverse public reaction to the Excise Tax proposal would cut deeply into the political strength of Walpole and his lieutenants. This was as true with regard to Sussex at it was in those counties with less of a record of allegiance to the ministerial cause. The Earl of Chesterfield wrote with evident satisfaction to the Earl of Marchmont:

> The Duke of Newcastle will probably be beaten in Sussex; the Duke of Dorset most certainly will in Kent, and so of very many other places, where the court used formerly always to carry it.[36]

The southern secretary was as acutely aware of these dangers as his opponents. National prominence ultimately rested upon strength in the boroughs. The appointment of Burnet was one step toward safeguarding this local hegemony. The selection of two other Sussex friends and supporters for colonial sinecures constituted a further extension of the same program. Nathaniel Cruttenden, one of the eight Jurats of Hastings, was named Vendue Master in South Carolina; and Peter Forbes, another of the Duke's servants and election agents, was appointed Pro-

[35] Nulle, *Thomas Pelham-Holles*, 36, 140-41.

[36] October 5, 1733, Rose, ed., *Marchmont Correspondence*, II, 2-3. Fierce opposition in the country and the threat of riots in London eventually forced Walpole to abandon this plan to raise revenue by means of indirect taxes on spirits and certain other commodities.

vost Marshal of Jamaica, a post worth £600 per annum.[37] As both of these offices could be served by deputy, they provided a considerable revenue with a minimum of effort. In effect, Newcastle was subsidizing his election expenses in Sussex through the judicious allocation of colonial places.

The sinecures given to Burnet, Cruttenden, and Forbes were not the only American posts utilized by the southern secretary for electoral purposes. In 1732, Newcastle appointed Matthew Concanen as Attorney-General of Jamaica. This "hired scribbler for the Daily Courant," as Pope labeled him in the *Dunciad*, edited the *British Journal* on behalf of the administration Whigs.[38] And in 1733, on the eve of the election, Newcastle asked Governor Hunter of Jamaica to assist Rose Fuller, an important Sussex freeholder who had various investments in the islands.[39]

The support of the local aristocracy and gentry was equally crucial in Nottinghamshire. From his uncle, Newcastle had inherited the predominant influence over three seats, two in the town of Nottingham and one at East Retford. Two other elections were controlled by the Tories and the remaining three were managed by independent country gentlemen. By combining forces with Lord Howe in 1722, the Duke ousted one of the Tory

[37] "List of the Major Jurats . . . of Hastings," no date, Add. MSS 33058, fol. 485; Newcastle to Hunter, April 9, 1730, C.O. 137/53, foll. 213-14. Cruttenden was appointed in 1735; Forbes succeeded his father in 1730.

[38] Theophilus Cibber, *The Lives of the Poets of Great Britain and Scotland*, London, 1753, V, 27; Yonge to Delafaye, July 10, 1732, C.O. 137/53, fol. 358; Concanen to Newcastle, April 4, 1733, C.O. 137/43, foll. 202-204; Hunter to Newcastle, April 14, 1732, C.O. 137/54, fol. 72, complains of the Governor's loss of patronage.

[39] Hunter to Newcastle, April 1, 1733, C.O. 137/54, fol. 192.

representatives for the county. In a second political bargain, Newcastle arranged for the Duke of Rutland to have a post in the King's bedchamber and to be made a member of the Order of the Garter. In return, Rutland allowed the young aristocrat to nominate his cousin James Pelham for one of the seats at Newark.[40] Neither of these understandings testified to Newcastle's personal political power. One was dependent on the continuing good will of a local landowner, while the other was contingent on the availability of ministerial patronage.

In the Nottinghamshire election of 1727, the opposition counterattacked with considerable skill and regained the ground lost to the Duke five years before. As part of a bargain with the local Whigs and country gentlemen, the Tories did not oppose the incumbent members for the county, Lord Howe and Sir Robert Sutton. In return, they were given the nomination of one of the two candidates in both Nottingham Town and East Retford.[41] This local agreement cost the southern secretary the disposal of one of the seats in the town of Nottingham. Borlace Warren, a Tory, replaced the Duke's election agent, John Plumptre, in Parliament. The balance of power in the county had reverted to that of 1714. Once again Newcastle controlled completely only three of the eight seats in Nottinghamshire.[42] The Duke's personal influence was no match for a local alliance between Whig gentlemen and Tory squires.

[40] Stebelton H. Nulle, "The Duke of Newcastle and the Election of 1727," *JMH*, IX (March 1727), 16-19; "Mr. Truman's Bill of Expenses . . . 1714," Add. MSS 33060, foll. 13-18; Newcastle to the Duchess, March 28, 1722, Add. MSS 33073, fol. 15.

[41] Sutton to Newcastle, September 4, 1727, S.P. 36/3, foll. 61-62.

[42] John Stanhope, Thomas White, and James Pelham sat for Nottingham Town, East Retford, and Newark respectively.

Even before the election of 1734, Newcastle sought to reestablish his primacy in the county. The target of his efforts was Lord Howe, the M.P. for the county and a political associate since 1721. Howe's estate was burdened by a heavy load of debt; he was the perfect man to tempt with the offer of a lucrative American post. The opportunity came in February, 1732, with the death of Walter Chetwynd, whom Walpole had recently appointed to the government of Barbados in return for his support in Staffordshire politics.[43] By May, the First Lord of the Treasury had been brought to acquiesce in Newcastle's scheme. For his part, the new Governor saw to it that his part of the agreement was fulfilled. "All those that call themselves my friends & would have me believe they are really so," Howe assured the southern secretary, "will do all they can to serve Yr. Grace's Interest. . . ."[44] In the by-election of 1732 and again in the general poll two years later, Thomas Bennet, one of the Duke's agents in Nottinghamshire, was returned for the county in Howe's place. Even the colonists in Barbados were pleased by the bargain. Once nominated to the government of the island, Howe did all in his power to secure the passage of legislation long-desired by the planters. "I hope the Sugar Bill will pass your House," the Governor wrote to the Duke of Rutland early in 1733; "If it does not, and no relief is

[43] In 1727, Walpole had removed John Chetwynd from the Board of Trade and his brother William Richard from the Admiralty Board and from his parliamentary seat for Plymouth, an Admiralty borough. Then, in 1731, the first minister sought to regain the political support of the family. See Edgecumbe to Walpole, no date, W.C., no. 3240.

[44] Howe to Newcastle, November 5, 1733, C.O. 28/45, foll. 275-76; T. Pelham to Newcastle, May 4, 1732, S.P. 36/26, fol. 331; Howe to Newcastle, May 13 and 16, 1732, Add. MSS 32687, foll. 453-54, 455.

given to this island, it will be ruined."[45] Rarely had an appointment made for domestic political reasons worked out so well for the colonists in the West Indies.

For the southern secretary the result was no less salutary. The Duke could now boast complete control of four of the eight seats in the county. Furthermore, with the seduction of Howe, Newcastle had seized the initiative in Nottinghamshire. Robert Clifton, the M.P. for East Retford since 1727, offered to trade his seat in return for the government of New York. "It is not everybody," Clifton reminded the Duke in 1736, "that would give up their Seat in Parlmt & go abroad, or could be sure of Chuseing another to supply their place to the mind of the Ministry. . . ."[46]

Although this bargain was never struck, it indicated the effective use which could be made of American patronage and the degree to which the availability of colonial posts had become known. It represented, moreover, the apogee of Newcastle's influence in Nottinghamshire during the first half of the eighteenth century. The death of Lord Howe in 1735 and of Thomas Bennet two years later renewed the conflict between the Duke's supporters and the independent country gentlemen. John Plumptre reported to his patron shortly after Bennet's death that

> The Whigs amongst the middling People of this Town, who are, most of them, Freeholders in the County, seem to have No Notion of being against the Howe Interest, or, indeed, of its being separate

[45] January 28, 1733, H.M.C., *Twelfth Report*, pt. V, 194; Frank W. Pitman, *The Development of the British West Indies, 1700-1763*, New Haven, 1912, 264.

[46] July 22, 1736, S.P. 36/39, fol. 37; in 1745 Clifton sought another place, this time on the Board of Trade: Add. MSS 32704, fol. 184.

> from that of the Whigs. . . . In our minds we make the Torys the Compliment to think they will not be so mad as to break among themselves as we have done.[47]

The political forces in the county were so finely balanced that in "ordinary" times Newcastle had to share control of the Nottingham boroughs with the other influential landholders. On the three occasions during his career when Newcastle did increase his parliamentary representation from three to four, the price was paid outside the county. A Garter and a post in the bedchamber extracted a seat from the Duke of Rutland in 1721; the West Indian governorship displaced Howe in 1732; and an appointment as a Commissioner of the Excise persuaded William Mellish to relinquish his seat in 1751.[48] Of the three, the transatlantic appointment was undoubtedly the most effective. It did not require an expansion of domestic places, a move which would have been condemned and opposed by the country gentlemen in Parliament. Nor did it put Newcastle as deeply in debt to his colleagues as a domestic appointment of comparable value. The governorship came from the southern secretary's own department and, more important, it was outside the normal field of political patronage.

[47] Plumptre to Newcastle, October 29, 1737, Add. MSS 32690, foll. 406-407; Newcastle to Plumptre, August 24, 1731, Add. MSS 32687, foll. 405-406 recounts the previous history of these factional disputes.

[48] A Commissionership of the Customs for William Levinz in 1747 was yet another instance, but Levinz's successor was not a devout Pelhamite. See Add. MSS 32707, foll. 308, 320-21; Add. MSS 32710, foll. 246, 485; and J. B. Owen, *The Rise of the Pelhams*, London, 1957, 307. Lewis B. Namier and John Brooke, *The House of Commons, 1754-1790*, London, 1963, I, 114-17, provide a general survey of politics in Nottinghamshire.

American posts had been used in the past to reward those whose lives or fortunes had been expended in the "national" interest. Service to the Crown in war, in diplomatic negotiations, in the bureaucracy; noble birth or influential connections; economic hardship because of national financial policy—these had been the acknowledged criteria for a colonial sinecure. Now a new category of eligibility, political allegiance or service to an individual minister, had appeared on the scene. By the 1730's, this political exploitation of the administrative resources of the colonies was becoming widespread and, even more significantly, was becoming closely integrated with local English politics.

This interaction between the political systems of the old and new worlds came to affect Scottish affairs as well. The union of England and Scotland in 1707 opened up America for Scottish settlement. The subsequent migration of thousands of Scotsmen into the middle and southern continental colonies relieved the pressure of population on the meager resources of the homeland. It also provided an outlet for the upper classes. Like its counterpart in Ireland, the social elite of Scotland was not readily accepted by the English governing class. Indeed, there was a pervasive dislike of Scots among all segments of the English population during the eighteenth century. The Duke of Richmond wrote to Newcastle of Solicitor-General William Murray, the future Lord Mansfield:

> The only objection that can be made to him, is what he can't help, which is that he is a Scotchman, which (as I have a great regard for him) I am extremely sorry for.[49]

[49] Quoted in Yorke, *Life of Yorke*, I, 307n. Desmond Clarke, *Arthur Dobbs, Esquire: 1689-1765*, London, 1955, mentions simi-

Rebuffed at the seat of empire, the sons of the Scottish upper classes sought their fortunes in America. In the colonies they could use the political influence stemming from representation at Westminster to secure places of profit and authority in an even more "provincial" part of the British empire. There was a definite hierarchy of accent and culture among the constituent parts of the empire, just as there was a stratification of power and prestige within each of them.

The infiltration of the Scottish governing class into American administrative positions was facilitated by a bureaucratic rearrangement in 1725. In that year Walpole dismissed the Duke of Roxburgh as the Secretary of State for Scotland because of his connection with the Sunderland Whigs. Instead of appointing a successor to Roxburgh, the chief minister vested the duties of the office jointly in the two main secretaries of state. In practice, however, the bulk of the responsibility fell on Newcastle. These new duties brought the Duke into close contact with the Duke of Argyll and the Earl of Islay, the allies of Walpole who controlled Scottish patronage, and provided a natural bridge between the politics of Scotland and America. In 1733, for example, the banker John Drummond approached the southern secretary about a position in South Carolina:

---

lar prejudice against Dobbs, an Anglo-Irishman who became Governor of North Carolina in 1753. Twenty years before, a correspondent had told Newcastle that there were four "nations" resident on the island of Jamaica: English, Scots, Irish, and Jews (April, 1733, C.O. 137/54, foll. 368-70). The implications of cultural diversity and provincialism are suggestively outlined by John Clive and Bernard Bailyn, "England's Cultural Provinces: Scotland and America," *WMQ*, 3rd ser., XI (April, 1954), 200-13.

> The Very Small employment which I used the freedom to sollicit your Grace for in favor of Mr. James Wedderburn, a younger Son of Sir Peter Holket Wedderburn, formerly a member of Parliament for the County of Fife . . . is Clerk of the pleas in South Carolina, which allwye goes along with two Small patent places which patents *I bought of Mr. Lowdes.* . . .

"I humbly hope," the banker continued, "that I shall not be refused Soo Small a favor for him, the election of that County being very much in his Fathers power who is my relation and a Sincere friend to Sir John Anstruther. . . ."[50] Within two weeks Newcastle had secured a royal warrant directing the appointment of the younger Wedderburn.

This nomination was just one of a series. From 1707 to 1737 the government of Virginia was held by George Hamilton, the Earl of Orkney. His deputy for part of this period was Alexander Spotswood, another Scotsman. The Surveyor-General and later Lieutenant-Governor of New York, Cadwallader Colden, was a Scottish physician who emigrated to the colonies when he failed to break into London society. The new royal provinces in the Carolinas were overburdened with Scottish administrators. John Montgomery and James Abercrombie were appointed Attorney-General in North and South Carolina, respectively. And Robert and James Wright were named as Chief Justice and Remembrancer Clerk in the southern province. Indeed, the web of patronage linking Scotland with the Carolinas had become sufficiently strong by 1732 for Abercrombie to offer to resign his post to Benjamin Whitaker, a deserving ministerial supporter. In return Abercrombie asked for the place of Assistant Solicitor to the

[50] April 14, 1733, C.O. 5/383, fol. 204, italics in the original; Thomson, *Secretaries of State*, 35-37; Riley, *English Ministers*, chap. 16.

Crown in the Court of the Exchequer in Scotland, a Treasury post worth £200 per annum.[51]

The movement of officials between the two sections in time reached a level which caused Newcastle some concern. When he dispatched Lord Cathcart as head of a military expedition against Spanish positions in the West Indies in 1740, the southern secretary felt obliged to add a warning. "Give me Leave, as a Faithful Friend, and servant," the Duke wrote to the Scottish aristocrat,

> to hint to you, That, in the future Disposition of Commissions, You should endeavor to remove the Opinion, which many People (however unjustly) have conceived, of your giving the Preference to one particular Part of His Majesty's Subjects.[52]

Newcastle's cautionary note was tinged with hypocrisy. His own use of American positions to placate his Scottish friends and to establish political alliances had been far more significant. The Duke's utilization of colonial patronage had served to increase his influence in Scotland no less than in Nottingham and Sussex.

These coups were not completely bloodless. The political use of American offices avoided the disruption of the carefully balanced hierarchy of power and authority in

[51] Abercrombie to Walpole, December 16, 1732, W.C., no. 1936; Leonidas Dodson, *Alexander Spotswood* . . . , Philadelphia, 1932, 6; Alice Mapelsden Keys, *Cadwallader Colden* . . . , New York, 1906, 1-3; and Gerrit P. Judd, *Members of Parliament, 1734-1832*, New Haven, 1955, 53: "Here is evidence that the Scots, underprivileged as a nation, were flocking to the professions as a means of climbing up the social ladder. . . ."

[52] October 2, 1740, Add. MSS 32695, foll. 192-95. Shy, *Toward Lexington*, 179 and 352-54, notes that the Scots were overrepresented among the officers serving in the British army in America in the 1760's and 1770's.

England but only at the cost of the destruction of the subsidiary equilibrium in America. The patronage demands of the ministry could be satisfied only at the expense of the colonial governor or assembly. Eventually this encroachment on local prerogatives affected the character of the colonial relationship. "With respect to Carolina," General Oglethorpe reported in 1736, "the Assembly are so angry at the Offices being filled up in England, that they have lessened all the Officers Fees so that the Deputies can afford to give but very little."[53] In the short run this curtailment of income worked to the disadvantage of those whom Newcastle had attempted to aid; over the longer term this appropriation of American resources for English political purposes exacerbated the tensions inherent in a dependent relationship and contributed to its breakdown.

III

Just at the time that Newcastle was expanding his control over American patronage, his interest in the internal politics of the colonies declined sharply. This paradox was more apparent than real. The enthusiasm with American affairs engendered by the Duke's first taste of executive power had waned with the passage of time. Moreover, with Townshend's departure from the ministry in 1730, Newcastle diverted much of his energy into the intricate and demanding stream of European diplomacy. Preoccupied by more important matters of state, the southern sec-

[53] Oglethorpe to Stone, July 3, 1736, C.O. 5/654, fol. 74. Haffenden, "Colonial Appointments," 428, denies that "lesser colonial offices were reserved in any way for the granting of political favors or systematically developed to serve political purposes" by Newcastle in the years before 1739, but the available evidence does not support his argument.

retary ignored the colonies except when domestic patronage was at stake.[54]

One result of Newcastle's abdication of responsibility was to increase the leverage of the lower strata of the colonial bureaucracy. On the death of Lieutenant-Governor Wentworth of New Hampshire in 1730, for example, the Board of Trade immediately recommended the appointment of David Dunbar, the Surveyor of the King's Woods in New England. "We apprehend this would increase Mr. Dunbar's Authority in those Parts," the board explained to Newcastle, "and greatly contribute to the Preservation of his Majesty's Woods."[55]

It was unlikely that this was the sole motivation. In picking upon Dunbar for the post of Lieutenant-Governor, the board deliberately passed over Henry Shelburne, the candidate suggested by Jonathan Belcher, the joint Governor of Massachusetts Bay and New Hampshire. This direct repudiation of the new chief executive was prompted by Belcher's continued requests for permission to accept an annual salary from the Massachusetts Assembly. If the Governor was intent upon sacrificing imperial policy, then the Board of Trade was determined to deny him patronage and to install an advocate of the prerogative of the Crown in a position of authority.[56]

[54] Beginning in 1732, Newcastle's letter books for the southern department change both in tone and in content. Routine requests to the Board of Trade replace specific inquiries; there are few references to intra-colonial issues or problems; and the emphasis is now upon colonial trade and defense. See S.P. 44/128-32, and above, chap. 1, note 24.

[55] February 10, 1731, C.O. 5/931, fol. 113. Dunbar owed his surveyorship, a Treasury post worth £800 per annum, to Walpole. See W.C., nos. 1375, 1473, and 1890.

[56] The board knew of Belcher's preference before recommending Dunbar. See Belcher to Newcastle, December 15, 1730, C.O. 5/898, foll. 344-45, received February 9, 1731.

Following the recommendation of the advisory body, Newcastle secured a royal warrant constituting Dunbar the Lieutenant-Governor of New Hampshire. On the same day the southern secretary informed the board of the receipt of letters from Belcher describing a number of severe jurisdictional disputes with the diligent Surveyor of the Woods. The Duke therefore asked the board to "let me know whether you are still of the same Opinion as to Colo Dunbar's having that Government."[57] Newcastle understood clearly that the Governor's position in New England would be severely undermined by the promotion of his leading opponent; it was for this reason that the southern secretary took the unusual step of requesting a further review of the matter. When the board reaffirmed its choice of Dunbar, however, the Duke immediately acquiesced in the decision. He had no personal interest to serve in this case and was therefore content to abide by the verdict of his subordinates.[58]

It was Belcher's perception of Newcastle's new attitude which determined the Governor's next move. He sought to replace Dunbar with Anthony Reynolds, the son of the

[57] February 27, 1731, S.P. 44/127, p. 211; Board to Newcastle, March 5, 1731, C.O. 5/931, foll. 116-17. Malone, *Pine Trees and Politics*, chap. 6, offers a much too unfavorable view of Dunbar's role in these disputes.

[58] Newcastle was not so solicitous of the Governor's position when it conflicted with his own desires. In 1731, on the request of Joseph Danvers of the Royal African Company, the Duke named Spencer Phipps as Lieutenant-Governor of Massachusetts Bay, passing over Belcher's candidate. Danvers was the M.P. for Bramber in Sussex, an old associate of Newcastle, and a firm supporter of the ministry. See H. and J. Palmer to Danvers, April 19, 1732, C.O. 5/898, fol. 442; Danvers to Newcastle no date, C.O. 5/10, foll. 315-16; and Belcher to Newcastle, March 6, 1732, C.O. 5/898, fol. 440. Haffenden, "Colonial Appointments," 421, offers a more favorable interpretation of Newcastle's conduct in this case.

Bishop of Lincoln. A completely incompetent official, even as a placeman, Reynolds had the advantage of an interest in England, something that Shelburne lacked completely. When the Bishop refused to intervene with Newcastle on his son's behalf, Belcher resolved upon a direct appeal to his adversaries within the ranks of the colonial bureaucracy. "Perhaps £150 properly placed with Bl - d - n or P - pp - le," the Governor suggested to his agent in London, "might do the business without D-b-r's leave."[59]

Belcher's attempt to bribe the secretary of the Board of Trade and its leading member failed as decisively as his effort to win the support of the Bishop of Lincoln. The governor therefore turned his attention once again to the higher levels of the ministry. "I find Coll B - - - n is my enemy . . . ," Belcher wrote to Richard Partridge in April, 1732, "we must therefore constantly apply to their superiors. . . ."[60] Two years later he was still attempting to secure political support. Belcher wrote to his son and brother-in-law in August, 1734:

> I intend to follow Lord Townshend's advice, and apply myself directly to Sr. R.W. in the case of D - b - r . . . Bl - d - n I am sensible is a fast advocate to D - b - r, and I must expect no favour while he is at the Board of Trade; but were the D - v - l there I shou'd expect justice under British Constitution corroborated with the Hannover Succession. . . .
>
> I have known many instances of things going quite contrary at the Privy Council to what they wou'd have done at the Board of Trade. Had they known when I solicited to their superiours for the

[59] Belcher to Partridge, April 23, 1733, MHS, *Collections*, 6th ser., VI, 269-71.

[60] April 27, 1732, ibid., VI, 120-23.

governmt they (say Bl - d - n) would have done all in his power to have hindered it. I say I had rather on all occasions have recourse to the King in Council than have any thing of mine decided before the Board of Trade.[61]

Unlike the question of an annual salary grant or the matter of Belcher's own appointment, this matter was not of sufficient importance to come automatically to the attention of the committee of council. The Governor finally resigned himself to an accommodation with the members of the bureaucracy in London. He agreed to cease his harassment of the Surveyor-General and to allow Dunbar one-third of the governor's salary in New Hampshire in addition to the fees of the office. In return for these concessions, Belcher sought to win Bladen's support in another patronage decision. "I know," the Governor confided to his agent, "Collo Bl - d - n can greatly assist with Sr R.W. and D.N.C. to regain me the Naval Office. . . ."[62] Beaten by Belcher on the salary question, Bladen and the Board of Trade had secured a measure of retribution with their successful defense of Dunbar's position and perquisites.

Given the devolution of effective power over many colonial matters to the lesser officials within the English government, it was significant that a more purposeful approach to American problems was not forthcoming. In part this lack of energy and of accomplishment can be traced to the constant decline in the abilities of the members of the Board of Trade. In 1727, for instance, Richard Plumer was removed from the advisory body because of

[61] August 7, 1734, ibid., VII, 94-108.

[62] December 6, 1734, ibid., VII, 173-74.

an adverse vote in Parliament.[63] Sir Orlando Bridgeman, his replacement, was a fourth-rate politician infamous for his accumulation of debts.

The mediocrity of the new official was all too familiar. During Walpole's twenty years as chief minister, hardly a man of note was named to the board. During this period the burden of administration was borne by those named between 1715 and 1721. Two of these "activists," John Chetwynd and Paul Docminique, served until 1728 and 1735. The Earl of Westmoreland, the prime figure in the extension of royal control over the Carolinas, resigned in the mid-1730's.[64] By this time only Thomas Pelham and Martin Bladen remained to carry on the struggle against the fractious colonists. In 1734 Belcher was outraged that "Coll Bladen took upon him[self] the management of the whole hearing."[65] But this was not unusual. When he appeared before the board in 1737 on behalf of the Georgia trustees, the Earl of Egmont found that Bladen was in complete control. And, Admiral Norris noted in his journal two years later, Bladen "was supposed to have the most generall knowledge of all the plantations" of anyone in England.[66] Bladen's hegemony was misleading; it signified the decline of the Board of Trade rather than its growing strength. As age and death had taken their toll of the members appointed during the early years of the

[63] Plumer to Walpole, July 31, 1727, W.C., no. 1462; Plumb, *Walpole*, II, 213, 242, 243.

[64] Two other first-rate men, Joseph Addison and Daniel Pulteney, served between 1714 and 1721.

[65] Belcher to J. Belcher, Jr., August 7, 1734, MHS, *Collections*, 6th ser., VII, 94-103.

[66] December, 1739, Add. MSS 28132, foll. 111-12; February 9 and April 20, 1737, Egmont, *Diary*, II, 344, 391; Wolff, *Colonial Agency*, 61; Haffenden, "Colonial Appointments," 421-22, 429-30.

Hanoverian period, the activism of the advisory body and its commitment to a reform of the colonial system had faltered as well. Always an office filled with due regard for political allegiance, the Board of Trade had now become a repository for sterile placemen and shabby politicians.

One indication of the decline in the board's fervor for reform was its own use of patronage. In 1726, the advisory body had suggested to Newcastle that he appoint Bryan Wheelock, for many years its Deputy-Secretary and Chief Clerk, as Clerk of the Markets in Jamaica. This appointment was intended as a reward for Wheelock's long service and as compensation for the board's inability to secure his promotion to the secretary's post, a preserve of the Popple family since 1696. On the death of the elder Wheelock in 1735, the board asked the southern secretary to appoint the clerk's son to succeed him.[67] This second and more dubious request came from the members of the board in their "private" capacities, a tacit admission of the impropriety of its action. The board had long recommended the abolition of patent posts served by deputies. Now, with very little justification, it had resorted to the very evil which it deplored when practiced by others.

With such a fallible guardian of the morals of the colonial system, it was not surprising that officials on all levels of the administrative hierarchy continued to act as their own personal advantage demanded. Following the example of the secretaries of state, minor officials built up a personal following in America and sought places and profit for themselves and their friends. Charles Delafaye, Undersecretary of State for the southern department from

[67] April 10, 1735, C.O. 137/48, foll. 13-15.

1717 to 1734, had connections in New York and Jamaica. In 1719 his intervention with Governor Hunter secured the command of an independent company for his brother-in-law, John Riggs. In return, Delafaye supported the New York Governor in his effort to win the ratification of several other nominations by the home authorities. This Anglo-American connection did not end with Hunter's departure from New York. His successor named Riggs's son to a lieutenant's post in 1724; and in 1727, at the time of Colonel Montgomery's appointment, Delafaye secured yet another promotion for his nephew.[68] As long as Delafaye remained in his key position in London, the advancement of his relatives in America was assured.

The Undersecretary also benefited personally from his post in the colonial bureaucracy. "I have wrote to Colonel Bladen," Governor Hunter of Jamaica informed Delafaye; "You must Send over a power of Attorney to some body to receive and remitt your money."[69] With a stake in the island, probably in the form of rent from a patent post, the Undersecretary became its ardent supporter within the administration. In a letter to Walpole in 1732, he argued strongly in favor of the duty imposed by the Assembly on slaves imported into the island.[70] Delafaye contended that the provision of an adequate revenue was more important than the burden placed on the merchant interest. In this case, the intervention of the Undersecretary was offset by the determined opposition to the tax by the

[68] See the material in C.O. 5/1092, foll. 17-18, 23-24, 60-61, 165; also Montgomery to Newcastle, December 18, 1728, C.O. 5/983, foll. 10-11.

[69] July 17, 1729, C.O. 137/53, foll. 166-67; Trelawney to Stone, September 22, 1739, C.O. 137/56, foll. 255-56; Thomson, *Secretaries of State*, 140.

[70] August 26, 1732, W.C., no. 1899; Delafaye to Newcastle, October 18, 1734, Add. MSS 33689, foll. 463-64.

South Sea Company. It was only when there was no outside pressure or when there was a balance of power between competing ministers or interest groups that a junior administrator could hope to have a decisive influence.

Nevertheless, royal officials in America found it very helpful to have a voice within the home bureaucracy. During the first half of the eighteenth century minor bureaucrats such as Delafaye were called upon by those in the colonies to mediate between themselves and the ministry. The utilization of these officials on a mutually profitable basis was simply another informal strand binding one part of the empire to another. This was the positive side of the equation. There was a negative aspect as well. At the same time that Governor Hunter of Jamaica was arranging for one of Undersecretary of State Temple Stanyan's friends to receive the income from an office in the colony, he asked Stanyan to ease the objections of the senior ministers to a revenue bill which he had just negotiated with the assembly.[71] The satisfaction of private interests had become inextricably intertwined with the formation of public policy.

By the early 1730's this "informal" imperial administrative system had assumed the character it was to retain until the eve of the outbreak of the Seven Years' War. Many American politicians, office-holders, and merchants had tacit understandings with strategically-placed individuals in England. In addition, many of the colonies employed permanent "agents" to represent their interests in the mother country. The power of these spokesmen and agents depended in the first instance on their access to influential members of the ministry. Those without a firm

[71] Hunter to Stanyan, March 7 and May 17, 1728, C.O. 137/53, foll. 24, 56-57; also Nicholson to Stanyan, August 25, 1724, C.O. 5/387, fol. 137.

"interest" did not bother to accept colonial posts. In 1729 and 1731, Micajah Perry had secured the appointment of councillors in Virginia and New Jersey by virtue of his friendship with Newcastle. By 1734, however, the London merchant was informing his correspondents in America that,

> it is my misfortune at present to be so much out of favour that my appearance at ye Council board would rather do you hurt that good. . . . I am in great disgrace with the present powers. . . .[72]

As Perry's experience indicated, there was a premium on those intermediaries with a personal attachment to the Walpoles or the Pelhams. Indeed, men of this description soon began to dominate the informal mechanism of empire. John Sharpe, the Solicitor to the Treasury, and Peter Leheup, a Treasury clerk and private secretary to Horace Walpole, were among the most popular of this new breed of middlemen. Jonathan Belcher informed Governor Talcott of Connecticut in 1730 that "Mr. Sharpe is one of the ablest Sollicitors in Engld, and imployd by almost all the Plantations."[73] With the clerks of the Board of Trade pro-

[72] Perry to Colden, March 19 and August 30, 1734, NYHS, *Collections*, I, 105-106, 111-12. Perry was in disfavor because of his opposition to the excise tax. See H. Walpole the younger to H. Mann, June 17, 1742, Mrs. Paget Toynbee, ed., *The Letters of Horace Walpole*, Oxford, 1903-05, I, 238-40; Elizabeth Donnan, "An Eighteenth Century English Merchant: Micajah Perry," *Journal of Economic and Business History*, IV (1931), 70-98; Perry to Newcastle, May 12, 1731, C.O. 5/1344, fol. 17; Plumb, *Walpole*, II, 182.

[73] April 23, 1730, CHS, *Collections*, IV, 197-98. Sharpe's brother Horatio became Governor of Maryland, as did Bladen's nephew, Thomas Bladen. The proprietors of Maryland were obviously determined to court the favor of those in key administrative positions in London.

hibited from accepting colonial agencies after 1726, the minor bureaucrats in the Treasury had become the leading agents and spokesmen for colonial interests.[74]

The remaining positions were appropriated by the southern secretary for his own associates. On Newcastle's request, Governor Johnson of South Carolina secured the appointment of Peregrine Fury as agent for the colony in 1731. Two years later, the Duke made a similar overture to Lord Howe when he dispatched his Nottinghamshire associate to Barbados. "It is not in my power to Obey Yr Graces Commands this Year," Lord Howe wrote in reply, "But yr Grace may be assur'd I will do all I can to get Mr. Teissier in, the next." Six months later the Governor reported that

> I hope I have now got the Assembly to Consent to pass an Agents Bill to your Graces Satisfaction (Mr. Sharp, Teissior, and Leheup), there are still some that object to Mr. Leheup but . . . your Grace was pleas'd to order me to do what I cou'd to get him nam'd and . . . Mr. Walpole was very desirous and very pressing to have him continued. . . .[75]

And in 1734 Charles Delafaye used his influence with the Legislature of Jamaica to seek the continuation of his friend John Sharpe as agent.[76] Simply in the provision of places of profit for friends and associates, the colonial agencies served the ministry well.

These appointments had a wider significance as well.

[74] This regulation was made in 1726 after Arthur Sanderson, the Third Clerk of the board, had become joint agent for the colony of Massachusetts Bay with Francis Wilks.

[75] Howe to Newcastle, April and December, 1733, C.O. 28/45, foll. 224-25, 283-84.

[76] Sharpe to Delafaye, May 18, 1734, S.P. 36/32, fol. 1; Hunter to Newcastle, March 11, 1733, C.O. 137/55, fol. 13.

The installation of the personal acquaintances of the chief administrators in the interstices of the colonial bureaucracy affected profoundly the character of Anglo-American politics. Informal machinations and agreements took on an increased significance as a result of this siphoning-off of authority from the regularly constituted bureaucratic institutions. There were fewer opportunities for issues to be given a clear-cut formulation by the quasi-professional administrators of the Board of Trade. Debates over principles were smothered in a cloud of private understandings among friendly antagonists. Predictably enough, the dispute between the Crown and the Assembly of Massachusetts Bay—the one controversy which had developed into an ideological and constitutional confrontation—had been managed in England by a merchant and by two Dissenters from the colony. Elsewhere, the minor bureaucrats who served as colonial agents mitigated the impact of the inevitable clash between American and English interests. There was a thin line to be walked between the antagonistic demands of their two employers. If only because of their own personal financial interest, the colonial agents had come to serve as buffers between the colonies and the mother country.

It was not accidental that such a smooth-flowing and trouble-free administrative machine came into operation during Newcastle's long tenure in the southern department. Nor was it surprising that Anglo-American politics became more personal and less susceptible to rational organization; or that imperial problems were solved increasingly through the cultivation of individual influence rather than through formal bureaucratic procedures. These results were virtually inevitable, given the interlocking network of personal relationships which had come to constitute the core of the imperial administrative system. The sequel was equally predictable. The crumbling of this elaborate structure of personal influence and informal understandings following Newcastle's departure in the late 1740's was an important factor in exacerbating the new imperial conflicts which appeared during the following decades and in hampering their peaceful resolution.[77]

IV

These developments were far in the future. In the 1730's the imposing web of informal administrative control was still being constructed, and Newcastle's attempt to staff the colonial bureaucracy with men of his own choosing was bringing him into increasing conflict with the other members of the ministry. At first these disputes were muted in tone and accidental in occurrence, the natural result of overlapping administrative jurisdictions and of the incessant search for new sources of patronage. In 1735, for example, Sir Robert Walpole secured the appointment of James Gordon as Chief Justice of St. Christophers, a post formally under Newcastle's control.[78] Then, within the space of a few years, Walpole was petitioned for the secretary's place in New Jersey, command of two independent companies in Jamaica, a councillor's post in South Carolina, the Naval Office of New Hampshire, and a seat on the Board of Trade.[79] Although Newcastle successfully

[77] See Michael G. Kammen, *A Rope of Sand: The Colonial Agents, British Politics and the American Revolution*, Ithaca, 1968.

[78] Memorial of Patrick Heron, no date, W.P., vol. 42, no. 63; Matthew to Coope, July 30, 1735, and Coope to Newcastle, October 3, 1735, Add. MSS 32690, foll. 101-103. This was the first time this post had been filled from London, a usurpation protested by local officials.

[79] See W.C., nos. 1914, 2157, 2195, and 3143; W.P., vol. 42, nos. 101 and 119.

asserted his control over most of these posts, he could never ignore the paramount political position of the chief minister. Because of his predominant status, Walpole was a constant target for ambitious place-hunters and was under a continual temptation to extend his control over all aspects of policy. When Richard Partridge formulated his report to the Governor of Rhode Island on the struggle against the Molasses Act, he felt obliged to note that "our opposition . . . was attended with the more difficulty in that the Ministry with Sir *R W* appeard on the divission in the House of Commons against us. . . ."[80]

The power of the Treasury chief was illustrated again in a dispute in South Carolina. Complaints had been lodged against Governor Robert Johnson and Lord Craven had approached Newcastle about the position for his son. Additional support for the candidacy was forthcoming from the Duke of Montagu, Lord Halifax, Horatio Townshend, and James Brudenell of the Board of Trade. The complaints and this impressive roster of supporters notwithstanding, no action was taken by the ministry. The interest of the incumbent with Walpole and Archibald Hutcheson placed him in a nearly impregnable position. The southern secretary could only inform the petitioners that there was no vacancy at present. "Indeed," Newcastle felt obliged to add even before the complaints against Johnson had been heard, "I am not sure there will be any."[81]

Walpole was not the only minister with an influence in colonial affairs which on occasion approached that of the

[80] Partridge to Wanton, March 3, 1733, Kimball, *Rhode Island Correspondence*, I, 25-26.

[81] Newcastle to Solicitor-General, June 22, 1733, C.O. 5/383, fol. 209; Newcastle to Craven, June 22, 1733, C.O. 5/383, fol. 207; Brudenell to Newcastle, June 12, 1736, Add. MSS 32690, fol. 128.

southern secretary. Lord Wilmington, the President of the Privy Council, also exercised considerable power. Sir Robert's authority stemmed from his omnipotence in domestic politics; Wilmington's, by contrast, derived from his strategic position within the administrative hierarchy. As titular head of the Privy Council, Wilmington presided over the committee for plantation affairs. This placed him at the center of every important debate over colonial policy and put him in a prime position to win favors and preferment for his associates.

Wilmington's reputation was such that a number of colonial governors sought his friendship and assistance. Belcher wrote continually to Wilmington from Boston, and Governor Cunningham sought to win the Lord President's backing for his nominations to Council during his brief administration in Jamaica. Edward Trelawney, his successor, was even more solicitous of Wilmington's favor and enjoyed a considerable measure of success. "Mr. Sharpe acquaints me," the Governor wrote to Wilmington in 1739,

> how much I am obliged to your Lordship for my success in the five Councillors I recommended, a point of great consequence to me in the beginning of [my] Administration; nor am I a little obliged to your Lordship for the great share you had in the order of Council whereby I had a discretionary power to pass the Bill wherein the Jews were taxed for the current year.[82]

In conjunction with Walpole, Wilmington represented a considerable check on Newcastle's authority within his

[82] November 12, 1739, H.M.C., *Eleventh Report*, pt. IV, 301; Cunningham to Wilmington, December 27, 1735, ibid., pt. IV, 297; Trelawney to Newcastle, November 6, 1739, C.O. 137/56, fol. 264.

own department. If the interests of the two ministers coincided, their wishes would almost certainly prevail over those of the Duke. In 1732, for example, they joined hands to dispose of an office in the West Indies. On Wilmington's request, Walpole secured the deputy's place for the Clerk of the Markets in Jamaica for the son of Alderman Floyer. As Wilmington and Sir Richard Lane had written to the Treasury chief, Floyer was "a popular man with us at Worcester."[83]

Sir Charles Wager, the First Lord of the Admiralty and the other senior minister with an interest in American affairs, did not represent a direct threat to Newcastle's political ambitions, whatever his demands on colonial patronage. Wager was the nephew of John Hull, a London merchant who had settled in Newport, Rhode Island, and by whom he was adopted. As a young naval officer in the western Atlantic, Wager built up an extensive personal following in the colonies. It was these friends, many of them fellow officers, whom Wager attempted to serve when he became First Lord in 1733. Although he was dependent on Walpole for whatever power he might hope to exert within the ministry, Wager had a distinct set of associates to oblige in America.[84]

Within two years of his promotion, Wager had placed two of his friends in the South Carolina establishment. In 1734 the Clerkship of the Markets was bestowed upon

[83] Lane and Wilmington to Walpole, April 4, 1732, C.O. 137/53, fol. 131. Wilmington and Walpole were more often rivals than allies. They had struggled for the position of primacy within the ministry in 1727, and this battle left a lasting mark. See Owen, *Rise of the Pelhams*, 12-14.

[84] Kimball, *Rhode Island Correspondence*, I, 76n.; Colman to Talcott, October 29, 1739, CHS, *Collections*, v, 172-75; Wager to Walpole, July 12, 1731, W.C., no. 1852; Baugh, *Naval Administration*, 66-68.

John Beswicke, a personal friend of Wager who had suffered financially while Deputy-Consul at Tripoli.[85] In the following year Wager again intervened in the affairs of the southern department, this time to secure the post of Deputy Naval Officer for John Cleland of Charleston. Because the Admiralty chief "was very desirous of ye thing for Mr. Cleland . . . ," Samuel Wheatley informed Undersecretary Andrew Stone,

> The deputation is given to Mr. Cleland['s] Friends in order to be transmitted to Him for three Years Onely & He to pay me Ninty pounds p annum by two Sufficient Securities. . . .[86]

By this adroit manipulation Newcastle was able both to oblige Wager and to continue to provide for a political supporter at home.

As these developments indicated, the disposition of patronage did not consist simply in the initial allocation of office. It was also necessary to protect those in office from the attacks of their political enemies and from the intrigues of place-hunters with good connections. The dangers facing an incumbent were particularly acute in America, given the intense factionalism of colonial politics. The safe tenure of those in provincial commands was dependent upon strong support from their patrons in England.

Newcastle confronted this problem for the first time in 1731, when George Burrington came under attack in North Carolina. "I have used my endeavours to settle this Government as commanded by the King's Instruc-

[85] Wager to Delafaye, June 12, 1734, C.O. 5/383, fol. 211.

[86] October 25, 1735, S.P. 36/36, foll. 183-84; W.C., nos. 944, 1302, 1784, and 2214.

tions . . . ," the recent appointee reported to the southern secretary, but

> Mr. Smith the Chief Justice, Mr. Ashe and Mr. Porter Councillors violently opposed me . . . Smith . . . is gone to England to complain against me. . . . I have reason to think this ungrateful youth was seduced by Mr. Rice Secretary of this Province Coll: Bladen's Brother in Law. . . .[87]

The Governor was particularly worried that Bladen would use his position at the Board of Trade to undermine his position. "It is commonly reported here," Burrington confessed to Newcastle, "That upon any complaint I shall be dismissed, and Rice promoted to the Government by Mr. Bladen's interest." The Governor made matters even worse for himself by questioning the judgment of his patron. "The Chief Justice and Attorney General of this Province ought to be Men of understanding and Lawyers," Burrington complained in a letter to the Duke; "neither of the persons your Grace bestow'd these places upon in this Government ever knew Law enough to be Clarke to a Justice of the Peace."[88]

Such an indictment, even if true, was unlikely to make friends for Burrington in London. And these were what he needed most. In December, 1731, William Smith lodged a complaint against the Governor on behalf of the Assembly; nine months later Rice, Montgomery, and the members of the Council submitted yet another.[89] Few governors could hope to remain on friendly terms with all

[87] July 1, 1731, C.O. 5/308, fol. 29.

[88] March 1, 1732, ibid., fol. 176.

[89] Report, December 17, 1731, C.O. 5/21, foll. 9-10; "Memorial," September 16, 1732, C.O. 5/306, foll. 45-50.

groups and factions while carrying out their royal instructions. But it was a supreme failure of leadership to earn the opposition of the Assembly, the Council, and one's subordinates without winning any increase in the prerogatives of the Crown. By the spring of 1732, Burrington's position had deteriorated to such an extent that petitions from potential replacements began to flow into the southern department.

As the Governor was his own nominee, Newcastle was understandably hesitant to be rushed into hasty action. The removal of Burrington after two years in office would suggest at the least that the southern secretary had severely misjudged his ability. Moreover, the Governor's replacement by an associate of another minister would betray political weakness as well as administrative incompetence. Questions of personal loyalty intruded also. "It is a known attribute of Your Greatness," a placehunter wrote subsequently to Newcastle, "to take a pleasure in supporting those Creatures of your own making who profess . . . an entire duty, devotion, & gratitude to your Grace."[90]

Newcastle's unwillingness to abandon Burrington was indicated by his unsympathetic reaction to a campaign mounted to secure the governorship for Christian Cole. In October, 1732, the Duke of Manchester approached the southern secretary on behalf of Cole, a former government representative at Venice. This petition was seconded by the Duke of Kent. "His misfortune," Kent explained, "has been to have Lost in the South Sea, and Again Lately in the Charitable Corporation, which makes him desirous to leave his own Country, and to goe

[90] George Jackson to Newcastle, February 3, 1742, Add. MSS 32699, fol. 46.

abroad. . . ."[91] Additional support for the erstwhile diplomat came from Lord De la Warr, a member of the Privy Council, and Lord Torrington, the First Lord of the Admiralty.[92]

The weight of Cole's interest was not as great as it appeared at first sight. Certainly the favors owing to Manchester, his chief advocate, were not as substantial as he had suggested in his letter to Newcastle. A friend of Manchester's father, Savile Cust, was already serving as Secretary of the Leeward Islands. More important, Manchester was dependent on the southern secretary for support in borough elections. Prior to the elections of 1734 and 1741, Manchester requested the Duke's assistance in securing the support of Lord Lincoln, the Pelhams' brother-in-law, in the Huntingdonshire poll.[93] Finally, misfortune in the South Sea Bubble no longer represented an obligation which the administration felt obliged to fulfill. The years of expiation had passed.

In the end, however, it was less the weakness of Cole's interest than the appearance of a stronger candidate which broke the stalemate. The widespread dissatisfaction in North Carolina had found an influential spokesman in the person of Lord Wilmington. As President of the Council, Wilmington sat at the head of the committee which would consider the various complaints against the Governor. He had a personal interest to serve as well. Wilmington

[91] Kent to Newcastle, October 12, 1732, Add. MSS 32687, fol. 510; Manchester and Torrington to Newcastle, October 10 and 12, 1732, ibid., foll. 501-05.

[92] De la Warr to Newcastle, October 16, 1732, C.O. 5/306, foll. 61-62.

[93] Manchester to Newcastle, August 16, 1733 and October 26, 1739, Add. MSS 32688, fol. 117 and Add. MSS 32692, fol. 423.

owed a political debt to Gabriel Johnson, Professor of Ancient Languages at St. Andrew's University, for his writings in the Whig cause.[94] Now the Scottish scholar wished to extract his reward. With a guarantee of Wilmington's support at the committee for plantation affairs, Johnson informed Brigadier John Tyrell, Newcastle's ally in the politics of Yorkshire and Nottinghamshire, of his candidacy. In May, 1732, Johnson asked Tyrell to remind the southern secretary "How much more advisable it was to remove Mr. Burrington now, than to wait till His uncommon Conduct, had raised a still greater Clamour. . . ."[95] Newcastle had no choice but to acquiesce. Burrington was not even given an opportunity to defend his record in office before the home authorities. In March, 1733, the southern secretary informed the Board of Trade of Johnson's appointment as Governor of North Carolina.[96]

This incident illuminated the extent of the authority over colonial appointments exercised by various members of the ministry. It illustrated as well the role played by the formal administrative bodies in the settlement of an American dispute. The real influence both of the Board of Trade and of the Privy Council committee to which it was subordinate stemmed from the personal influence wielded by its members. It was the adoption of the cause of one party to a dispute by an eminent politician-*cum*-bureaucrat that usually decided a controversy. The resolu-

[94] Blackwell P. Robinson, *The Five Royal Governors of North Carolina*, Raleigh, 1965, 12-13; Johnson to Wilmington, June 2, 1737 and March 1, 1739, H.M.C., *Eleventh Report*, pt. IV, 264.

[95] May 28, 1732, S.P. 36/26, foll. 360-61.

[96] March 27, 1733, C.O. 5/294, fol. 66; Burrington to Newcastle, June 1, 1734, C.O. 5/306, fol. 42; Charles G. Sellers, Jr., "Private Profits and British Colonial Policy: The Speculations of Henry McCulloh," *WMQ*, 3rd ser., VII (October, 1951), 536-37.

tion of a colonial dispute became less a balancing of objective arguments than a decision in favor of a particular interest group.

In the present instance, Martin Bladen undoubtedly contributed to the Governor's downfall because of his close personal relationship to the faction headed by Smith and Rice. But if Bladen could bring down a governor by his machinations at the Board of Trade, he could not make a new one. This was the prerogative of the more important members of the Whig oligarchy and increasingly of the southern secretary. The recall of his appointee was a severe blow to Newcastle's efforts to bring the management of American affairs completely under his control. Burrington's incompetence, Bladen's factional ties, and Wilmington's political debts had combined to thwart the Duke's first bid to maintain a man of his own choosing in a major colonial post. As southern secretary, Newcastle might have been able to resist any one, or even two, of these pressures for a change of governors. Coming together, they overwhelmed his tenuous authority. If there was a lesson to be learned for the future, it was simply the necessity of dividing the opposition while using the formal powers of his office to retain personal control of the situation.

Much more quickly than he must have wished, Newcastle found another of his clients at the center of a colonial controversy. Upon his arrival in New York, Colonel Cosby had suspended Chief Justice Lewis Morris from his office. Morris had supported the claim of Rip Van Dam, the President of the Council and acting Governor, to one half the governor's salary for the period preceding Cosby's arrival. The Governor's bitter opposition to Van Dam's request completely disrupted the harmony of the province. Political allegiance polarized between those who supported the new chief executive and those who were determined to secure his removal.

Early in 1734, the optimism of the faction headed by Morris, Van Dam, and Cadwallader Colden was heightened by the rumor that Cosby was to be recalled in favor of James Brudenell of the Board of Trade. "This Brudenell," Morris' son informed Colden,

> has a post of a £1,000 pr ann. which I suppose will be given to Cosby. he is a member of Parliament no Soldier nor Sailor a man of Letters and one who has Dipped pretty much in the Study of Laws. he is at Present Recorder of The town of Chichester So that I flatter my Self that in the next Reign polite Literature will be Introduced Instead of a God Dam ye.[97]

Like Cosby, Brudenell had close ties to Newcastle. He had secured his position in Chichester from the Duke of Richmond, the chief ally of the Pelhams in Sussex politics. His marriage to a daughter of the Duke of Montagu had won his promotion to the Board of Trade in 1730. There was no indication, however, either that Brudenell was seeking the New York governorship or that the ministry was likely to recall Cosby.

Morris therefore decided to travel personally to England to undermine the position of the Governor at home. Once in London, the former Chief Justice quickly became aware of the extent of Cosby's support within the ministry. He reported to Colden's Scottish patron, the Marquess of Lothian, that the Governor "thinks himself secure by the great interest of the Dukes of New Castle,

[97] January 17, 1734, NYHS, *Collections*, LI, 100-101. This controversy is treated in great detail in Katz, *Newcastle's New York*.

Montague and Lord Halifax to be protected in the doing of Every thing. . . ."[98]

This impressive array of backers did not deter Morris. After a discussion with Lothian, the New Yorker was sanguine about his chances. Colden's influence in Scotland might win the support of the Duke of Argyll, the overlord of Scottish patronage in the ministry.[99] Less valuable, but none the less welcome, was the encouragement Morris received from two members of the opposition, Lord Carteret and Micajah Perry. His progress since his arrival in London, Morris reported to Colden in April, 1735, "Promises me hopes of Success unless the whole ministry Should Joyne in Cosby's favour, wch I have reason to believe they will not do. . . ."[100]

As yet Morris possessed only an imperfect understanding of the English political situation. His letter to Colden betrayed his failure to realize that it was his own side rather than Cosby's which would need the backing of an overwhelming majority of the members of the Board of Trade and the Privy Council. It was Morris who was attempting to secure a major change; Cosby's friends had only to fend off the attacks of the dissident colonials. And it would require a greatly superior force to oust the solidly entrenched supporters of the Governor.

The first step in the accumulation of such an overwhelming interest came in the summer of 1735 with the adherence to the Morris faction of Sir Charles Wager.

[98] March 26, 1735, NYHS, *Collections*, LI, 128-29.

[99] Colden's father had written to Lothian, Islay, and Argyll in 1732 asking them to recommend his son to the new Governor: A. Colden to C. Colden, August 5, 1732, ibid., V, 72-80. In April, 1735, F. J. Paris told Morris that Lothian wished to help him but would have to follow the lead of Argyll, ibid., LI, 135-36.

[100] April 11, 1735, ibid., LI, 135-36.

Wager's support proceeded primarily from the naval connections of Lewis Morris. Two daughters of the former Chief Justice had wed naval men. One son-in-law was Captain Vincent Pearse, a relative of a Commissioner of the Navy; the other was Captain Matthew Norris, the son of Sir John Norris, the Admiral of the Fleet.[101] The marriage of yet another daughter into the Ashfield family of New York provided Morris with a valuable connection to a third naval man, Captain Long, who served as an intermediary with Wager. By the end of June, 1735, the New Yorker had secured Wager's tacit support for his cause.[102]

This alliance brought an immediate dividend. Wager's intervention was a crucial factor in winning Morris a hearing before the Privy Council committee on plantation affairs. As Robert Hunter Morris, the son of the Chief Justice, wrote in his diary for August 6, 1735,

> Sr. Charles Wager came to wait on my father on my fathers cause at present before the council, wch Sr. Charles said the[y] were resolved to Hear after the Vacation, He Having spoke to my Lord President about it tho he said they Had rather let it Alone, but hear it they would.[103]

Newcastle and the other supporters of Cosby within the ministry had not remained on the defensive. At the same time that they attempted to block Privy Council consideration of the controversy, the Governor's friends initiated a

[101] Beverly McAnear, "An American in London, 1735-1736," *PMHB*, LXIV (April, 1940), 171.

[102] Morris, "Diary," June 30 and August 24, 1735, *PMHB*, LXIV, 203-204, 372. The Chief Justice also sought the interest of Joseph Jekyll, the Master of the Rolls, and John Hanbury and David Barclay, the Quaker merchants and bankers, ibid., 282-83.

[103] Ibid., 365-66.

successful counterattack against the faction headed by Morris. Using their influence at the Board of Trade, they secured a report endorsing Cosby's removal of the Chief Justice and two of his associates from the New York Council. Newcastle had long urged this confirmation of the Governor's action, but it was only with the death of Paul Docminique and the resignation of the Earl of Westmoreland from the board that the southern secretary could command a majority in the advisory body.[104]

The divisions within the Board of Trade were mirrored in the Privy Council committee. Only here it was the friends of the Chief Justice who held the balance of power. The committee refused to accept the board's recommendation confirming the dismissals from the New York Council. Now it was Newcastle and his associates who lacked the power to implement a "positive" program. Suddenly aware of the precariousness of his position, the southern secretary attempted to strike a bargain with Morris. The Chief Justice's son noted on November 4, 1735:

> It is worthy of remembrance that this day about 11 oClock Mr. Gashe[r]y, Sr Charles Wagers Secretary, came to wait on my father & told Him that Sr Charles Had been with the Duke of New Castle, and, talking of my father, the Duke said that, if Mr. Morris would Drop the Complaints Against Cosby and Put of[f] the Hearing that was apointed to be the next day, He would Joyn with Sr Charles in asking the government of New Jersie for him. . . .[105]

[104] Docminique was one of the original proprietors of New Jersey and a member of the West Jersey Society. In 1735, his son was Treasurer of the Society, and Morris was its agent in America, ibid., 359 and 359n.

[105] Ibid., 383-85.

Once before Morris had been this close to the governorship of New Jersey. During the reign of Queen Anne, he had nearly secured the chief executive's post for his services in winning the surrender of the proprietary charter. On that occasion the Earl of Rochester had intervened to create a joint governorship for New York and New Jersey in order to increase the prestige and income of his nephew, Lord Cornbury, the chief executive of New York.[106] Now it was Morris who refused the post; to accept under these circumstances would be to betray Van Dam, Colden, and his other supporters in New York.

It was not merely unselfish altruism which motivated the former Chief Justice. His political instincts told him he was on the brink of complete victory. There was no need to compromise when the Privy Council committee was certain to overturn his dismissal. Peter Collinson, one of his supporters, reported the outcome to James Alexander:

> The Duke of Newcastle was a strenuous friend in the governor's interest, and also Lord Halifax who is a relation of the governor; but the governor's spleen, pique, and prejudice were so notoriously seen through the whole charge, that there was no supporting it.[107]

[106] Morris to Newcastle, June 2, 1732, C.O. 5/983, foll. 35-6. Since 1730, the Assembly of New Jersey had been attempting to secure a separate governor for the province. Thomas Smith, William Keith, and Morris had all applied for the post, but Newcastle had told Keith that the provinces would not be divided during Cosby's administration. See the correspondence in C.O. 5/983, foll. 18-27, 64; S.P. 36/32, fol. 232; and S.P. 36/39, fol. 1.

[107] Quoted in William A. Whithead, ed., "The Papers of Lewis Morris . . . ," New Jersey Historical Society, *Collections*, New York, 1852, v, 26. Cosby was apparently supported by Newcastle, Halifax, and Fitzwalter, the new President of the Board of Trade; Morris' side was probably taken by Wager, Jekyll, and Islay. It was

Led by Wager, the Privy Council committee had administered a stinging rebuke to Cosby and dealt a strong blow to the authority of the southern secretary. For the second time within as many years, Newcastle had not been able to protect a client from the attacks of his enemies.

Cosby was more fortunate than his colleague in North Carolina. Newcastle was able to muster enough influence to maintain the New York official in power. Lord Islay, Morris' Scottish patron, informed the Chief Justice that the Council "intended to continue Him governor, since there was nothing appeared Against Him."[108] Even more disappointing to the New Yorker was the outcome of his own case. For the decision of Council did not automatically reinstate him as Chief Justice. And Newcastle, utilizing his prerogative as southern secretary, refused to present the matter to the King in Council for the necessary ratification.[109] The peculiar equilibrium of forces within the

---

the sentiments of the relatively uncommitted members of the committee—Walpole, Wilmington, Hardwicke, Henry Pelham, and Arthur Onslow—which decided the issue.

[108] R. H. Morris, "Diary," December 19, 1735, *PMHB*, LXIV, 395-96; Donald L. Kemmerer, *Path to Freedom . . .* , Princeton, 1940, 151-52. There were rumors of Cosby's recall in early 1736, R. H. Morris to L. Morris, Jr., February 13, 1736, *PMHB*, LXIV, 399-400.

[109] Morris to Newcastle, March 21, 1736, C.O. 5/1093, foll. 386-87. In 1720, Deputy-Governor Spotswood of Virginia removed William Byrd from the Council of the colony. This action, like Cosby's dismissal of Morris, Van Dam, and Alexander, was approved by the Board of Trade, but failed for lack of support in the Privy Council committee. Moreover, the agitation in England of Byrd and of James Blair, the Commissary of Virginia, resulted in the removal of the Governor in 1722. Blair seems to have persuaded Horace Walpole to have the Earl of Orkney recall his deputy. Spotswood had friends on the Board of Trade but no protector similar to Newcastle in the higher ranks of the government. The de-

administration had made it impossible either for Morris or Cosby to triumph completely.

Indeed, all parties to the contest had lost more than they had gained. Newcastle had sacrificed his prestige in an unpopular cause; Cosby had severely compromised his position at home; and Morris had only a moral victory to show for his years of agitation. But more important than any of these results was the impact of the controversy on the changing domestic political situation. The factional politics of New York had been temporarily duplicated within the government of the mother country. The differences in temperament and outlook between Newcastle and the other members of the administration had found concrete expression in a substantive issue. The growing rifts within the once-united ministry had been accentuated. The New York controversy was at once a contributing cause and a significant result of the growing instability of the English political scene.

The increasing antagonism and competitiveness within the Walpole government was fully revealed in a series of developments involving a third client of Newcastle. In 1733, the Duke had written a strong letter of recommendation to Governor Belcher on behalf of William Shirley, a former resident of Sussex with close ties to one of the branches of the Pelham family there. With the backing of the southern secretary, Shirley was named Advocate-General for the Treasury in Massachusetts Bay. Within a few months of his appointment, Shirley was

---

tails and the outcome of the Cosby case were different, but it conformed to a larger structural pattern. A colonial governor was ill-advised to become involved in a dispute with the assembly or with his subordinates in America unless he possessed the strong backing of the Board of Trade and enjoyed the confidence of a number of the leading ministers. See Dodson, *Alexander Spotswood*, 260, 270-75.

complaining to Newcastle that the fees of the non-salaried office were insufficient and was requesting a more lucrative position. In November, 1734, he proposed that the jurisdiction of his office be expanded to include New Hampshire and Rhode Island and that a salary be attached to the post. Two years later Shirley's wife arrived in England to solicit personally on her husband's behalf. In March, 1736, she asked Newcastle to bypass the Admiralty board and to refer the salary request to the lords of trade, "they being well Inform'd of ye Affair, & much dispos'd to assiste me in it. . . ."[110]

There were two reasons behind this request. Thomas Pelham of Stanmer, a member of the Board of Trade, was a close friend of the Shirley family. More important, the Board of Trade had consistently supported the expansion of royal jurisdiction in the colonies. Just as regularly the Admiralty had opposed the creation of new American offices and the diversion of naval funds for colonial use.[111] The confidence of the Shirleys was not misplaced. In May, 1737, the Board of Trade recommended the expansion of Shirley's authority and a salary of £300 per annum, to be paid "in the like manner as your Majesty's Surveyor General of the Woods, by the Treasurer of the Navy."[112] All that remained now was to secure the grant from the naval department. "I beg leave to Return my Most grateful Thanks, for ye Reference your Grace was so good to make to ye Lords of Admiralty in

[110] March 2, 1736, Add. MSS 32690, foll. 261-62; John A. Schutz, *William Shirley, King's Governor of Massachusetts*, Chapel Hill, 1961, 3-7, 10-11.

[111] In the 1720's, the Admiralty had refused to underwrite the post of Surveyor-General of the Woods. See Wentworth to Board of Trade, August 20, 1723, C.O. 5/869, foll. 33-35 and Malone, *Pine Trees and Politics*, chaps. 5 and 6.

[112] Report, May 19, 1737, C.O. 5/752, foll. 304-305.

the Affair of Mr. Shirley's Salary . . . ," the wife of the Advocate-General wrote to Newcastle,

> [it] was in such terms I thought they cou'd not have Refused it, but I was inform'd Yesterday they have, & after all ye trouble & Expence I have been . . . I am just where I was wh[en] I first came Over, & must return broken . . . unless your Grace will be so good to do something for us. . . .[113]

The southern secretary did his best to reverse the decision of the Admiralty chiefs. In November, 1737, Newcastle directed his private secretary to take Mrs. Shirley's latest petition into Norfolk in order that he "& Mr. Pelham may find an opportunity of conversing with Sr Robert on the Subject of it."[114] Ordinarily, the intervention of both Pelhams would have been sufficient to secure an exception to the tight-fisted financial policy defended by those in the minor ranks of the bureaucracy. By this time, however, the traditional stinginess of the Treasury and the natural antagonism among competing sections of the bureaucracy had been accentuated by conflicts among the chief ministers. As Hervey wrote in his diary in September, 1737,

> Sir Robert told Mr. Williams, too, that the Duke of Newcastle was making great court to my Lord Chancellor, and that he proposed by that means to work himself into more power at present, and to be able to form a ministry of his own with my Lord

[113] No date, S.P. 35/65, foll. 21-22; Thomas Pelham to Stone, July 21, 1737, S.P. 36/41, foll. 210-11.

[114] Thomas Pelham to Stone ?, November 3, 1737, C.O. 5/752, fol. 325.

Chancellor in case any accident happened to Sir Robert.[115]

Fully aware of the machinations of the southern secretary, Walpole was no longer prepared to make an exception to established policy to oblige his colleagues. Shirley's petition was decisively rejected by the Treasury chief.

The hopeful note of administrative reform upon which the decade of the 1730's had opened had now been overwhelmed by loud demands for American offices. With the continued decline of the Board of Trade, the pursuit of patronage had superseded the implementation of policy as the dominant tendency within the ranks of the colonial bureaucracy. Newcastle's own vision had also narrowed during these years. The unity of the Walpole administration was crumbling in the face of the Duke's attempt to create an alternative government through a liberal distribution of places to his supporters. The peculiar distribution of power within the ministry which had produced an inconclusive outcome to the struggle for power in New York, and which had constituted the basic framework within which all of the colonial questions of the 1730's had been resolved, was also coming to an end. His patronage, power, and prestige as southern secretary had placed Newcastle in a position where he could challenge Walpole for the leadership of the government.

[115] September 18, 1737, Sedgwick, *Hervey's Memoirs*, 830.

CHAPTER 4

The Great Struggle for Power *1737-1741*

IT WAS within this framework of an increasingly bitter rivalry among the factions led by Walpole, Wilmington, and Newcastle that the colonial problems bequeathed by the stalemated battles of the middle of the 1730's were finally resolved. Before this domestic struggle came to a head, colonial patronage had been largely neglected for two years because of its potentially disruptive effect on the unity of the administration. At least five colonial governorships remained vacant at the beginning of 1737 because of these divisions within the ministry.

It was the threat of war with Spain in America which precipitated an all-out struggle for power within the English government and which made it imperative that more attention be paid to colonial affairs. In 1736, following a minor dispute between Spain and Portugal in Brazil, Horace Walpole criticized Newcastle for his neglect of the defensive posture of the West Indies:

> Believe me, my Lord, you doe not know what may be ye consequence in all respects of your great indolence and neglect of this Point . . . when there is danger of a Rupture we are frightened out of our witts; ye Admiralty and ye board of Trade are talked with and councils summoned, but if, while they meet and deliberate, that danger seems to blow over, all thoughts of ye W. Indies are over too, and nothing is done.[1]

[1] Quoted in Williams, *Carteret and Newcastle*, 111.

Walpole's charges were largely justified. The Duke's concern with colonial developments had flagged after the resignation of Townshend in 1730 had opened up the wider field of continental diplomacy. It was the convergence of European and American affairs in 1737 which brought Newcastle's attention back to the western hemisphere. Within a year of Walpole's reprimand, the southern secretary was giving the highest priority to colonial questions. In the process, the Duke was marking out a stand on diplomatic and military strategy which threatened to shatter the ministerial equilibrium of the preceding period and to bring him into a direct confrontation with the Walpole interest.

The factors underlying Newcastle's growing disenchantment with Walpole and his consequent adoption of an independent position within the ministry are not completely clear, but they seem to have concerned disagreements over policy as well as patronage. In 1731 and 1732, the Duke had assumed a completely submissive attitude when the chief minister rejected his advice on two important questions of foreign policy. Despite Newcastle's pleas, Walpole refused to honor the terms of the treaty of Vienna and to intervene on the side of the Austrian Emperor in the war of the Polish Succession. At the same time, the Treasury chief declined to sanction reprisals against Spain for that nation's interference with English trade in the West Indies.[2] Five years later, when the merchants renewed their complaints against the depredations of the *guarda costas* and when the settlers in Georgia began to protest against Spanish harassment, Newcastle took a more determined stand on behalf of his own principles.

[2] Ibid., 94-98; Harold W. V. Temperley, "The Causes of the War of Jenkins' Ear, 1739," *Transactions* of the Royal Historical Society, 3rd ser., III (1909), 197-236.

The first complaints from the colonists and the merchants were registered at the Board of Trade in February and March, 1737; by June, Walpole and Newcastle had already quarreled over the proper course of action to be pursued.[3] The First Lord of the Treasury, never over-friendly with the merchant interest, was determined to preserve peace and domestic financial stability; Newcastle was concerned lest a tepid foreign policy should encourage the ambitions of France and Austria. "I have long suspected that those Two Powers have been jealous of the Figure England has formerly made in Europe," the southern secretary warned Horace Walpole in July, "And are now determined to take the Government of the world into their own Hands, without Regard to any other Powers. . . ."[4]

Newcastle's aggressive stance reflected as well his concern with his own record in the southern department. The alleged infringements of English territorial and trading rights had taken place in America and seemed to confirm Horace Walpole's recent judgment of his administrative performance. By October, when the merchants presented their first major petition on the Spanish depredations to the King, the Duke was clearly troubled. He confided to Lord Chancellor Hardwicke, his closest advisor, that he expected a personal attack on his conduct by the parliamentary opposition.[5]

By this time there were other issues which divided Walpole and Newcastle. Early in 1737 the Duke had joined Hardwicke in demanding stern retribution against those

[3] Richard Pares, *War and Trade in the West Indies, 1739-1763*, Oxford, 1963, 46.

[4] July 22, 1737, S.P. 36/41, foll. 221-22; Plumb, *Walpole*, II, 186-87, 239.

[5] Pares, *War and Trade*, 44, argues that fear of domestic criticism was a crucial factor in Newcastle's adoption of a belligerent attitude.

involved in the Porteous riots in Edinburgh. The chief minister had resisted the imposition of draconian measures, in part because of the threat they would pose to his political alliances in Scotland, and this rebuff had angered his colleagues. This quarrel was immediately aggravated by another. Strongly supported by Hardwicke and Pelham, Newcastle attempted to persuade Walpole to seek an accommodation between the King and the Prince of Wales. The Pelhams argued that the political position of the ministry would be weakened if the recent dispute over the Prince's monetary and personal dependence upon his father were to result in a permanent estrangement. With the heir apparent at their head, the Whigs in opposition would be immune from the charge of Jacobism which Walpole had employed so effectively against them in the past. Even more disturbing to the Pelhams was the possibility that the leadership of the Prince would create a sense of unity and common purpose among the fractious members of the opposition. The chief minister took a different reading of the situation. Confident of his power in the House of Commons, Walpole preferred to safeguard his link with the King. He would use the anger of George II against his son to discredit still further the political allies of the Prince.[6]

[6] Porteous, the Captain of the City Guard, had been found guilty of the murder of members of a crowd gathered to watch the execution of a smuggler who enjoyed considerable public sympathy. When he was pardoned by higher authorities, a disciplined "mob" had taken Porteous from jail and hanged him. The political repercussions are examined in the entries for Porteous and for the chief ministers in the *D.N.B.*

The text of Hardwicke's long conversation with Walpole in September, 1737, on the dispute between the King and the Prince is in William Coxe, *Memoirs of the Life and Administration of Sir Robert Walpole . . .* , London, 1800, II, 475-81. Walpole

Neither at Court nor in the country was Walpole's strategy greeted with much success. His policy of conciliation toward Spain did not find favor in Parliament; and the death in November, 1737, of Queen Caroline, his friend and ally, undercut his once impregnable position in the palace. These setbacks only served to confirm Newcastle in his growing opposition to the chief minister. The Duke had loyally supported Walpole at the time of the Excise Crisis in 1733 and had helped to maintain him in power in the general election which followed. Now, his ambition stimulated by the thought of greater power and his confidence shaken by the caution of the chief minister in foreign affairs and by Walpole's arrogant disregard of the domestic opposition, Newcastle was no longer willing to support a diplomatic policy which ran counter not only to his own sentiments but also to those of a considerable part of the political nation.[7]

---

acknowledged the wisdom of the Pelhams' position in January, 1742, when he made an abortive attempt to reunite the royal family and thus to save his own ministry by securing the parliamentary support of the followers of the Prince. See Owen, *Rise of the Pelhams*, 29.

[7] Plumb, *Walpole*, II, 280, notes Newcastle's earlier loyalty. In 1737, Walpole had begun to pursue certain diplomatic objectives behind the back of the southern secretary, a practice that had aroused Newcastle's anger several times in the past and which had prompted the Duke to offer his resignation in 1728. See Reginald Lucas, *George II and His Ministers*, London, 1910, 281.

Beginning in February, 1737, Lord Hervey, who hated Newcastle, sought to persuade Walpole that the Duke was seeking his downfall. Hervey's *Memoirs* have to be read with some caution, but they clearly point to a decline in the internal unity of the ministry. See Sedgwick, *Hervey's Memoirs*, 653, 701, 734, and 829-30.

Finally, it should be noted that Egmont, who was not unfriendly toward Newcastle, observed in March, 1737, that Walpole was planning a general reshuffle of the ministry: "Mr. Sands is talked of for Secretary of State in the Duke of Newcastle's room . . . and

I

Just as important issues of foreign policy and domestic political strategy threatened to split the ministry, the backlog of colonial business reached a dangerous level. When the first complaints against the Spanish were lodged at the Board of Trade early in 1737, nearly one half of the royal colonies in America were without a proper chief executive. No appointments had been made to major colonial positions for over a year, perhaps because of the controversy created in the Privy Council committee for plantation affairs by the struggle in New York between Cosby and Morris. News of the death of Lord Howe in Barbados reached England in June, 1735, but his successor was not nominated until two years later.[8] There was an identical delay in South Carolina. A replacement for Robert Johnson, who died in the summer of 1735, was not named until June, 1737.[9] Similarly, it took from May, 1736, until April of the following year to appoint a

Lord Carteret . . . President of the Council in Lord Wilmington's room . . ." (Egmont, *Diary*, II, 364). Horace Walpole the younger argued somewhat later that Hardwicke had joined Newcastle in seeking to supplant Walpole as the King's minister following the death of the Queen in November, 1737: *Memoirs of the Reign of King George the Second*, ed., Lord Holland, 2nd ed., London, 1846, I, 160, 164.

Further evidence of the split between Walpole and Newcastle during the course of the year 1737 is in Donald Grove Barnes, "Henry Pelham and the Duke of Newcastle," *JBS*, no. 2 (May, 1962), 69-70, and Thomson, *Secretaries of State*, 38-39.

[8] Dottin to Newcastle, April 16, 1735, C.O. 28/45, fol. 331, received June 15, 1735. Orlando Bridgeman was named in June, 1737.

[9] Board of Trade to Newcastle, June 24, 1735, C.O. 5/383, fol. 225; Oglethorpe was appointed Commander-in-Chief of South Carolina and Georgia two years later.

substitute for Colonel Cosby, who died in New York just as his cause triumphed in England.[10] Once these nominations were made, the ministry moved quickly to fill the chief executives' posts in Virginia and Jamaica, which had been vacant for one and two years respectively.[11] After a hiatus lasting several years, six American governorships were filled within the space of as many months.

Some of this delay in the making of American appointments may be traced to the personality of the King. George II was more obstinate than his father in catering to the patronage plans of his ministers. This was especially the case in military affairs. The King often rejected the friends and relatives of members of Parliament suggested by Walpole, and later by Newcastle.[12] He preferred to make his own appointments on the basis of loyalty and ability and possessed a keen knowledge of the available applicants. In other fields, George II did not insist on the right of an alternative nomination; instead, he often deferred taking any action on a recommendation when the applicant was unknown to him. Hervey attributed this behavior by the King to "a natural dilatoriness in his temper, joined to a particular backwardness in giving . . . and his liking nobody well enough to have any

[10] Clark to Newcastle, March 16, 1736, C.O. 5/1093, foll. 342-45, received May 10, 1736; De la Warr received his patent as Cosby's successor only in August, 1737, but he had been chosen for the post in April: Memorandum, April 13, 1737, S.P. 36/40, foll. 232c-33.

[11] The Earl of Orkney died in England on January 29, 1737. Albemarle received his patent as Orkney's successor on November 4, 1737. News of Governor Cunningham's death in Jamaica reached England by the end of 1735; Trelawney received his patent for the post on August 31, 1737.

[12] H. Walpole to R. Trevor, February 22, 1740, H.M.C., *Fourteenth Report*, pt. IX, 40.

pleasure in preferring them. . . ."[13] In 1736, the monarch postponed the filling up of a great number of commissions in the army; and this reluctance may have carried over to colonial appointments as well, especially if his ministers could not agree.[14]

Whatever its origin, the termination of this period of inactivity was the result of Walpole's taking a new interest in the formulation of American military policy and in the disposition of colonial patronage. In June, 1737, the chief minister sought to install one of the King's friends in the government of Barbados, vacant since the death of Lord Howe in 1735. This was Sir Orlando Bridgeman, a close associate of George II and his Auditor-General while he was still Prince of Wales. In 1727, Walpole and Townshend had ousted Richard Plumer from the Board of Trade in order to appoint Bridgeman and so win the favor of the new monarch.[15] Ten years later, the Commissioner's incompetence and extravagance had outrun his stipend of £1,000 per annum. He resigned from the board on Walpole's promise of the much more rewarding governorship of Barbados.

[13] May 22, 1736, Sedgwick, *Hervey's Memoirs*, 556-57. It took four years for Newcastle to win the King's permission to form the independent companies in Jamaica into a regiment and to secure Trelawney's appointment to its command. "The King is very nice in making new Establishments in the Army," the Duke told the Governor in 1740, "and consequently This Proposal may meet with great Difficulties." Newcastle to Trelawney, April 18, 1740, C.O. 137/56, foll. 313-14. There are further details in C.O. 5/5, fol. 214; C.O. 137/56, foll. 338-39; and Add. MSS 32703, foll. 69-70.

[14] Hervey to Henry Fox, November, 1736, Ilchester, ed., *Hervey's Friends*, 255-56, suggests the existence of such a stalemate within the administration, but there is no conclusive evidence on this point. The King was in Hanover from May, 1736, to January, 1737, but his absence from England is not an adequate explanation.

[15] See above, chap. 3, note 63.

Here was the classic case of the debtor placeman and fourth-rate politician named to an important colonial administrative position during the Walpole era. One supporter had replied to Sir Robert's request for a cooperative effort with Bridgeman in the crucial election of 1734 that "Proposalls made to a Man, who is neither cautious or secret, may ruin my Interest."[16] Even the attempt to shunt this burden upon the colonists was doomed to failure. As Egmont recorded in his diary in October, 1738,

> Sir Orlando Bridgman, who, instead of going to his Government of Barbados conferred on him last winter, made his escape (as he hoped) from the world, to avoid his creditors, by pretending to make himself away, and accordingly gave it out that he had drowned himself, was ferreted out of his hole by the reward advertised for whoever should discover him, and was seized in an inn at Slough, where he had ever since concealed himself.[17]

Only in 1739, four years after Howe's death, was an official sent out to replace him.

The abortive appointment of Bridgeman to the government of Barbados has been preceded in April, 1737, by the nomination of Lord De la Warr as the chief executive of the provinces of New York and New Jersey. On the death of Colonel Cosby in March, 1736, the government of New York had devolved temporarily on George Clarke,

[16] Duckett to Walpole, August 17, 1733, W.C., no. 2021.

[17] Egmont, *Diary*, II, 510. G. E. Cokayne, *The Complete Baronetage*, Exeter, 1899-1906, IV, 55-56, reports that Bridgeman was "found drowned in the Thames, near Limehouse, 10 June 1738," and also the fact that a Sir Orlando Bridgeman was buried in 1745. The latter entry is the correct one. Bridgeman was nominated for the Barbados post and the customary "bounty" money of £1,500 was paid to him, but a patent was never issued.

the President of the Council. An Englishman by birth, Clarke had come to New York in 1704 as Secretary of the province, an appointment arranged by his cousin, William Blathwayt.[18] Subsequently, Clarke served as deputy to Horace Walpole, his cousin's successor as Auditor-General of the Plantation Revenues. It was Clarke who finally won from the New York Assembly an acknowledgement of the right of his office to audit all of the accounts of the provincial government. Now, in return, the Secretary asked Horace Walpole for his recommendation to Newcastle to succeed to the vacant government; at the same time he sought permission to resign his post as Secretary to his son.[19] Whatever the sense of obligation felt by the younger Walpole, his brother realized that the rewards of the New York post were simply too considerable to be left in the hands of a man with only his colonial service and an old relationship with Blathwayt to recommend him. Upon the return of the King from Hanover in January, 1737, the chief minister took up the struggle for the governorship at Court.

Two factors prompted Walpole to seize upon De la Warr as his candidate for the post. Since 1732, the Earl had been an effective spokesman for the ministry in the House of Lords and a devoted supporter of the chief minister. Equally important in Walpole's eyes was the fact that De la Warr, like Bridgeman, occupied a position of prestige within the royal entourage, having served as Treasurer of the household since 1731. Indeed, the new Governor's influence was such that by September, 1737, he had man-

[18] Add. MSS 9732, foll. 262-63; Gertrude A. Jacobsen, *William Blathwayt; A Late Seventeenth Century English Administrator*, New Haven, 1932, 348.

[19] Clarke to H. Walpole, March 16, 1736, C.O. 5/1093, foll. 342-45; "Reasons . . . ," no date, C.O. 5/1086, fol. 81c.

aged to extract a lucrative military command from the King, thus sparing himself, as Hervey put it, "from his disagreeable exile to the West Indies."[20]

In the same month yet a third American government was bestowed upon a friend of the King. The government of Virginia had been vacant since the death of the Earl of Orkney in January. This important position was now given to the Earl of Albemarle, a spendthrift aristocrat with some military abilities. This preferment was the first of many. George II raised the absentee Governor to the rank of Brigadier-General in 1739, promoted him to Major-General three years later, and subsequently dispatched him to Paris as Ambassador.[21]

The appointments of Albemarle, Bridgeman, and De la Warr—none of whom ever went to America—pointed up the fact that for the second time during his reign George II was playing a major role in the disposition of colonial governorships. Immediately following his accession to the throne in 1727, the new monarch had won the nomination of John Montgomery, a longtime associate, as the chief executive of New York. Montgomery's appointment, as well as a great number of others in various branches of the

[20] Hervey to Fox, September 13, 1737, Ilchester, ed., *Hervey's Friends*, 271; C. Colden to Mrs. Colden, September 11, 1737, NYHS, *Collections*, LI, 179; Sedgwick, *Hervey's Memoirs*, 713; Katz, *Newcastle's New York*, 24-25. The entry for De la Warr in the *D.N.B.* notes his support of Walpole in Parliament until the very outbreak of the war; thereafter the Earl sought to win Newcastle's favor using Hardwicke as an intermediary. See Add. MSS 32697, foll. 31, 54-57.

[21] Sedgwick, *Hervey's Memoirs*, 713. Both Walpole and Newcastle had come to Albemarle's aid in 1736: see Add. MSS 32690, foll. 8 and 174. Since Orkney had served as an absentee Governor for thirty years, Albemarle's failure to go to Virginia had the sanction of tradition.

administration, had been arranged by Walpole and Townshend in order to demonstrate their ability to serve the King's friends and so preserve their position of primacy.[22] A decade later the motivation was much the same. In a divided ministry the only safe candidates were those who enjoyed the favor of the monarch as well as the support of an influential patron. Through an astute selection of nominees, Walpole had placed three of his friends in major American posts.[23]

Walpole's intervention into the affairs of the southern department was not limited to matters of patronage. In February, 1737, the chief minister met with General James Oglethorpe, who had recently returned from a military reconnaissance of the frontier province of Georgia. Confessing that he "was at a loss what to do in American affairs with respect to the security of our Colonies," Walpole sought Oglethorpe's advice on "some plan or scheme." On the grounds of expense, the First Lord of the Treasury immediately rejected the General's proposal that regular troops be dispatched to America. Walpole was more favorably disposed toward the suggestion that each colony raise five hundred volunteers and place them under the command of a captain general. But as a first step, the Treasury chief proposed that Oglethorpe assume the vacant governorship of South Carolina. This would provide the General with personal financial support and with a

[22] Plumb, *Walpole*, II, 169-70.

[23] The extant materials do not provide explicit confirmation of this interpretation. The argument is therefore based on strong circumstantial evidence: the obvious change in the type of men appointed to American positions in 1737; the heated debates in the Privy Council committee for plantation affairs in 1735 and 1736; the subsequent hiatus in colonial appointments; and the growing hostility between Walpole and Newcastle during 1737.

convenient geographical base from which to manage the defense of the southern colonial frontier.[24]

There were compelling domestic political considerations underlying this proposal. The territorial integrity, perhaps even the existence, of the infant colony of Georgia was threatened by the pacific, compromising foreign policy which Walpole had decided to pursue. Yet many of the trustees of the colony were supporters of the ministry in Parliament and had to be mollified. Oglethorpe's appointment would neutralize temporarily the Georgia "lobby" in the House of Commons while preserving the option of surrendering the province to Spain if this was required to keep the two nations at peace. Whatever its superficial brilliance, Walpole's plan was not without its own dangers. Putting the security of Georgia in the hands of a well-known expansionist and imperialist such as Oglethorpe was a serious gamble. The General's aggressiveness might easily precipitate an incident with the Spanish in Florida and bring the two kingdoms to the brink of war. Indeed, the Spanish government warned Walpole that Oglethorpe's appointment itself would signify an aggressive design and bring about a further deterioration in the relations between the two countries.[25] In the end, the need to calm Parliament, aroused by merchant agitation against the Spanish depredations, overrode the chief minister's qualms about Oglethorpe's suitability for the post.

In fact, Walpole was so intent upon safeguarding his domestic position that the General was able to dictate his own terms. He refused to accept the government of South

[24] February 6, 1737, Egmont, *Diary*, II, 339.

[25] August 10, 1737, ibid., II, 429; Pares, *War and Trade*, 51; Newcastle to Oglethorpe, July 2, 1736, C.O. 5/654, foll. 64-65; Trevor R. Reese, "Georgia in Anglo-Spanish Diplomacy, 1736-1739," *WMQ*, 3rd ser., xv (April, 1958), 168-90.

Carolina both because he wished to retain his seat in Parliament and because he hesitated to identify himself completely with the larger and more prosperous colony. Instead, Oglethorpe relied on his interest with the King to demand the military command of both Georgia and South Carolina. He would go on "no other terms," the General declared to Walpole in May, 1737. Within a month the monarch, himself a strong supporter of a belligerent policy, had appointed Oglethorpe as the Commander-in-Chief of all the military forces in the two colonies. This gave him effective control of the entire region, the General subsequently explained to Egmont, because

> it will not be worth the while for any gentleman to apply for the government of South Carolina, all their pay arising from the salary of Captain General, which is now in him, there being no profit from the civil government of South Carolina. He therefore hoped that Colonel Horsey will succeed in his application to be appointed Civil Governor, to whom he will out of his own pocket allow a salary. It is of great consequence to Georgia that whoever is Governor of South Carolina should be a dependent, or at least a friend to Georgia and such is Colonel Horsey. . . .[26]

The luckless Horsey was named to the emasculated post in August, 1738; within two weeks of receiving the long-sought-after patent, the Colonel was dead. His patron had not fared much better. Walpole's appointment of Oglethorpe had not only undermined Newcastle's control of the patronage of the southern department, but it had also

[26] June 29, 1737, Egmont, *Diary*, II, 417-18; Amos Aschbach Ettinger, *James E. Oglethorpe, Imperial Idealist*, Oxford, 1936, 199. The Place Bill of 1705 had prohibited colonial governors from sitting in Parliament.

deprived the Duke of the support of the Georgia trustees in the immediate formulation of an aggressive foreign policy.[27]

The most the southern secretary could achieve under the circumstances was a more definite commitment by the home government to the military defense of the threatened colony. It was the strong stand taken "by all the Scots's lords and Harry Pelham, as also the Earl of Pembroke . . . and Sir Joseph Jekyl" which secured the dispatch of an English regiment to Georgia in October, 1737. Walpole had been "backward" in the affair, Egmont reported, "partly from not much affecting our Colony, and partly from fear of disobliging the Spaniards. . . ."[28] It was left up to the Pelham faction to press the point over the objections of the chief minister.

Walpole's difficulties were still minor ones. His commanding position within the administration gave him a decided edge over his associates. The chief minister always had an alternative policy to fall back upon, a luxury that was often denied to his subordinates. He acceded to the demand for an English regiment in Georgia only in the face of a nearly unanimous representation by his colleagues, and then only because his own less expensive plan for transferring the independent companies in Jamaica had been strongly opposed by Governor Trelawney and Sir Charles Wager.[29] It was merely a question of maximizing the return of the various resources at his disposal.

[27] Egmont, *Diary*, II, 506-507. The trustees of Georgia were dependent on Walpole for parliamentary support and hoped that the chief minister would gradually assume a more belligerent stance.

[28] September 21, 1737, Egmont, *Diary*, II, 434; Jekyll to Hardwicke, October 4, 1737, Add. MSS 35586, fol. 37.

[29] July 20, 1737, Egmont, *Diary*, II, 424; Trustees to Walpole, June 22, 1737, C.O. 5/654, fol. 109. In 1729, the protests of the Governor and of the merchants trading to the Leeward Islands had

It was worth more to Sir Robert to placate the new Governor of Jamaica than to save the Treasury the cost of shipping a regiment to Georgia. For Trelawney was as important as Oglethorpe to Walpole's domestic political strategy. Upon the recommendation of Wager, now his chief ally in the cabinet, Walpole appointed Trelawney to the West Indian post in August, 1737, in order to bolster his parliamentary position. In return for the governorship and an annual stipend of £500 to Sir John Trelawney, the First Lord of the Treasury took control of the family's boroughs of East and West Loos in Cornwall. As long as Trelawney stayed in Jamaica, "sometimes Four Freinds [of the ministry] were chosen, & sometimes Three."[30] Coming hard on the heels of his maneuvers in South Carolina and Georgia, Walpole's nomination of Trelawney showed his intention of bolstering his political strength at home by placing loyal associates in key positions in the American colonies.

II

The increased concern of the chief minister with developments in the western hemisphere was completely justified; for by 1738 national politics had become virtually synonymous with American affairs. The increasing agitation by the merchant interest in the House of Commons had become the overriding concern of the administration. The bitter debates which ensued gave the members of the

---

reversed a decision to transfer the independent companies there to the Bahamas. See S.P. 36/11, fol. 34; S.P. 36/12, fol. 61.

[30] Memo, 1754-55, Add. MSS 33055, foll. 336-37; Newcastle to Harry Trelawney, March 23, 1754, Add. MSS 32734, foll. 314-15; George Metcalf, *Royal Government and Political Conflict in Jamaica, 1729-1783*, 58-59.

opposition some reason to think that the internal unity of the ministry would crumble under the weight of this external attack. "I love the Chancellor [Lord Hardwicke] much," Bolingbroke wrote to his fellow Tory Sir William Wyndham in February, 1738,

> and I should therefore be very sorry to see him become the crutch of a battered minister. If he has engaged to a certain degree with the Pelhams, and if the Duke of Newcastle's breach with Walpole is irreconcilable, why should not these circumstances be improved?[31]

By this time the stakes of the struggle had become clear to the southern secretary as well. He could defer to Walpole in the formulation of foreign policy and thereby hope to retain some measure of control over colonial affairs and ecclesiastical appointments. Alternatively, he could attempt to oust Walpole and gain complete power for himself, thus ensuring control of policy as well as patronage. Given the restless ambition of the Duke, there was little doubt as to his choice. Still, the definite nature of the final goal did not automatically bring its fulfillment. Walpole had decided to "rub on" with the competing factions within his government. Newcastle now faced a similar choice. Should he break decisively with his colleagues in an attempt to bring down the aging chief minister, or should he work from within toward a position of dominance?

To some extent this tactical question had already been decided by the personality of the southern secretary. Temperamentally the Duke was not prepared to go into opposition. Newcastle treasured power too much to stand on

[31] Quoted in Yorke, *Life of Yorke*, I, 192; Coxe, *Walpole Memoirs*, III, 114-18, describes the erosion of Walpole's authority within the cabinet.

principle or to risk a sojourn outside the government. Lord Waldegrave commented at the height of the Duke's career that he lacked "the smallest particle of that elevation of mind, or of that dignity of behaviour, which command respect, and characterise the great statesman."[32] Once in office, Newcastle was never able to give it up. He served continuously from his first appointment as Lord Chamberlain in 1717 until he was ousted by Bute in the 1760's. The Duke was the only major political figure who was never in opposition during the reign of the first two Hanoverians.

If an inner craving for the trappings of power and prestige was one factor influencing Newcastle's conduct, economic necessity was another. The Duke's finances never really recovered from his early extravagance. Contemporaries believed that he spent as much as £100,000 in the Hanoverian cause in the year following the death of Queen Anne.[33] This great monetary commitment to the Whig cause was the mainspring of Newcastle's rapid ascent to the highest ranks of the government. Yet the Duke must have wondered occasionally if it had been worth the price. For this expenditure had mortgaged his political future. On more than one occasion during his long career, Newcastle had to remain in the ministry to save himself from bankruptcy.[34] He had lost his freedom of action.

The Duke had only himself to blame for this state of affairs. Proper financial management of the large annual income from his estates would have allowed him to redeem

[32] James Earl Waldegrave, *Memoirs from 1754 to 1758*, London, 1821, not paged.

[33] This was the estimate of Bishop Atterbury, a hostile Tory; in fact, the Duke probably spent one third or one half of this amount. See Barnes, "Henry Pelham and the Duke of Newcastle," 65.

[34] See above, chap. 1, sec. I.

his mortgaged property and to accumulate a sizeable reserve. His younger brother had done as much. After his appointment as Secretary of War in 1724 and his marriage to the daughter of the Duke of Rutland two years later, Henry Pelham curbed his expensive tastes and began to create a private fortune. Marriage and authority worked no such miracle on the elder Pelham. The compulsive aristocrat continued his spendthrift ways until his death.[35]

The precarious state of Newcastle's finances had a far-reaching effect on his struggle with the Walpoles. Just at the time that the controversy with Spain was beginning to occupy the attention of the country, the southern secretary encountered another economic crisis. "The Draughts upon Mr. Hoare coming pretty thick upon us," Peter Forbes wrote in a "very Private" letter to a friend in January, 1737, "His Grace wants a thousand pounds to be borrowed for one year. . . ."[36] In the previous year Newcastle had spent over £13,000 in Sussex alone, and £9,000 of that had been borrowed. "Why not as plainly say, for that is what you must know," Henry Pelham rebuked his brother, "that you have spent more than your income. . . ." The younger Pelham could only lament that "the best natured man that ever was born [was] running headlong to his own destruction."[37]

The southern secretary was preserved from bankruptcy only by his government salary of £5,000 per annum. Without this regular source of income, the Duke's credit would

[35] Barnes, "Henry Pelham and the Duke of Newcastle," 68-69. Pelham held the lucrative position of Paymaster of the Forces during the 1730's.

[36] Forbes to Dr. Burnet, January 15, 1737, Add. MSS 33065, foll. 144-45.

[37] January 14, 1737, Add. MSS 33065, foll. 142-43; R. Burnet's "Account Book of Sussex Expenses, 1734-1742," Add. MSS 33157, 72 folios.

have collapsed immediately. The bankers taking four per cent on Newcastle's growing debt were certain to demand the principal if this asset should vanish. An advisor's comment during a subsequent crisis summed up as well the situation in 1737: "If the Run shou'd begin, there are no means of stopping it: There is no resource left."[38]

Given his financial weakness, Newcastle found that his political options were severely limited. The adoption of a completely independent position would bring financial disgrace as well as political defeat. Even his considerable interest in the House of Commons was of little use in the face of personal economic disaster. Newcastle was susceptible to pressure; his newly-found assertiveness could be slowly eroded without fear of resignation. By judicious management, Walpole could retain the Duke's votes in Parliament and pursue a pacific foreign policy; all that

[38] William Murray to Newcastle, November 5, 1752, Add. MSS 33066, foll. 341-47. In 1737, the Duke set up a "Scheme" to cut his expenses to the size of his income (S.P. 36/44, fol. 198). Newcastle's annual income from 1741 to 1751 was £11,500. Of this amount £5,000 came from the office of southern secretary and the remainder from his estates. During the same period the Duke spent an average of £17,600 per annum.

At first, however, the "Scheme" of 1737 cut Newcastle's expenditures by a considerable amount. In 1736, he spent £13,000 in Sussex; in 1737, £4,500; in 1738, £1,400; in 1739, £2,500; and in the pre-election year of 1740, £4,000. After the financial crisis of 1737, therefore, the Duke had to rely more on local supporters to finance his election campaigns and to maintain his reputation for generosity in the county. These debts to his associates and clients would be paid off in patronage during the course of the succeeding decade.

Detailed statements of Newcastle's finances are in Burnet's "Account Book," Add. MSS 33157, 72 folios; James Waller's "Account Book," Add. MSS 33321, 47 folios; the Trustee Accounts, Add. MSS 33322, 84 folios; and "Election Bills . . . ," Add. MSS 33058, foll. 343-44.

was required was the correct blending of threats with favors. "In the situation Things are in," Newcastle confessed to Hardwicke in June, 1738,

> the Event of my being out of Employment may very soon happen and it would be a very great alteration to be reduced then, & perhaps that so very soon, to £7000 p. ann. But as these necessities are the consequences of my own Follies, I will & must cheerfully submit to them, if there be no Remedy.[39]

The Duke fooled only himself; he lacked the courage to push the dispute with the First Lord of the Treasury to the breaking point. There was no alternative but to submit to Walpole's continued predominance.

The chief minister had reasons of his own for hesitating to break the southern secretary upon the rock of the Duke's extravagant past. The old statesman had begun to groom Henry Pelham as his successor. "Sir Robert Walpole," Hardwicke commented perceptively a few years later,

> had the art early to detach Mr. Pelham from his brother; told the former he should be his successor . . . and said they could not stand without one another; they always talked of going out together; convinced it would be the ruin of the Whigs.[40]

For Walpole to expel Newcastle would endanger his pact with the younger Pelham. More than the fate of a friendship was at stake here. Walpole keenly appreciated the necessity of being succeeded by those he could trust. Other-

[39] June 10, 1738, Add. MSS 33065, foll. 272-73.

[40] February 14, 1748, quoted in Yorke, *Life of Yorke*, I, 629-30; Marchmont Diary, November 15, 1744, Rose, *Marchmont Papers*, I, 84.

wise, his fortune and his person would be at the mercy of a new and possibly vindictive ministry. In the last analysis, Walpole was as dependent on the Pelhams as they on him. There was no alternative but co-existence.

III

It had taken slightly more than a year to reveal the true dimensions of the shift in the distribution of power within the ministry. The outcry in the country against Spain, the death of the Queen, and the split between the King and the Prince of Wales had combined to weaken the position of the First Lord of the Treasury. At the same time, the addition of Hardwicke to the cabinet as Lord Chancellor and the growing prestige of Henry Pelham had increased the political leverage which the restive Newcastle could bring to bear in the councils of state. For the first time since the ouster of Townshend in 1730, Walpole's power had been challenged from within the ranks of the administration.

The gradual alteration in the locus of authority within the government was first apparent in the affairs of the southern department. When the Earl of Fitzwalter resigned his place at the head of the Board of Trade in 1737, he was succeeded as President by Lord Monson, a favorite of the King and a close political associate of the Pelhams.[41] Within a few months of his own appointment, Monson emerged as the chief patron of Alured Popple, the Secretary of the Board of Trade, in his quest for the

[41] Monson had been raised to the peerage by George II in 1728 and had served subsequently as Captain of the Board of Gentlemen Pensioners. Like the men appointed to American governorships in 1737, Monson received his promotion because of his connection with the King; unlike the others, however, he was a Pelhamite.

governorship of Bermuda. With the support of James Brudenell of the Board of Trade and of Newcastle, Monson won Popple's nomination to the American post.[42]

Secretary Popple played a crucial role in securing his own appointment. His strategic position at the Board of Trade placed him in a position to prevent the mobilization of domestic political support for John Pitt, the incumbent official. "Complaints of a very strong nature, with proper Proofs, were sent from Bermuda against him," Popple informed Andrew Stone, Newcastle's undersecretary, on the eve of his own appointment,

> These Papers were brought to me, for my perusal, but as I then knew his Grace's kind intentions with regard to me, & that the Island could be rendered easy by a new Governor, I have hitherto kept them in my Custody, judging it would be more agreeable to Mr. Pitt's Friends. . . .[43]

[42] Popple to Stone, September 16 and October 16, 1737, S.P. 36/42, fol. 242 and S.P. 36/43, fol. 153.

[43] September 16, 1737, S.P. 36/42, fol. 242. After spending ten years in the islands, Pitt had requested a leave of absence. The bitter antagonism between Walpole and William Pitt may have deprived the Governor of his original patron at this crucial moment. In the 1740's, the Pelhams named John Pitt to the Board of Trade in order to win the favor of his influential relative.

The Popples had many friends in the ministry because of their diligent service at the Board of Trade. William Popple, Alured's grandfather, served as Secretary of the board from the time of its creation in 1696 until 1707 when he resigned his post to his son. Alured's father, the Secretary from 1707 until 1722, had been rewarded for his efficiency by a gift of land in the West Indies and by permission, given in the face of opposition from the Board of Trade itself (which wished to name its own secretary), to convey his office to his son. Alured's brother then succeeded him as Governor of the Bermudas. See S.P. 44/121, pp. 69, 88; S.P. 36/43, fol. 14.

Newcastle and his associates supported Popple in his bid for the West Indian government in order to create a vacancy at the Board of Trade. In Popple's place the southern secretary inserted Thomas Hill, a minor poet with good political connections. Hill left Cambridge, wrote one contemporary, "having a good patrimony from his father, and has ever since lived with the Duke of Richmond. . . ."[44] It was on Richmond's request that Newcastle filled Popple's important office with this administratively incompetent man of letters.[45] With Hill as Secretary of the Board of Trade and the ineffectual Monson at its head, the southern secretary had brought the advisory body firmly under his own control. There would be little chance now that the board would initiate any policy which might endanger the Duke's management of colonial affairs.

The dominance of Pelhamites on the Board of Trade constituted a first step toward ending the traditional fragmentation of imperial administrative power. Events in New Jersey demonstrated, however, that the Walpoles continued to exercise considerable authority over developments in America. On the death of Colonel Cosby in 1736, William Keith and Lewis Morris had revived the proposal of the colonial assembly for the creation of an entirely autonomous government in New Jersey.[46] The prospects for a complete separation of the chief executive's post from that in New York was enhanced in the follow-

[44] Joseph Welch, *The List of the Queen's Scholars of . . . Westminster . . .*, London, 1852, 239.

[45] Richmond to Newcastle, August 30, 1743 and February 26, 1746, Add. MSS 32701, foll. 62-65 and Add. MSS 32706, foll. 219-20.

[46] Keith to Newcastle, July 1, 1736, S.P. 36/39, fol. 1; Keith to Wilmington, July 5, 1736, H.M.C., *Eleventh Report*, pt. IV, 297-98.

ing year by the appointment of Lord De la Warr as absentee Governor of the larger province. De la Warr's nomination aligned Horace Walpole on the side of the New Jersey Assembly; the Auditor-General still hoped to secure the government of New York for George Clarke and believed that this aim would be facilitated by the division of the two commands.

By 1738, the interests of Clarke and of Morris, both opponents of Newcastle, had become complementary. One memorandum in the files of the plantation office described the connection in explicit terms:

> It is thought immediately Necessary for the Peace of the Government of New York that Lewis Morris Senr Esq; the late Cheif Justice there, be made Governor of New Jersey; and that Mr. Clark the Lieut: Govr of New York be continued so, untill the arrival of Lord Delaware or some other Governor. . . .[47]

The alliance of Clarke and Morris in America was sealed by an agreement between their patrons in London. In March, 1738, Horace Walpole and Sir Charles Wager joined forces first to secure the approval of the Privy Council committee for the complete division of the two governments and then to place their clients in the new posts. "I cannot easily Express the Obligation I think myself under to you," a grateful Lewis Morris wrote to Wager on learning of his appointment, "& am sensible of those I owe to Mr. Walpole & would be gladly serviceable to Mr. Clark or any friend of his or yours."[48] Without

[47] Memo, no date, no author, C.O. 5/1092, fol. 166.

[48] May 10, 1739, NJHS, *Collections*, v, 40-41. Subsequently Morris attempted to secure the agent's post for New Jersey for Wager's private secretary. See Morris to Clarke, May 25, 1739, ibid., v, 46-47.

Newcastle's approval Wager and Horace Walpole had pushed through a significant change in the structure of the colonial system.

The weakness of the southern secretary continued for over a year. As long as the First Lord of the Treasury was successful in his policy of accommodation with Spain the Duke was powerless. By December, 1738, Sir Charles Wager and the Walpoles had again combined to dispose of a major American post. This was the government of Barbados, which was bestowed upon Robert Byng, one of the commissioners of the navy, in order to create a vacancy on that board for one of Wager's friends. Admiral Norris noted in his diary that Walpole had begun to give "all his influence to Sr Charles Wager" in the determination of naval affairs and this preference carried over to colonial matters as well.[49]

Both in Barbados and in New Jersey Wager had cleverly exploited the antagonism between Walpole and Newcastle to his own advantage. Since his emergence as the effective head of the southern department in 1730, Newcastle had never been able to control completely the patronage within his formal jurisdiction. Previously, however, the encroachments of the other ministers had been cautious and circumspect. Now the First Lords of the Treasury and of the Admiralty were prepared to intervene openly and actively into the affairs of Newcastle's province. The Duke had provoked a quarrel with his col-

[49] Norris, "Journal," May 2, 1740, Add. MSS 28132, fol. 183. The Earl of Kinnoull, a client of Newcastle, also applied for the post. For details of the incident see Wager to Newcastle, December 2, 1738, Add. MSS 32691, fol. 502; Wager to Walpole, December 13, 1738, W.C., no. 2820; Kinnoull to Newcastle, August 4, 1738, Add. MSS 32691, foll. 284-87; and Dupplin to Newcastle, December 29, 1740, Add. MSS 32695, foll. 529-30.

leagues and was paying the price. Indeed, for a short time it seemed as if the road to colonial preferment lay through Wager rather than Newcastle. As "an old Friend of Forty years acquaintance," William Byrd wrote to the Admiralty chief to ask him to put in "a good word for me to your Friend S'r Robert" for the Deputy-Governorship of Virginia.[50] And in 1739 William Sharpe reminded Newcastle of Governor Trelawney's suggestion that the office of Receiver-General in Jamaica be given to "Sr Charles Wagers Friend."[51]

By that date Wager had lost his influence over colonial affairs as a result of the erosion of Walpole's own power and prestige during the course of the preceding year. In May, 1738, the House of Commons had demonstrated its determination to protect the rich possessions in the West Indies by offering on its own initiative the money needed to complete the purchase of the strategic Bahama Islands from the proprietors.[52] In the same month, Newcastle secured the dispatch of a squadron under Admiral Haddock to the Mediterranean. This was followed early in June by a ministerial order for a general impressment of sailors, a plain sign of impending war.[53] In the midst of these bellicose preparations, Walpole mustered his remaining political resources and resolutely initiated negotiations with Spain. The outbreak of armed hostilities had been delayed, but it was now clear that the chief minister and his dwindling band of supporters—Wager, Godol-

[50] July 2, 1736, *Virginia Magazine of History and Biography*, IX, 124. Byrd and Wager had become acquaintances during Byrd's sojourn in London in the 1710's.

[51] September 13, 1739, Add. MSS 32692, fol. 294.

[52] Stock, *Proceedings*, IV, 575, 605-608. A bill to this effect was finally brought before the House in February, 1741, ibid., V, 100.

[53] Temperley, "War of Jenkins' Ear," 213-14.

phin, and Devonshire—constituted only a minority of the cabinet in any vote on the continuation of peaceful relations with Spain.[54]

By the end of 1738, there were definite signs that the anti-war coalition painstakingly constructed by Walpole within Parliament was also coming apart at the seams. Among the first to rebel were the Georgia trustees. In common with the parliamentary supporters of the South Sea Company, the trustees feared that their best interests would be compromised by Walpole in his continuing negotiations with the Spanish government. By December, the Earl of Egmont had been encouraged by the other trustees to take the lead of a movement designed to safeguard the territorial integrity of the infant colony.[55]

Egmont pursued two lines of attack, one within and the other outside the administration. His first move was to feel the pulse of the opposition Whigs. In January, 1739, he waited on Lord Carteret "to know his sense of Georgia" and to seek his support. Carteret had a direct interest in the preservation of the southern frontier because of his holdings in Carolina. Moreover, it was very likely that the former Secretary of State would soon be back in the government. Both Walpole and Newcastle were considering a rapprochement with the brilliant orator and diplomatist. Carteret's support for Georgia would be invaluable; yet it was still impossible to accede to his demand for immediate support in the House of Commons. The trustees, Egmont explained to a friend,

> were in a difficult situation, the minority threatening to be against supporting us unless we joined with

[54] Coxe, *Walpole Memoirs*, III, 116.

[55] The fears of the trustees were justified. See, for example, the cautious instructions given to Oglethorpe in May, 1738, C.O. 5/654, fol. 133.

them *tête baisse* against the ministry and inflamed the House, and on the other hand, no money to be expected if Sir Robert were disobliged. . . .[56]

Egmont had no choice but to explore an alternative way of guaranteeing the safety of Georgia. The imperialist ideology and patriotism of the opposition Whigs could be counted upon to bring them to the defense of the threatened colony; what was more urgent and more difficult was a similar pledge from the ministry. Egmont's strategy was to involve a prominent member of the administration with the welfare of the province. In September, 1738, he recommended the appointment of James Glen to the government of South Carolina.[57] Glen was the ideal man for Egmont's purposes. He was married to the daughter of Lord Wilmington, the President of the Council and a possible successor to Walpole. There were already rumors in February, 1739, that Wilmington and a number of Newcastle's associates intended to go over to the minority and thus precipitate the fall of the ministry. Either way, Glen's presence in South Carolina would bolster the position of the infant colony to the south. With the backing of Newcastle and Wilmington, Glen was named to the government in April, 1739.[58]

Egmont's success in securing Glen's appointment coin-

[56] January 31, 1739, Egmont, *Diary*, III, 15; Jean O. McLachlan, *Trade and Peace with Old Spain, 1667-1750*, Cambridge, 1940, 114ff; Richard S. Dunn, "The Trustees of Georgia and the House of Commons, 1732-1752," *WMQ*, 3rd ser., XI (October, 1954), 551-56.

[57] Egmont to Newcastle, September 19, 1738, Add. MSS 32691, foll. 362-63; Egmont, *Diary*, II, 516.

[58] Oglethorpe to Walpole, November 22, 1738, W.C., no. 2814; Egmont, *Diary*, III, 28; Glen to Wilmington, April 29, 1740, H.M.C., *Eleventh Report*, pt. IV, 264-65; Greene, *Quest for Power*, 134.

cided with the outbreak of the war with Spain, which Walpole had struggled so long and so hard to prevent. This was more than a symbolic defeat for the chief minister. His majority in the House of Lords had fallen to nineteen in the vote on the Convention of Pardo and in the Commons to a mere twenty-eight.[59] No sooner had Walpole surmounted these hurdles than Newcastle raised what proved to be an insuperable barrier by winning cabinet approval for new naval orders. Admiral Haddock was directed to remain with his squadron at full strength off the coast of Spain, a provocation which provided the Spanish plenipotentiaries with a convenient pretext to break off negotiations.[60] Walpole's parliamentary majority had dropped from more than one hundred to less than thirty in a few short years, and now he seemed to lack the authority to restrain his own colleagues.

The chief minister had been forced, much against his will and better judgment, to go to war. From the ranks of the opposition Egmont now noted the existence of

> three parties in the Court—1. Lord Chancellor, joined by the Duke of Newcastle, Hen. Pelham and their followers. 2. Lord Wilmington, Duke of Dorset and their friends. 3. Sir Robert Walpole, Duke of Devonshire, Duke of Grafton and all Sir Robert's posse.[61]

[59] The vote was 95 to 74 in the Lords and 260 against 232 in the Commons: Coxe, *Walpole Memoirs*, III, 67, 85. As late as 1741, Walpole could normally count on a majority of 42 in a full house, Owen, *Rise of the Pelhams*, 6.

[60] Pares, *War and Trade*, 55-56, 58. Temperely, "War of Jenkins' Ear," 228-30, 233-35, argues that Newcastle's initiative at this point "caused the war." He suggests that Walpole acquiesced in this decision because news of a rapprochement between Spain and France, but his evidence on this point is not conclusive.

[61] May 13, 1740, Egmont, *Diary*, III, 141.

"I know," wrote another well-placed observer, "Sir Roberts confidence is not in the strength of his own party, but in the disunion of his opposers. . . ."[62] The imminent disintegration of the ministry, anticipated by the opposition since 1738, finally seemed at hand. It was the general opinion of London, Robert Trevor wrote to Horace Walpole, "of the Chancellor's and the Duke of Newcastle's having not only a set of ideas, but of friends too, distinct from those of your Excellency and your brother."[63]

The tactical advantage accruing to the Pelhams following the outbreak of war was immediately reflected in the disposition of colonial patronage. In the autumn of 1739, Newcastle ignored General Oglethorpe's nomination of Andrew Rutledge as Chief Justice of South Carolina; instead, he appointed Benjamin Whitaker to the post. Requests for other positions in the colony flowed into the Duke's office, a drastic change from the situation in the preceding year. The increase in the number of applications for patronage served as a rough barometer of Newcastle's growing strength.[64]

A second index yielded the same result. The increasing authority of the Pelhams was reflected in the outcome of colonial disputes before the Board of Trade and the Privy Council committee. Early in 1740, Governor Trelawney of Jamaica removed Rose Fuller and Mathew Concanen from the Council because of a political dispute within the colony. When the Governor sought ratification of his action at home, he ran into difficulties with Newcastle. The

[62] Earl of Stair to Earl of Marchmont, August 15, 1739, Rose, ed., *Marchmont Papers*, II, 134-36.

[63] August 28, 1739, quoted in Yorke, *Life of Yorke*, I, 192.

[64] Jefferies to Scrope, March 1, 1739, S.P. 36/47, fol. 111; Whitaker to Jefferies, October 17, 1739, S.P. 36/48, fol. 216; Munro to Newcastle, December 15, 1739, Add. MSS 32692, foll. 521-22.

southern secretary had personally appointed Concanen Attorney-General in the West Indian colony in return for his literary efforts. Fuller was even more closely attached to the Duke because of his political influence in Sussex. By August, John Sharpe, William Murray, and Andrew Stone had advised the Governor to restore the deposed councillors as this was "the disposition . . . [of] the Lords of Trade and Members of His Majesty's Council."[65]

To counter the growing dominance of the Pelham faction in the ranks of the ministry, Walpole attempted to introduce his sharp-tongued friend Hervey into the cabinet. When this maneuver failed, the Treasury chief sought to use the Bishop of Chichester, a long-time friend of the Pelhams in Sussex, to mediate the dispute and decrease the tension within the government. "Sr R.," the prelate reported to Newcastle in November, 1739, "said a great deal of matters between you & him for three years past, and how hard it was for him to serve with you." "As those misunderstandings," the Bishop continued,

> as far as I can judge, seem all to have arisen from Yr Grace's uneasiness that he should have the lead, and be first in the King's favour, give me leave My Lord, since this is the *Rock* Great Men oftener split upon than any other, to say two things to yr Grace, which make to be most certain truths, one is, that while Sr R. is in the King's Service, you can be but second; the other, that whenever his death or any other Incident shall make it be thought necessary to take in any of the Patriots, they will never suffer you to be first.

"The consequence from these Premises," the man of God concluded, "is plainly this, yt yr Grace should unite again

[65] Trelawney to Sharpe, November 25, 1740, Add. MSS 32695, foll. 435-40; Trelawney to Newcastle, July 26, 1740, C.O. 137/56, foll. 381-82.

heartily with Sr R & with ye same intimacy as formerly in support of the common cause, & live upon a good foot with his friends. . . ."[66]

This was intelligent, if impossible, advice. The Pelhams had gone too far to return to a condition of complete subordination to Walpole. They might decide, for the sake of expediency, to stay in the administration and to preserve it from an immediate overthrow; but they would continue to pursue a deliberate and open policy of building up an alternative ministry from within the ranks of the government. And this meant that the acquisition of places for potential supporters was more necessary than ever. An expectation had to be created in the minds of placemen and politicians that their own personal advancement was intimately involved with the success of the Pelhams. The decline of the First Lord of the Treasury had to be accelerated, if only to dislodge him as the source of all favors and rewards. Newcastle, Pelham, and Hardwicke had to establish themselves as the natural heirs of the aging minister. Patronage had to be accumulated and a sense of legitimacy had to be created if the Pelhamites were to step successfully into the political vacuum which would be created by Walpole's departure.[67]

[66] November 8, 1739, Add. MSS 32692, foll. 450-51. The Pelhams had threatened to resign if Hervey was brought into the cabinet. Hervey eventually became Lord Privy Seal in April, 1740, and his appointment produced a violent argument between Walpole and Newcastle. See Newcastle to Hardwicke and others, October 4, 1739, Add. MSS 32692, foll. 377-84; Harrington to Newcastle, July 20, 1740, Add. MSS 32694, foll. 197-99; and Coxe, *Walpole Memoirs*, III, 143-45.

[67] Walpole resigned only after seven adverse votes in the House of Commons and then only because his associates flatly refused to support him. "The panic was so great among—what shall I call them?—my own friends," Walpole complained to Devonshire on

III

Newcastle's part in this effort was to preserve his new position of hegemony within his own province. The southern department was to serve the Pelhams as a citadel from which their influence could be gradually extended. It was imperative for the brothers to hold a commanding position in the Secretary of State's office for another reason as well: the war was being fought in the West Indies, not in Europe. After years of neglect, America had become the prime concern of the Pelhams and of the English nation. The dissent of the Newcastle faction from Walpole's pacific foreign policy had been fully as important as the merchant agitation in bringing about a resort to arms. Victory in war would both justify the past conduct of the Pelhams and aid their future prospects. For nearly a decade, the fate of the governors, assemblies, and inhabitants of the colonies had rested in Newcastle's hands; now the situation was reversed. The continued advancement of the Duke in English politics depended to a considerable degree on the willingness and ability of the American settlers to support the war effort and to administer a sharp blow to the military power of Spain in the West Indies.

Everyone in England counted on the colonists to carry

February 2, 1742, "that *they all* declared that my retiring had become absolutely necessary, as the only means to carry on the public business with honor and success."

By this time Hardwicke, Newcastle, and Henry Pelham had emerged as the "natural successors" and had captured the loyalty of the "old corps" of Walpole supporters. The Pelhams then approached the leaders of the Whig opposition factions to arrange a ministerial coalition. In the process of establishing their own legitimacy the Pelhams undermined the position of their mentor, but this was not their primary intention. See Coxe, *Walpole Memoirs*, III, 288, 245-55, and Owen, *Rise of the Pelhams*, 7-8, 27-35, 91.

the brunt of the war effort. "By raising troops in our colonies of America, headed by a very few regular troops sent from Britain . . . ," the Earl of Stair declared in 1739, "I do not know what we are not able to do in America."[68] Lord Cathcart, the prospective commander of the West Indian expedition, told Newcastle in 1740 that it was "the very great Number of very good men that is in our Collonies . . . wch made me propose to be appointed Governour General of Our Continent of America."[69] Alexander Spotswood, the man appointed to take charge of the American levies before Cathcart's arrival, had estimated more than a decade before that eight or ten thousand troops could easily be raised on the mainland for an attempt upon the Spanish possessions.[70]

Newcastle was less sanguine about the number and eagerness of military recruits in America. From Martin Bladen and from his subordinates in America, the Duke knew that the prosperous economy of the continental colonies would discourage a massive call to arms. From the very beginning, the southern secretary realized that the colonists would have to be managed with care if the war effort was to succeed. His patronage policy reflected this understanding. The Duke informed Spotswood that the selection of officers would not be made from home but rather would be vested in the hands of the governors "as an Encouragement to Them to exert Themselves in making their Levys, and as a Means to induce the Council, and principal People of each Province, to assist Them

[68] Memorial in Stair to Marchmont, December 9, 1739, Rose, ed., *Marchmont Papers*, II, 170-73.

[69] No date but 1740, Add. MSS 32692, foll. 544-45.

[70] Spotswood to Townshend, 1727, Add. MSS 32694, foll. 3-8; Newcastle to American governors, January 5, 1740, C.O. 5/1337, fol. 220; Hardwicke to Newcastle, December 10, 1739, Add. MSS 32692, foll. 510-11.

in it."[71] The disposition of military appointments and victualling contracts would also allow the colonial chief executives to bolster their majorities in the assemblies. Those few nominations which were reserved for the home administration gave Newcastle a similar opportunity. In April, 1740, the southern secretary asked Spotswood to appoint Edward Martin, a nephew of the influential Lord Fairfax, as captain of a company of troops in Virginia.[72]

This nomination, based on personal influence rather than demonstrated achievement, was consistent with the traditional criteria governing the disposition of colonial patronage. But even as this appointment was being made, the standards of selection were changing. With the future of the Pelhams dependent on the successful conclusion of the war in America, it was crucial that only qualified officials be dispatched for service there. As long as the war persisted, the colonies would not be used as a dumping-ground for impecunious relations and friends or needy placemen.

The emergence of a different and an administratively superior set of criteria for the allocation of colonial places was clearly seen in the selection of a new governor for the Bahama Islands. Since 1735, James Colebrooke, a London merchant and a friend of the southern secretary, had been attempting to oust Richard Fitzwilliam and to install his brother in the government. Three years of agitation by the Colebrookes achieved no more than the referral of the complaints against Fitzwilliam to the committee of the

[71] Newcastle to Spotswood, April 5, 1740, C.O. 5/5, fol. 159; Norris, "Journal," December, 1739, Add. MSS 28132, foll. 111-12; Clarke to Newcastle, July 25, 1740, C.O. 5/1094, foll. 141-42. Bladen had estimated the size of the colonial militia at 100,000 men. Greene, "Bladen's Blueprint," 523.

[72] April 5, 1740, C.O. 5/5, fol. 157.

Privy Council for plantation affairs. There they made little progress because of the support given to the Governor by Lord Wilmington.[73] Even when Fitzwilliam returned to England on personal business in 1738, he was not replaced. The Governor's return, however, did engender new applications for the post. J. Frontin wrote to his patron, the Earl of Essex, in December, 1739:

> I am encouraged to apply for the government by Mr. Burrel, Governour of the South Sea Company. . . . Mr. Edward Walpole has assur'd me, that he will recommend me to his father the very first opportunity, and advised me to get my self immediately propos'd for it to the Duke of Newcastle, in whose province it is . . . the only hitherto named for it has been Mr. Tinker . . . but I have heard so many reasons against his going thither, that I am persuaded it will never happen.[74]

Essex immediately petitioned the southern secretary on behalf of Frontin, "a very Honest good sort of Man & extremely unfortunate." The Duke of Devonshire, Essex continued, "knows him & has lately been very good to him." Within a short time, Frontin acquired a formidable list of supporters. In addition to Burrell, Devonshire, Essex, and a son of the chief minister, Frontin could count James Colebrooke as a supporter.[75]

[73] See the extensive material in S.P. 36/35, foll. 57, 248; C.O. 23/14, foll. 231-34; Add. MSS 32690, foll. 111-12; Fitzwilliam to Newcastle, February 18, 1737, C.O. 23/14, foll. 282-83; Fitzwilliam to Wilmington, 1737, H.M.C., *Eleventh Report*, pt. IV, 300.

[74] December 26, 1738, Add. MSS 32691, foll. 533-34.

[75] Essex to Newcastle, December 28, 1738, Add. MSS 32691, foll. 535-36; "Some Particulars of the Bahamas," no date, C.O. 23/14, foll. 227-30.

John Tinker, the other applicant for the Bahama post, had much less interest, though what influence he did have was strategically placed. Tinker was the son-in-law of Martin Bladen, of the Board of Trade. Bladen first approached Newcastle on Tinker's behalf in September, 1738, while the complaint lodged by Colebrooke against Fitzwilliam was pending before the board. "The Motives that induce me to take the Freedom of recommending Mr. Tinker to Your Grace," the Commissioner told his superior,

> are his Capacity for the Employment, and his Ability to do His Majesty and the Publick good Service, by venturing part of his own Fortune, which is not inconsiderable, in promoting the several Improvements and Advantages, the Publick may expect from the Settlement of the Bahamas, after the Expense they have been at in the Purchase of them from the Proprietors.

This was a unique argument, if not a compelling one. Frontin and the great majority of candidates for colonial posts pleaded financial hardship as a prime qualification for their appointment. Bladen advanced the opposite case in putting forward his son-in-law. "He would also be Supported in these Undertakings," the Commissioner assured the Duke,

> by his Relations in the City of London, who are some of the most considerable there; and I apprehend it is virtually impossible, these Islands shou'd ever be Settl'd, unless they are put under the Government of some Person of Substance and Experience in Trade. . . .[76]

[76] Bladen to Newcastle, September 25, 1738, Add. MSS 32691, foll. 374-75.

Despite this attractive proposition, the southern secretary took no action until March, 1740, when Fitzwilliam offered to surrender his post. The Governor explained to Newcastle that a lawsuit would continue to require his presence in England and would make it impossible to return to the West Indies "so soon as the Kings Service may require the presence of a Govr there."[77] Years of agitation by his enemies had been unable to dislodge Fitzwilliam; now his own sense of the national interest impelled him to resign.

This consideration figured as well in the choice of his successor. Because he had managed the affairs of the South Sea Company at Portobello and Panama, John Tinker was the most experienced of the candidates for the post. In September, 1739, he and his father-in-law had appeared before the Privy Council to advocate the establishment of a strategic military settlement on the isthmus of Darien, a scheme first advanced by Bladen the preceding June.[78] It was this knowledge of the colonies, so rare among applicants for American positions, which was one factor in winning Tinker's appointment as Governor in May, 1740.

Equally important in determining Tinker's selection was his relationship to Martin Bladen. Bladen had become virtually an *ex officio* member of the cabinet because of his great knowledge of the West Indies. He sat regularly with senior ministers in the formulation of military strategy, personally masterminding the expeditions against

[77] March 8, 1740, Add. MSS 32693, foll. 90-91.

[78] Bladen to Harrington, June 12 and 18, 1739, Add. MSS 32694, foll. 21-30; "Proposal," September 10, 1739, ibid., foll. 31-32. The plan was referred to the Admiralty for a detailed logistical report but was ultimately discarded, Norris, "Journal," September 17, 1739, Add. MSS 28132, foll. 29-31.

Cartagena and Havana in early 1740.[79] The Colonel could also count on the support of the Pelhams. He owed his early political advancement to Walpole, but since 1730 he had benefited considerably from his connection with the southern secretary, especially in the distribution of American patronage.[80] The coming of war in 1739 tended to confirm Bladen's connection with Newcastle, for his defense of English rights in America as a Commissioner of Trade had helped to undermine Walpole's policy of peaceful accommodation.[81] Now Bladen was indispensable to the war effort. Backed by the Pelhams, the Colonel's personal authority and prestige had reached its apogee. Two years after Tinker's appointment in the Bahamas, Bladen's nephew was named Governor of the proprietary colony of Maryland.

Bladen's transfer of allegiance from Walpole to Newcastle was symptomatic of a more general alteration taking place within the English bureaucracy. Before 1739, the First Lord of the Treasury had been essential to the King

[79] Cabinet and Council Minutes, June 19 to 26, 1740, S.P. 36/51, foll. 116-92, *passim*; "List of Papers," December 19, 1739, S.P. 36/49, foll. 21-22; Bladen to Newcastle, January 9, 1740 and November 10, 1741, C.O. 5/752, foll. 348-49 and C.O. 5/654, fol. 368.

[80] Bladen to Walpole, April 19, 1716, W.C., no. 734. From 1714 to 1734, Bladen was M.P. for Stockbridge in Hampshire; in 1734, he was returned for the Treasury borough of Maldon in Essex; and in 1741, he was named for the Admiralty borough of Portsmouth.

[81] Thus, when preparing a report on the boundaries of Carolina for Newcastle's use in 1739, Bladen told Stone that he could "only consider these Matters for his Service, as a Private Gentleman, not as a Commissioner of Trade." See Bladen to Stone, April 20, 1739, S.P. 36/47, foll. 191-92; Bladen to Courand, May 2, 1739, C.O. 5/306, fol. 133; Bladen to Newcastle, March 18, 1738, C.O. 137/28, foll. 42-43.

because he was indispensable in the House of Commons. Forced to fight a war in which he had never believed, Sir Robert ceased to function as an effective link between King and Commons, both of whom strongly supported the recourse to arms. This crucial mediating role was assumed more and more by the Pelhams, whose sentiments on the Spanish depredations more closely mirrored those of the country as a whole. Faced with this shift in the balance of power and authority within the government, an increasing number of ministerial supporters attempted to safeguard their positions by siding with Newcastle and his brother. As Bladen's conduct indicated, the disenchantment with Walpole was not limited to the fringes of the ministerial coalition, but extended into the hard core of the "Court and Treasury party." Eventually, this alienation was reflected in parliamentary divisions. When the Treasury chief came under severe attack in the House of Commons in 1741 and 1742, Bladen was one of a dozen or so Whigs in political office who deserted their original benefactor on the eve of his fall.[82]

During the three years between the outbreak of the war with Spain and the fall of the Walpole ministry, the Pelhams thus built up an alternative administration from within the ranks of the ministry. Their strategy was to isolate the chief minister and his brother within the cabinet and diminish their effectiveness as a source of government patronage. This policy achieved considerable success. "It is indeed come to that pass," Horace Walpole complained to Newcastle in April, 1740,

[82] Owen, *Rise of the Pelhams*, 24n., 39-40. Steele, *Politics of Colonial Policy*, 152n., seeks to explain this defection by suggesting that Bladen had been a client of Newcastle since 1717, but there are alternative explanations which are more convincing.

> that neither My Brother Walpole nor my selfe dares propose any thing, or speak in favour of any person directly where your Grace is concerned, but are obliged to take some means to have it intimated to you indirectly, knowing that an recommendation purely for being ours must be a clog to ye thing, & a prejudice to ye person. . . .[83]

The validity of Walpole's charge was quickly demonstrated. When George Clarke, Jr. arrived in London in June, 1740, to seek the governorship of New York for his father, he proposed, with the full backing of Horace Walpole, that Lord De la Warr arrange with Newcastle to transfer the government to his lieutenant. "I shall upon such Appointment," the younger Clarke assured De la Warr, "immediately pay your Lordship One Thousand Guineas. . . ."[84] This proposition held out a certain attractiveness for Newcastle, for an increase in Clarke's authority could be expected to bolster his efforts to mobilize the province for war. These potential gains were outweighed in Newcastle's mind by the domestic political consequences; the promotion of Clarke would indicate the continuing ability of the Walpoles to win preferment for their clients.

The southern secretary therefore gave fresh thought to the request for the New York governorship from Commodore George Clinton. Clinton was the second son of Francis, the 7th Earl of Lincoln, a close political ally of the Duke. Indeed, Newcastle's youngest sister Lucy had married Clinton's elder brother, the 8th Earl, and this connection had already won Clinton the naval governorship of Newfoundland and appointment as Commo-

[83] April 13, 1740, Add. MSS 32693, foll. 203-204.
[84] June 20, 1740, C.O. 5/1094, foll. 130-31.

dore of the Mediterranean fleet. At this point, however, the southern secretary was not willing to elevate the naval man to the chief executive's post in New York or to put him in Clarke's place as Lieutenant-Governor. The West Indian expedition had just gotten underway, and it was more important to Newcastle to have continuity in this key American government than to depose a friend of the Walpoles.[85]

Clinton was not the only solicitor for colonial preferment who was stymied by Newcastle's determination to give the highest priority to the successful prosecution of the war. Since the refusal of the Admiralty to fund his post of Advocate-General, William Shirley had been seeking the government of Massachusetts Bay. The Sussex native made no more progress than Clinton. For over eighteen months Newcastle refused to entertain any suggestion that Governor Belcher might be removed from his post. The Duke advised Shirley in July, 1738, that he would be wise to rest content with a lesser position.[86]

By the end of 1739, however, Newcastle had become more amenable to Shirley's candidacy as a result of political developments both at home and in New England. Shortly before the outbreak of war, John Thomlinson had petitioned the Crown for the separation of the governorship of New Hampshire from that of Massachu-

[85] There was a constant flow of petitions for preferment from Lady Lincoln and from Clinton. See Add. MSS 33064, foll. 322-23, 415-22, 469-70; S.P. 36/36, foll. 113-14, 121-22; Add. MSS 32691, foll. 159-60; Add. MSS 32693, foll. 245-48, 398, 414-15; Add. MSS 32695, foll. 24, 32, 533. In April, 1740, the southern secretary told Clinton that he had no intention of appointing him to the government of New York; in June and again in September the Duke advised the naval man to seek advancement at sea.

[86] Newcastle to Mrs. Shirley, July 13, 1738, Add. MSS 32691, fol. 262.

setts Bay. The recent success of the inhabitants of New Jersey in securing a chief executive of their own was one factor underlying this request by the London merchant; another was the alleged favoritism of Governor Belcher to the larger colony of Massachusetts Bay in the adjudication of a boundary dispute. The issues in the dispute were familiar ones. By virtue of his situation the governor of two provinces was tempted to discriminate in favor of the larger and more prosperous colony. It was this consideration, among others, which had convinced those in London of the wisdom of separating the governorships of New York and New Jersey. Now the same analysis was applied to New England. In its report on the settlement of the boundary dispute, the Board of Trade agreed with Thomlinson and his American clients that Belcher had unduly favored the larger colony. The board then proceeded to recommend that New Hampshire be given a chief executive of its own.[87]

By this time, Shirley's prospects were closely tied up with the movement to divide the two colonies. In November, 1739, Joseph Windham Ashe, a supporter of the ministry in the House of Commons, asked Newcastle to bestow the proposed government of New Hampshire on Benning Wentworth, a native of the province and a member of the Council. Ashe argued that the small size of the colony and the great expense of the boundary litigation meant that the province could not support a "Gentlemen of this Kingdom." He and Benjamin Keene,

[87] Council Meeting, December 27, 1739, C.O. 5/10, fol. 112; Jere R. Daniell, "Politics in New Hampshire under Governor Benning Wentworth, 1741-1767," *WMQ*, 3rd ser., XXIII (January, 1966), 76-81; Malone, *Pine Trees and Politics*, 118-20, notes the support given to Thomlinson by Ralph and Joseph Gulston, the principal mast contractors for the royal navy.

therefore, recommended Wentworth for the position. "I am well assured," Ashe wrote to Newcastle in December, 1739, with Shirley's candidacy in mind, "that the worthy Gentm in New England, to whom it is Supposed your Grace is Engaged, desires only the Government of the Massachusetts Bay."[88]

Even in the aftermath of the Board of Trade's critical report on Belcher's conduct and the requests from Ashe and Keene for Wentworth's appointment in New Hampshire, Newcastle did not move to displace the incumbent Governor from either of his posts. Belcher still had the support of Lord Wilmington within the ranks of the ministry.[89] More important to the southern secretary was the success of the West Indian expedition. In March, 1740, the Duke informed Mrs. Shirley through Mr. Western, a mutual friend in Sussex, that any change in governors would be inappropriate. Newcastle was only willing to assure Shirley that if a change were eventually made, he would have the Duke's recommendation "in which I am persuaded, all the King's Servants will readily concur."[90]

The southern secretary may have been slightly optimistic in his evaluation of the situation. The respite granted to Belcher by the exigencies of war allowed him the opportunity to mobilize support in England. At the request of Richard Partridge, the Governor's brother-in-law, the Quakers of Minehead petitioned Francis Whitworth,

[88] Ashe to Newcastle, November 23 and December 30, 1739, Add. MSS 32692, foll. 475-76, 540; Schutz, *William Shirley*, 23-24, 34-35.

[89] Hutchinson, *History of Massachusetts Bay*, II, 398; Belcher to Partridge, November 26, 1739, MHS, *Collections*, 6th ser., VII, 247-50.

[90] April 5, 1740, Add. MSS 32693, foll. 177-79; Mrs. Shirley to Newcastle, March 13, 1740, ibid., foll. 123-24.

the absentee Secretary of Barbados, and Thomas Coram, the London merchant and philanthropist, to ask them to intercede on Belcher's behalf. In part, this was a repayment for the Governor's action in securing Assembly approval for legislation exempting the Quakers of Massachusetts Bay from a tax for the maintenance of the Established Church.[91] Belcher was properly thankful. "The uprightness & warmth with which your friends (the Quakers) have acted at this critical juncture for my service," he wrote to Partridge in May, 1740, "I shall ever bear the most grateful remembrance of. . . ."[92]

In the event, the issue was decided as much on the basis of imperial policy as of domestic political influence. Continuity in the government of Massachusetts Bay was producing an unintended result. The Governor had considerable difficulty in raising men for the military operation in the West Indies because of the increasing expectation in the colony that he would soon be replaced by Shirley. Chauncey Townshend, a London merchant, told Newcastle that Belcher had made himself "obnoxious to the leading men of the Massachusetts Collony" and warned that Connecticut might follow the lead of its northern neighbor in refusing to raise an adequate force.[93] The Governor's failure was offset by Shirley's success. In September, Mrs. Shirley reported to the Duke that seven of the eleven companies dispatched on the expedition had been raised by her husband. This was one more factor in

[91] Petition, January 29, 1740, C.O. 5/752, fol. 350. For another instance of Quaker electoral activity see the correspondence between Newcastle and Lord Tankerville, January-February, 1748, Add. MSS 32714, foll. 1-2, 96, 196-97, 210, 274.

[92] May 7, 1740, MHS, *Collections*, 6th ser., VII, 287-90.

[93] C. Townshend to Newcastle, March 28, 1740, Add. MSS 32693, foll. 121-22. Namier and Brooke, *House of Commons*, III, 536-37, describe Townshend's activities as a government contractor.

lowering Belcher's prestige in the minds of the home administrators. "It appears to me," Martin Bladen wrote to Newcastle in October, 1740,

> that Mr. Shirley has shewn a very laudable Zeal for the Publick, and that Govr Belcher has indulged his Personal Resentment against Mr. Shirley, to the Detriment of his Majesty's Service.
>
> But I look upon these Papers rather as Testimonials in favour of Mr. Shirley, than as Matters of formal Complaint against the Governor; who wou'd have a right, in that Case, to be heard in his Defense.
>
> However it would seem to me that there cannot be now any inconvenience in making an Alteration in that Government. . . .[94]

Newcastle was gradually accumulating support in the ministry for a change of governors in Massachusetts Bay and New Hampshire. In December, 1740, all the American governors, with the single exception of Belcher, were commended for their services in raising troops. Still, the southern secretary took no action and the Governor remained optimistic. As he wrote to his brother-in-law in England, "perhaps the great interest of the Quakers, together with the Dissenting Clergy, may be too hard for my stubborn enemies at last."[95] In November, 1740, the Quakers in Newcastle's home county of Sussex wrote on Belcher's behalf to the Duke and to Henry Pelham. At least two of those signing this latest petition had voted

[94] October 8, 1740, C.O. 5/899, foll. 524-26; Sharpe to Stone, December 3, 1740, Add. MSS 32695, fol. 448; Mrs. Shirley to Newcastle, September 20, 1740, C.O. 5/899, fol. 484; Shirley to Newcastle, May 12, 1740, Add. MSS 32693, foll. 279-80.

[95] January 26, 1741, MHS, *Collections*, 6th ser., VII, 361-66; Newcastle to governors, December 4, 1740, Add. MSS 32695, fol. 473.

for the younger Pelham and his associate, John Butler, in the county election of 1734.[96] Whatever their hopes for Shirley or their disenchantment with Belcher, the Pelhams could not afford to alienate too many of their Sussex supporters. The threat to the family's position in the boroughs was sufficiently strong to prompt Thomas Western, Shirley's prime supporter in the county, to assure Newcastle that "the Quakers & dissenters will be as well-pleased with Mr. Shirley's conduct towards them, as they possibly can have been with the present Governor. . . ."[97]

It was the convergence of developments in America with those in Sussex which finally broke the deadlock within the cabinet on the issue of Belcher's replacement by Shirley. The initiative in England came from Thomas Western, the long-time advocate of William Shirley. On April 24, 1741, the eve of the general election, Western told Newcastle that he had

> this day receiv'd a letter from a freeman of Shoreham in the name of a Majority of the rest, informing me that there is room for me in that Borrough. . . . Yr Grace must be sensible I have no other prospect or view of comeing into the house of Commons for any borrough in Sussex or indeed in any other, than by yr Grace's Interest. . . .

[96] Poll Book, 1734, Add. MSS 33059B, foll. 1 and 11; Petition, November 10, 1740, Add. MSS 35058, fol. 415. The voters were Ellias Ellis and John Gold. The names are common ones, but as both men "affirmed" before voting it is clear they were Quakers and thus probably the same men as those signing the petition.

[97] January 28, 1741, Add. MSS 32695, foll. 53-54. The Duke had been attempting to win the Dissenting interest at Lewes since 1736. See Stone to Burnet, January 29 and March 9, 1736, Add. MSS 33065, foll. 32-34 and 52-53.

"I cannot think of stirring a step," Western concluded, "without yr Grace's directions. . . ."[98] This proposal placed the Duke in a delicate position. To offend Western would jeopardize the chances of the Pelhams in Lewes, where Western's brother had an interest, and elsewhere in the county. Yet the incumbent members for Shoreham, Charles Frederick and Thomas Brand, were demanding that the southern secretary "dissuade Mr. Western from opposing us, since such an attempt can be of no service to him, and may be of some disservice to us. . . ."[99]

A master stroke was needed to satisfy both parties, and Newcastle rose to the occasion. By April 30, the southern secretary decided to appoint Shirley to the government of Massachusetts Bay, if he could secure the support of the Privy Council and the King. The only possible obstacle to this plan was the support of the Lord President for the incumbent. But by this time, Wilmington too had lost confidence in the Governor. The deciding event was the advocacy of the Massachusetts Land Bank by Richard Partridge, Belcher's brother-in-law and personal representative. With Partridge acting as the English agent for the proposers of the Land Bank, Wilmington could not believe that the Governor's opposition to the measure was genuine. It was Belcher's apparent duplicity as much as his willingness to accept a monetary policy with which Wilmington disapproved, which turned the Lord President against him.[100] Given Wilmington's change of heart,

[98] Add. MSS 32696, foll. 355-56.

[99] April 25, 1741, ibid., fol. 367; Ann Weston [Western] to Stone, November 30, 1747, Add. MSS 32713, fol. 509.

[100] Hutchinson, *History of Massachusetts Bay*, II, 398; Belcher to Partridge, July 3, 1741, MHS, *Collections*, 6th ser., VII, 402-403; J. Belcher, Jr. to Wilmington, May 23, 1741, H.M.C., *Eleventh Report*, pt. IV, 290-91.

Newcastle had little difficulty in pushing the change through the Privy Council.

In order to secure Western's prompt withdrawal from the poll at Shoreham, Newcastle sought to have Shirley appointed immediately to the government of Massachusetts Bay. The passing of the new Governor's commission through the various offices of the bureaucracy required extraordinary measures. The Board of Trade, whose formal approval was required for the appointment, was adjourned for the election. So Shirley's papers were signed by Lord Monson, the only member in London, and then carried by messenger into the country for the signatures of Bladen, James Brudenell, and Thomas Pelham.[101]

With Shirley's rapid appointment, all parties to the dispute were satisfied. Frederick and Brand had a clear field at Shoreham while the good will of Western was completely retained. "Had not I Imagined Your Grace would be entirely taken up with our Sussex business," Western wrote to Newcastle on May 14, "I should long before this have troubled Yr Grace with a letter with regard to Mr. Shirley . . . as it is an affair I have had more at heart than any thing I ever undertook. . . ."[102] The Duke was no less pleased with the transaction. His candidates at Lewes polled 156 and 154 votes against 117 for

[101] Board of Trade, *Journal, 1734/5-1741,* 381-82. There is no other reason which would explain the rapid confirmation of Shirley's appointment. Clinton and Wentworth were also named on April 30, but the board acted on their commissions only on May 20 and they received their patents on July 1. Shirley received his patent on May 16, only ten days after his nomination had been given final approval by the Privy Council.

[102] Add. MSS 32696, fol. 530. Schutz, *William Shirley,* indicates the relationship of the Shirley and the Western families but does not describe the role of Thomas Western in securing the governor's appointment.

Thomas Sergison, "the greatest victory that ever was known."[103] Henry Pelham and John Butler were likewise returned for the county with increased majorities. Thanks in part to the judicious use of colonial patronage, the Pelham interest in Sussex had been preserved intact.

Following the general election of 1741, the Pelhams remained in a prime position to aim for complete power in the event of Walpole's fall. Their strength in Parliament was unchanged, while that of the ministry as the whole had declined. The brothers had benefited from the initial success of British arms at Cartagena in the West Indies, and from their long identification with an aggressive foreign policy. America had figured yet another way in boosting the relative power of the Pelhams within the administration. Newcastle had used colonial patronage as a substitute for financial resources in maintaining the family interest in the borough elections. Shirley was not the only appointee with a political connection in Sussex. A host of the Duke's associates in the county were subsequently named to American posts in return for their efforts in the Pelham interest. [104]

In 1741, immediate rewards were given to Benning Wentworth in New Hampshire and George Clinton in New York. On the eve of the election, Clinton had made a final plea to the southern secretary. "I am told," he wrote to Newcastle,

> Mr. Walpole pushes very much in favour of Mr. Clark on account of Some business he does for him at New York, which I fancy I should be able to manage. . . . I have been advised to go and make an offer

[103] Newcastle to the Duchess of Newcastle, May 2, 1741, Add. MSS 33073, foll. 178-79.

[104] See below, chap. 5, sec. II.

> to Mr. Walpole but that can never be, for all that I can expect in this world is from your Grace, a Some little Share I hope of Mr Pelham's favour.[105]

It was less Clinton's obvious attempt to play one faction off against another than the influence of his nephew, the 9th Earl of Lincoln, which resulted in his appointment. The death of Lucy Pelham Lincoln and the 8th Earl had left Newcastle as the guardian of the young Lord. In his electoral activities, the southern secretary had continued to use the political resources of the Lincoln estates in Cambridgeshire, Huntingdonshire, Surrey, and Lincolnshire much as he had during the lifetime of the 7th Earl. Now with Lord Lincoln about to celebrate his twenty-first birthday, the Duke had to take steps to safeguard his control of this electoral influence. The concern of the nephew for his uncle was the key to Clinton's appointment in New York. Henry Pelham noted on a similar occasion eleven years later at the end of the naval man's tenure in America,

> Clinton will not, nor indeed should not, stay att New York; when he comes away, what else can be done for him? And if nothing is done for him; what a life will Lord Lincoln lead, and of consequence what lifes shall we lead also?[106]

[105] April 23, 1741, Add. MSS 32696, foll. 353-54.

[106] H. Pelham to Newcastle, October 13, 1752, Add. MSS 32730, foll. 108-13; Newcastle to Lincoln, October 18, 1753, Add. MSS 32733, foll. 97-98. On April 23, 1741, Clinton asked Newcastle for the New York post (or one on the Navy board) and reminded him of Lord Lincoln's birthday on the following day. On April 27, the Duke wrote to Lincoln, then in Italy, to wish him well and to inform him of the directions given to the election agents on his estates. Three days later Clinton was named to the New York governorship after a solicitation of three years. See New-

Clinton's appointment, no less than Shirley's, was determined by the needs of the Pelhams in the general election. Their long solicitations had been rewarded only when political developments on the local level in England forced Newcastle to take action. Previously, the desire to maintain continuity in the American governments during the war emergency, and the unwillingness to antagonize Walpole and Wilmington unnecessarily, had deterred the southern secretary. Only the preservation of the Pelhams' position in Parliament was sufficient to secure the displacement of two governors, the separation of a joint province, and the nomination of three chief executives in America.

The Duke was not an easy mark for patronage hunters. His generosity was matched by his political sagacity and his concern for larger questions of military and diplomatic strategy. The great goal of the family in 1740 and 1741 was power in Westminster and the palace and not the gratuitous disposition of colonial places. When American patronage could help to attain the wider aim, it was utilized with considerable effect; when it threatened to endanger that objective, it was withheld with finesse.[107] The guiding prin-

---

castle to Lincoln, March 16 and April 27, 1741, Add. MSS 33065, foll. 397-99, 412-13. In 1744, Lord Lincoln married his cousin, a daughter of Henry Pelham.

Newcastle's careful cultivation of Lord Lincoln brought an immediate and unexpected reward. "He came over all alive," Horace Walpole the younger wrote to Horace Mann of the newly-returned young aristocrat in November, 1741, "and not only his Uncle-Duke, but even his Majesty is fallen in love with him. He talked to the King at his levee, without being spoken to. That was always thought high treason, but I don't know how, the gruff gentleman like it. . . . In short, he says, *Lord Lincoln is the handsomest man in England.*" See Toynbee, ed., *Walpole Letters*, I, 127-31.

[107] This is not to deny Newcastle's largesse but only to place it in the proper perspective. "The truth is," one contemporary noted, "the Duke was a good natured man; he had not the courage to

ciple of self-interest provided a sure reference point for Newcastle and his brother. The decline of the Walpoles and the rise of the Pelhams was not a fortuitous development. The old ministers had found worthy successors.

say No, to anyone . . . and consequently promised more than he was ever able to perform." Occasionally Newcastle's weakness of character led him to prefer a persistent solicitor but for the most part the Duke displayed great political acumen in the dispensation of patronage. He may rarely have said "no" but those who lacked the proper connections lived on promises. The quotation is from Norman Sykes, "The Duke of Newcastle as Ecclesiastical Minister," *EHR*, LVII (January, 1942), 146.

CHAPTER 5

The Rewards of Victory

ON THE eve of his retirement as Secretary of State for America in 1772, Lord Hillsborough expressed his disappointment at the perquisites of the office he had held for the four preceding years. "The truth is," he told Lord Mountmorris,

> my Patronage is by no means extensive. All American Revenue offices which are indeed very numerous, are in the disposal of the Treasury, the Army in the Secretary at War; the Judge Advocates and other offices of the Navy in the Admiralty, Engineers etc. in the Ordnance; so that the Governments, the law offices and some patent offices constitute the principal part if not the whole of my Patronage. . . .[1]

Like Newcastle during the 1720's and 1730's, Hillsborough found the authority of the chief colonial administrator to be much less extensive than he had supposed. Yet the departing official had a great deal more power than his predecessor a generation before. By the 1770's the number of places in the disposal of the American secretary had soared to 226;[2] at the time of Newcastle's departure from the southern department in 1748, there were only 85

[1] Quoted in B. D. Bargar, "Lord Dartmouth's Patronage, 1772-1775," *WMQ*, 3rd ser., xv (April, 1958), 191-92.

[2] "Official Appointments in North America and West Indies," Add. MSS 22129, circa 1780, 36 folios. A total of 212 appointments in the western hemisphere are listed; 14 places are not included in this tabulation.

colonial offices in his gift.[3] What had not changed in the intervening period was the pressure for offices from applicants both at home and in the colonies. There were always too few posts at the personal disposal of the chief colonial administrator, while those that were under his formal control were sought eagerly by more senior ministers. Patronage, like the power which permitted it, was as fragmented in 1770 as it had been in 1740.

In 1772, as in 1742, a major alteration in the composition of the ministry effected a radical change in the distribution of Crown patronage in the western hemisphere. Lord Dartmouth, Hillsborough's successor, greatly extended the influence of his office over American patronage. His personal prestige gave him greater weight than his predecessor in the affairs of the administration and enabled him to encroach upon the colonial offices under the formal control of other departments. But it was Dartmouth's close family relationship with Lord North, the chief minister, which accounted primarily for the extension of the authority of the Secretary of State for American affairs.

A similar development had taken place thirty years before. The collapse of the Walpole ministry in 1742 bolstered the position of the Pelhams within the administration. This shift in the character of the government meant the end of two decades of diffused power and responsibility for colonial affairs. Newcastle's authority as southern secretary was augmented by the increased power of his family. On the death of the Earl of Wilmington in 1743, Henry Pelham became the First Lord of the Treasury, a position which bestowed upon him a certain primacy in the House of Commons and a leading role in the distribution of the

[3] "List of Places in the West Indies in ye Disposal of a Secy of State," November, 1747, C.O. 5/5, pt. II, foll. 273, 288-91; "List of Patent Offices," 1748-50, P.R.O. 30/50/39, foll. 56-57.

government's patronage. A decision of the southern secretary no longer faced the possibility of being reversed by the Treasury.[4]

With the death of Sir Charles Wager, also in 1743, the Pelhams achieved a position of complete hegemony over the administration of the colonies. The Board of Trade, the southern department, and the Treasury were now completely under their control, and they had a near majority on the Privy Council committee for plantation affairs. For the first time in the eighteenth century, there were no institutional or administrative obstacles to the purposeful management of the colonial system by a single official in England.

I

The question in the 1740's was not if the Pelhams would make use of colonial patronage, but rather how they would use it. Their friends and associates had no doubts on this point; requests for preferment in America poured into Newcastle's office in the aftermath of Walpole's resignation. In March, 1742, Lady Augustus Fitzroy reminded the Duke that with the death of Robert Burnet, the secretary's post in New Jersey was again vacant. As the daugh-

[4] Clinton took a year to depart for New York, largely because the Treasury would not approve his equipage money and an additional salary. See the series of letters from Clinton to Newcastle in Add. MSS 32697, foll. 261-62, 376-77, 411-12 and Add. MSS 32699, foll. 155, 394. On Shirley's appointment to the government of Massachusetts Bay, Newcastle himself advised the Governor's wife "to endeavour to get an Interest in Ld Wilmington's favour." See Shirley to Newcastle, May 4, 1742, C.O. 5/900, fol. 58.

Matters of policy were also affected by the power of the purse. The Treasury put a stop to its payments for General Oglethorpe's military expenses in America at one point, thus effectively deciding an issue of military strategy. See the papers of Herman Verelst, Oglethorpe's agent in England, in C.O. 5/655.

ter of Colonel Cosby, Lady Fitzroy was personally aware of the duties and the rewards of the post. She asked the southern secretary to "give it to a Man of my acquaintance, a particular friend of my Dear Papas, a native of that Province." "I must own to your Grace," confessed the oft-neglected wife of the 3rd Duke of Grafton, "It will be of a particular advantage to me. . . ."[5]

Newcastle apparently had no objection to this pernicious practice of a colonial officeholder paying a portion of his income to an English patron. In 1742, the Duke procured the deputy secretary's post for Lady Fitzroy's friend, just as some years before he had secured a patent at her husband's request for Joseph Warrell, the Attorney-General of New Jersey. Warrell already held a commission from the Governor, but wished a royal patent in order to increase his independence from the chief executive of the province.[6] The consequent transfer of authority benefited Newcastle as much as Warrell. Both men increased their hold on the office at the expense of the Governor. Control over a colonial position passed from the King's representative in the colony to an official in England.

The pressure on Newcastle to engage in a systematic appropriation of American positions for his own use increased in direct proportion to the growth of his authority within the ministry. Those with close political ties to the Duke were in a particularly good position to accumulate places of profit in America. Andrew Stone, Newcastle's private secretary and an undersecretary of state from 1734 to 1751, was among the chief beneficiaries. In 1737, Stone was appointed Clerk of the Court of Chancery in Jamaica. Then, in the general election of 1741, the Duke brought

[5] March 2, 1742, Add. MSS 32696, foll. 86-87.

[6] Lord Augustus Fitzroy to Newcastle, no date, C.O. 5/980, foll. 112-13.

his subordinate into Parliament for Hastings. Finally, in 1742, Stone was given a life patent as Secretary of Barbados. From American sources alone Stone's income amounted to more than £1,000 a year. Perhaps this was no more than his due. For over twenty years, Stone conducted Newcastle's political and financial affairs with great skill and success. In 1753, George II commented that Stone "knew all that he himself knew: that if he was a Peer, every body would think him proper to be Secretary. . . ."[7] Condemned by the accident of birth to play a minor, or at least an obscure, part in the management of the country's affairs, Stone succeeded in making his position a financially profitable one.

It was the demands of Newcastle's associates at home which accounted for the greater part of the requests for American posts. Each of his political supporters had patronage problems as important and complex as those of the Duke himself. In return for their continuing allegiance to the Pelham cause, the allies of the southern secretary sought a liberal allocation of places for their own use. Thus, in April, 1742, the Earl of Albemarle asked Newcastle to appoint "My Friend" William Adair to succeed John Carter as the Secretary of Virginia. As Albemarle wrote to the Duke, Adair "for many reasons greatly deserves from me this mark of friendship."[8]

There were a number of considerations which caused Newcastle to consider Albemarle's request with some care.

[7] Henry P. Wyndham, ed., *The Diary of the Late George Bubb Dodington* . . . , Salisbury, 1784, 218-22; Dr. Friend to Newcastle, October 8, 1735, S.P. 36/36, foll. 99-100. For Stone's own colonial patronage see Hamilton to Stone, October 1, 1737, S.P. 36/43, fol. 81; Nelson to Stone, September 21, 1747, Add. MSS 32713, fol. 98.

[8] April 20, 1742, Add. MSS 32699, fol. 201.

The post was an important one, not only because of its income but also because of the local patronage exercised by its holder. Edward Athawes, a London merchant trading to Virginia, cautioned the southern secretary that

> the place is very valuable from the Profit to be made & the influence of it. . . . If it should now as it was the last time, be purchased[,] there is Reason to believe it would be for your Graces benefit not to be too hasty upon the Occasion.[9]

The Duke was worried less about the price to be paid for the office than the recipient. There were two other applicants for the post besides Adair, and both had powerful backers. Lord Monson, the President of the Board of Trade, asked the post for James Abercrombie. Abercrombie's appointment in Virginia would allow James Wright, a relation of Monson, to succeed him as Attorney-General of South Carolina.[10] A family connection also figured in the third candidacy for the Virginia post: Richard Shelley was a nephew of the Duke himself and the son of Sir John Shelley, a devoted Sussex supporter.[11]

Newcastle's dilemma, if it could be called such, was a

[9] April 14, 1741, Add. MSS 32696, fol. 313. Athawes was London agent for the Carter family and perhaps hoped to keep the office in their hands. Robert Carter had purchased the office in 1721 from playwright Thomas Tickell. Tickell, an Undersecretary of State to Joseph Addison, had relinquished the post because of his reluctance to go to America and because he feared for his position as an absentee after the ouster of the Sunderland Whigs. See Louis B. Wright, ed., *The Letters of Robert Carter*, Chapel Hill, 1940, x-xi, and David Harrison Stevens, *Party Politics and English Journalism, 1702-1742*, Menasha, 1916, 93-94.

[10] Monson to Newcastle, October 25, 1742, Add. MSS 32699, foll. 481-82.

[11] Newcastle to Sir William Gage, November 26, 1743, Add. MSS 32701, foll. 271-72. Sir John Shelley had married the Duke's sister.

happy one. It was simply a question of choosing which of his own associates should be obliged in this particular case. The choice fell on William Adair. As Governor of Virginia, Albemarle had the most logical claim to the office, especially given its crucial importance in the internal administration of the colony. Then, too, Albemarle was in a position to perform a reciprocal service for the southern secretary. "Mr. Hanbury's recommendation in favour of Mr. Peyton Randolph to succeed Mr. Barradal as Attorney General of Virginia," the Governor told Newcastle in November, 1743,

> gives me the occasion to oblige him. But what gives me ye more particular satisfaction is ye opportunity it procures me of once more attoning to Your Grace for My pass'd faults . . . [and] to prove to mankind my inviolable attachment to Your Family.[12]

The predominance of the Pelhams in American affairs placed them in a position to extract some political advantage from practically every colonial appointment.

There was an aura of a family banquet surrounding this division of spoils. Lord Lincoln, the patron of Governor Clinton of New York, was a nephew of the southern secretary. So also was Richard Shelley, who received compensation for his disappointment in Virginia in the form of a life patent for the naval office in Jamaica. Lady Fitzroy was a more distant relation of Newcastle; Stone was an intimate friend of the Duke, practically a member of the family. The wife of Lord Albemarle, moreover, was the sister of

[12] November 18, 1743, Add. MSS 32701, foll. 265-66; Albemarle to Newcastle, July 25, 1739, and October 11, 1741, Add. MSS 32692, fol. 174 and Add. MSS 32698, foll. 122-23. Carter to Newcastle, January 22, 1727, C.O. 5/1337, foll. 97-98, indicates that the importance of the secretary's post was because of its control of the clerks of the county courts.

the Duke of Richmond, a political ally of the southern secretary in Sussex and the patron of Thomas Hill, the Secretary of the Board of Trade since 1738.

The essential absurdity of a system of colonial administration based solely on family connection and personal influence was illustrated in an appointment engineered jointly by Richmond and Lord Lincoln. This was the selection of Thomas Robinson as the Governor of Barbados in February, 1742. The relationship between Richmond and Robinson was an intimate one. "The whole town is to be tomorrow night at Sir Thomas Robinson's ball," Horace Walpole the younger reported to Horace Mann in October, 1741, "which he gives to a little girl of the Duke of Richmond's."[13] Robinson's interest with Lincoln had more of the characteristics of a business proposition. As the young Walpole wrote again to his friend in January, 1742,

> Sir Thomas Robinson is at last named to the government of Barbados; he has long prevented its being asked for, by declaring that he had the promise of it. Luckily for him, Lord Lincoln liked his house, and procured him this government on condition of hiring it.[14]

Robinson's appointment was spoilsmanship at its worst. The result should not have come as a great surprise. Within four years the Governor was recalled from his post because of the "great Heats and animosities" his administration had created in the Assembly and among the inhabitants of Barbados.[15]

Some of Robinson's difficulties in his government stemmed from a confrontation with another influential as-

[13] October 22, 1741, Toynbee, ed., *Walpole Letters*, I, 110-12.

[14] January 22, 1742, ibid., I, 162-70.

[15] Newcastle to Robinson, September 18, 1746, Add. MSS 32708, foll. 318-19.

sociate of the Pelhams. This was Edward Lascelles, a member of a large family of influential West Indian merchants. Throughout the 1730's, Lascelles held the contract from the Victualling Commissioners for the provisioning of the troops in Jamaica, Barbados, and the Leeward Islands.[16] One relation, Henry Lascelles, served for a time as Collector of the Customs at Bridgetown in Barbados; another, Colonel Thomas Lascelles, became chief engineer on the West Indian expedition headed by Lord Cathcart as the result of Lady Shelley's intervention with her brother.[17] An even more striking indication of the influence of the merchant clan came in 1745 when the Pelhams secured the appointment of William Smelt, the M.P. for Northallerton, as Receiver-General of the Casual Revenue in Barbados in order to create a vacancy in Parliament for Henry Lascelles. Lascelles bought the borough outright for £13,000.[18]

The varied interests of the Lascelles family in the West Indies placed it in a strategic position to affect the distribution of local patronage. In return for a percentage of the income from their posts, the English merchant house found deputies for patent officials and provided security for their performance in office and for the payment of their annual rent. For entrepreneurs like the Lascelles' brothers, these mediating activities were just another lucrative business transaction. Seen in a wider perspective, the family constituted yet another vested interest concerned to

[16] Baugh, *Naval Administration*, 401.

[17] Memorandum, 1733, Add. MSS 33028, foll. 378-85; Cabinet Council Minutes, June 12, 1740, S.P. 36/51, foll. 55-60; Lady Shelley to Newcastle, October 8, 1737, S.P. 36/43, fol. 133.

[18] Richard Pares, "A London West India Merchant House, 1740-1769," in Pares, ed., *Essays Presented to Sir Lewis Namier*, London, 1956, 78.

perpetuate the administratively debilitating patent system.[19]

It was this patronage activity which drew the family into the dispute between Governor Robinson and the Assembly of Barbados. Because of the Governor's refusal to allow a meeting of the Court of Chancery, the Deputy-Registrar of the court could neither collect his fees nor pay the rent of his office to the patentee in England. This burden fell on the merchant house. By 1746, over a thousand pounds was outstanding, and Edward Lascelles was forwarding papers to Newcastle in support of the Assembly's complaints against the Governor.[20]

The intervention of Lascelles, a prominent member of the West Indian lobby in Parliament, apparently confirmed the southern secretary in his decision to recall Robinson. There was a distinct possibility that this increasingly influential group would be brought to intervene in the controversy in Barbados. In 1744, the planters and merchants with West Indian interests had shown their power by combining with the Scottish and Irish members of the House of Commons to defeat the ministry's attempt to lay an additional duty on all sugar imported into Great Britain.[21] Now, John Sharpe, the agent for Jamaica and Bar-

[19] J. H. Parry, "The Patent Offices in the British West Indies," *EHR*, LXIX (1954), 200-25.

[20] "Paragraphs of Letters . . . ," May 30, 1746, Add. MSS 33029, foll. 32-33.

[21] In return the West Indians supported legislation taxing foreign linens. H. Lascelles to General Applewhaite, January 17, 1744, printed in Penson, *Colonial Agents*, 283-84. See also Penson, "The London West Indian Interest in the Eighteenth Century," *EHR*, XXXVI (July, 1921), 373-92, and Francis J. James, "The Irish Lobby in the Early Eighteenth Century," *EHR*, LXXXI (July, 1966), 543-57.

bados and the leader in the fight against the sugar duty, was in close contact with the faction opposed to Robinson.[22]

Newcastle could expect political difficulties at home unless Robinson was speedily removed. In this situation it was not possible to allow the colonial chief executive to present a defense of his conduct, a procedure which Robinson called "the right of an Englishman."[23] The Governor's multi-volume "History" of his administration lay unread at the plantation office at the time of his recall. All that could be done was to ease the blow as much as possible. The Governor's brother wrote to Richmond that the removal was "done in such a favorable manner, that his most sanguine Friends may see, the Powers that did it, mean him well."[24]

The Pelhams had been forced to hurt some of their friends in order to oblige others. In deciding between the two groups, the ministry was influenced to some degree by considerations of relative power. The great political influence of Lascelles and, behind him, the West India interest, outweighed the personal prestige of Richmond or even of Lord Lincoln.[25] Still, it was not obvious that an injustice had been perpetrated in the cause of political expediency; Robinson's follies by themselves were suffi-

[22] Blenman to Sharpe, December 24, 1745, January 30 and February 10, 1746, Add. MSS 32705, fol. 269, and Add. MSS 32706, foll. 69-70, 131-33.

[23] Robinson to Richmond, March 7, 1746, Add. MSS 32706, fol. 269.

[24] Richard Robinson to Stone ?, September 30, 1746, Add. MSS 32708, foll. 399-400. The Governor eventually received a pension out of the 4½% duty.

[25] There were only five West Indian merchants in the House of Commons before 1754, but twenty or more absentee planters. See Judd, *Members of Parliament*, appendix 19.

cient to warrant his removal. The intervention of the Lascelles family determined the manner and the timing of the Governor's recall, not its inevitability. It was simply the misfortune of the Pelhams that an incompetent appointee had threatened to undermine the domestic political position of the family. Even this was not such a disaster when seen in the perspective of the preceding decade. In the 1740's there was no danger that another minister would appropriate an American post for his own use. Now it was merely a matter of substituting one Pelhamite for another.

The only possible challenge to the hegemony of the Pelhams in American affairs was posed by the Walpole interest. Some of the associates of the former Treasury chief continued to hold positions in America, and Horace Walpole remained Auditor-General of Plantation Revenues until his death in 1757.[26] It was the younger Walpole who in June, 1746, took up once again the cause of Lieutenant-Governor Clarke of New York. It had been Clarke's misfortune to serve in a colony dominated by friends of the southern secretary. The Lieutenant-Governor, Walpole noted ironically in a letter to Newcastle,

> had ye good fortune to restore Peace & Union there after Coll Cosby had brought things into ye greatest confusion, & disorder; and what I think may encrease his pretensions to your Graces kindness is, that he was superceded to make room for one so nearly related to your family.[27]

[26] In 1751, Henry Pelham confided to Dodington that he and his brother "were afraid of the King, and of the party (the old Walpolians) nick named the Black-tan, & c." See Dodington, *Diary*, 136-37.

[27] June 16, 1746, Add. MSS 32707, foll. 318-19, and June 23, 1746, ibid., foll. 345-46.

Walpole proposed specifically that the Duke appoint Clarke to the government of New Jersey, now vacant by the death of Lewis Morris.

This application was no more successful than those in the past. This time Walpole's petition was checked by the intervention of Lord Chancellor Hardwicke, Newcastle's first and most steadfast ally in the long struggle for power. For some time Hardwicke had been solicited by Jonathan Belcher for a new appointment in America. The Lord Chancellor had taken a liking to Belcher's son, a solicitor in London, and procured for him first a position in Ireland and subsequently the post of Chief Justice of Nova Scotia.[28] This advancement by his son had rehabilitated the position of the elder Belcher sufficiently by 1746 that he was able to win Hardwicke's support for the government of New Jersey. This development confounded Horace Walpole. The Auditor-General reminded the southern secretary that Belcher "was removed for great misbehaviour." "I am persuaded," Walpole continued, "that Ld Chancellor is too impartiale, & equitable, even in a matter of favour, to decide for Mr. Belcher in preference to Mr. Clarke or his son."[29] Hardwicke's sense of equity, however, did not extend further than the law. Belcher was appointed to the New Jersey post in preference not only to Clarke but also to Robert Hunter Morris, the son of the late governor, and to a candidate proposed by the Duke of Bedford, the First Lord of the Admiralty.[30]

[28] Chesterfield to Hardwicke, November 28, 1745, Bonamy Dobrée, ed., *The Letters of Philip Dormer Stanhope, 4th Earl of Chesterfield*, London, 1932, III, 705-706; Chesterfield to Newcastle, March 11, 1746, ibid., III, 745-47.

[29] June 23, 1746, Add. MSS 32707, foll. 345-46.

[30] Bedford to Newcastle, 5 July 1746, S.P. 36/85, foll. 25-26; Kemmerer, *Path to Freedom*, 209n.; J. Belcher, Jr. to Hardwicke, November 4, 1742, and February 21, 1744, Add. MSS 35909, foll.

The appointment of the once-discredited Belcher to an American government was the most spectacular of the Lord Chancellor's intrusions into colonial patronage. Previously, Hardwicke had asked Newcastle to recommend a relation of a clergyman of his acquaintance as Chief Justice of Antigua. The southern secretary had immediately dispatched a strong letter to Lieutenant-Governor Mathews instructing him to appoint William Lavington "in the case of the Death, or other Incapacity, of Mr. Watkins, the present Chief Justice. . . ."[31] Subsequently, when Hardwicke inquired about an alleged competitor for the post, he was immediately reassured by Andrew Stone. "My Lord Duke's recommendation of Mr. Lavington to Governor Mathews was so strong," Stone declared,

> that it would be a very extraordinary Proceeding in Him, to appoint any other Person to succeed to that Office, there; And, as for any Application that may be made here, Your Lordship's Protection of Mr. Lavington will certainly make anything of that Sort, let it come from what Quarter it will, ineffectual.[32]

The comment of the Undersecretary was more than an indication of the influence of the Lord Chancellor. It reflected as well the predominant position of the Pelhams in American affairs in the years immediately following

---

92 and 94; Belcher to Hardwicke, March 19, 1746, Add. MSS 32706, foll. 314-15.

[31] February 14, 1743, C.O. 324/37, p. 205. See also the exchange of correspondence between Newcastle and Hardwicke in September, 1743, Add. MSS 32701, foll. 72-73, and Add. MSS 35407, foll. 259-60.

[32] January 23, 1744, Add. MSS 35408, fol. 1; Hardwicke to Newcastle, January 21, 1744, Add. MSS 32702, fol. 17; Hardwicke to Stone, March 14, 1746, Add. MSS 32706, fol. 298, reports that Lavington was appointed on Watkins' death.

Walpole's fall. Newcastle and Henry Pelham held all the strings of power. An application which did not bear their imprimatur was, as Stone suggested, "ineffectual." In the aftermath of victory, those who had supported the rise of the family to power claimed their reward. Naturally, many of these were relatives and close associates. They had formed the basis of the original "faction" or "party" which had been little more than a social connection. Hardwicke, Stone, Albemarle, and the others who now sought places for themselves and their friends had maintained this allegiance during the last half of the 1730's. It was during these crucial years that the weak family and personal network gradually coalesced into an effective political group, disciplined enough to vote and resign together.[33] That the amorphous links of the 1730's were forged into a more permanent connection by the chief colonial administrator left a certain mark on the new "party" and also on the American plantations.

II

The creation of a disciplined party owed as much to the secure establishment of the Pelhams in Sussex as to the support of friends and relatives on the national level. If anything, the devotion of those at the local level had been more steadfast and more costly. "For his Graces interest," Mr. Whitfield declared to a friend, "[I have] spent almost my whole time to quiet & calm ye opposition at Lewes. . . ."[34] Other supporters were deeply in debt.[35] They had used their personal financial resources to bolster

[33] Jacob M. Price, "Party, Purpose, and Pattern: Sir Lewis Namier and His Critics," *JBS*, no. 1 (January, 1961), 71-93.

[34] Whitfield to ?, no date, Add. MSS 33992, foll. 355-56.

[35] Poole to Newcastle, August 11, 1753, Add. MSS 32732, foll. 447-48.

those of their patron during the Duke's economic crisis in the late 1730's. It was their unselfish efforts which had preserved Newcastle's strong political base in Sussex and made possible the success of the southern secretary on the national level. The Earl of Egmont had commented in May, 1738, at a critical point in the Duke's struggle for power:

> The Report for some days past is that the Duke of Newcastle will be removed from Secretary of State, and Lord Harvey placed in his room, but I doubt it; for the Duke makes by his influence about fourteen members of Parliament who are all at the devotion of the Court, and there is no foregoing that point, otherwise Sir Robert Walpole is desirous enough (and has been so these five years) of dropping the Duke.[36]

Before 1742, few of these political agents had received payment for their services. It was not that Newcastle was an ungenerous employer—this was one charge that would never be leveled against the Duke—but simply that he no longer had the funds to cope with such contingencies. In the end, the political campaigns of the southern secretary were financed out of public funds. At least twenty "Sussex Gentlemen" were given government posts by the victorious Pelhams, ten of them in America.

One of the beneficiaries was William Kempe. Kempe, along with two other Sussex men, had been given charge of the Pelham interest in the town of Lewes in a drastic reorganization in 1738 and 1739. Mr. Poole of Hooke, a capable election agent, was named to oversee the campaign, while Mr. Stonestreet was given the "chief Conduct" of the town and instructed "to see what persons can be got off from the other Side; and by What Means. . . ."

[36] Egmont, *Diary*, II, 486.

Kempe's task was to fill up the houses recently purchased by Newcastle with those who would support the Pelham interest at the polls. He was also directed by the Duke to keep an "Enemys List."[37]

In 1746, Kempe petitioned Newcastle for a place on the royal establishment in America as compensation for his services. The Duke quickly responded by appointing Thomas Graham Receiver-General in Jamaica on the understanding that he would pay an annual rent of £300 to Kempe and Stonestreet. Then, on the death of Attorney-General Richard Bradley of New York in 1751, Kempe was named to replace him.[38] There was a certain perverse appropriateness to this nomination. The old Attorney-General had been appointed to his post as compensation for his

[37] See the elaborate political manual prepared at Newcastle's direction, "Considerations relating to the Town of Lewes," August 19, 1739, Add. MSS 33058, foll. 389-90, and Newcastle to the Duchess, August 21, 1739, Add. MSS 33073, foll. 133-34.

After easy victories in 1722 and 1727, Newcastle's candidates won by only 8 votes in the general election of 1734. Indeed, the poll was so close that the opposition contested the result in the House of Commons. After this scare the Duke began to buy additional property in Lewes; this expenditure helped to precipitate his financial crisis three years later. See Courand to Norris, February 24, 1736, Add. MSS 23157, fol. 5; the material in Add. MSS 33058, foll. 258-66, Add. MSS 32688, foll. 421-23, Add. MSS 33073, foll. 84-85; Nulle, "Election of 1727," 13-15; and above, chap. 4, note 38.

[38] Previously Kempe had refused the chief justiceship of South Carolina because of the meager return, and Newcastle had subsidized the lawyer by naming him to represent the Crown in Sussex litigation. Newcastle then ousted the Attorney-General appointed by Clinton, thus undermining the Governor's political position in order to aid Kempe. See Kempe to Newcastle, April 1, 1749, and March 22, 1750, Add. MSS 32718, fol. 153, and Add. MSS 32720, foll. 149-50; Clinton to Bedford, June 28, 1747, and August 31, 1751, C.O. 5/1096, foll. 124-26, 369-71.

losses in the South Sea Bubble, while his successor was rewarded because of his political activity in Sussex. The transition from Bradley to Kempe revealed in microcosm the changing uses of the administrative resources of America from the second to the fifth decades of the eighteenth century.

This transformation was particularly evident in the government of Jamaica. Matthew Concanen and Peter Forbes, two of Newcastle's associates, had served as Attorney-General and Provost Marshal respectively, since the early 1730's. Then, in 1737, Andrew Stone had been named Clerk of the Court of Chancery. In the following decade, these early appointees were joined by others. Richard Shelley, the Duke's nephew, became Naval Officer in 1743; Thomas Graham followed as Receiver-General in 1746. And in the following year, William Leech, a personal servant of the Pelhams, was named Vendue Master of the colony. There was hardly an office in Jamaica which was not held by an associate of Newcastle. Nor, for that matter, were many posts now served by the patentee rather than by deputy. The effects were soon evident. Forced to exploit his office to the utmost in order to support Kempe and Stonestreet as well as the absentee Receiver-General, the deputy appointed by Thomas Graham was soon stripped of his office by the Assembly for gross misbehavior. The Pelhams' exploitation of the colonial bureaucracy had led to abuse and to increased antagonism between the local assemblies and the representatives of the Crown.[39]

[39] "Mr. Graham's Case," 1752, C.O. 137/52, foll. 569-70; Knowles to Newcastle, June 6, 1754, Add. MSS 32735, fol. 394. When his deputy in Jamaica failed to render an adequate rent, William Leech was appointed as a King's Waiter in the domestic customs service, Memo, no dates, Add. MSS 33055, foll. 70, 306; Trelawney to Holderness, April 28, 1752, C.O. 137/59, fol. 195.

Nowhere else in America was there such a concentration of Pelhamites. Nevertheless, the sum total of those holding positions in the colonies was impressive. Christopher Coates, the Secretary of New Jersey since the death of Robert Burnet in 1742, was a Sussex man. So also was Apsley Brett, the new Naval Officer of South Carolina. He joined Nathaniel Cruttenden, a Jurat of Hastings, who had served as absentee Vendue Master of the colony since 1735. John Roberts, an Undersecretary of State, became Receiver-General of Virginia in 1748. John Courand, Roberts' colleague in the undersecretary's office, had been Naval Officer of the York River since 1743. Edward Fredcroft, yet another Sussex man, had been appointed to a similar position on the James River in the following year.[40] And the long tenure of Joseph Williard, the Secretary of Massachusetts Bay, was the result, in part at least, of his willingness to employ his influence in Nottingham in the Pelham interest.[41] The first British empire, like the second, was a great national system of relief for the privileged classes. Yet for a brief time in

[40] Murray to Brett, May 11, 1743, May 25 and September 21, 1745, Add. MSS 32700, fol. 121, C.O. 5/388, foll. 401-402, Add. MSS 32705, foll. 199-200; Glen to Stone, October 15, 1746, C.O. 5/388, fol. 425.

The Pelhams used the resources of all departments of the government to oblige their Sussex friends. The son of Sir Francis Poole of Lewes was recommended for military service in the West Indies, as was John Smith of East Grinstead. Sir John Miller, a relative and a supporter of the Richmond interest at Chichester, was a frequent applicant for military contracts. So was William Attersol, the man appointed by Newcastle in 1739 to supervise the acquisition of vacant properties in Lewes. And, on the recommendation of Henry Pelham, Governor Trelawney selected Mr. Man, another native of the county, to supply clothing to the military forces in Jamaica.

[41] Shirley to Newcastle, September 15, 1742, C.O. 5/900, foll. 67-68.

the 1740's and 1750's, the American colonies had become less a national than a Sussex preserve, operated by Newcastle for the political benefit of his family.

The potential uses of this Anglo-American relationship were manifold. During the 1740's, Newcastle used the rent from the collector's place at Antigua in the Leeward Islands to support Mr. Board, one of his political agents in Sussex. This was not a sinecure except perhaps in the strict sense of the word. For what came in from America was paid out in Sussex. As the agent explained to his patron on the eve of an important election,

> That I might contribute all that lyes in my power to the Success of my Ld Middlesex, I leave no Stone unturn'd to secure it; My House, wch I have taken Care to let all the Country know is allways open to Ld Middlesexs friends, is seldom without some or other of them, on some occasion or other, whom I bid all heartely well come to what my Table & Cellar affords.[42]

Board's hospitality and political influence played a large part in defeating the continued attempts of Thomas Sergison, a member of the local gentry, to capture one of the Pelhams' seats in the borough of Lewes.

The death of Mr. Board in 1746 made it necessary to safeguard the election in another way. William Poole, another political agent, warned Newcastle that Sergison's influence in the county was "a growing one, and will be more so in these parts, now Mr. Board is dead . . . there being none but my self to work against him. . . ."[43] Deprived of local support, the Duke decided to come to

[42] November 7, 1741, Add. MSS 32991B, foll. 9-10; Mrs. Board to Newcastle, April 22, 1746, Add. MSS 32707, fol. 83.

[43] April 15, 1747, Add. MSS 32710, foll. 440-41.

terms with his old enemy. By June, Poole reported that a "favorable turn in regaurd to his Brother Michael may Confirm and fixe him."[44] Sergison wanted the income from Board's place in Antigua to go to his brother. Even then he was not willing to come into Parliament as a dependent of the Pelhams. Poole informed Newcastle on the eve of the election of 1747 that Sergison "was still of Opinion, that you wanted from him a declaration how he would act in the House, which was a thing he would never make on any terms."[45] For ten years the Duke's American patronage had been sufficient to counteract the strong local support amassed by the leader of the opposition in Sussex. By 1747, this was no longer possible. In the general election Sergison came into Parliament for Lewes on his own interest, the first time in the eighteenth century that both seats in the borough had not been held by a Pelhamite.[46] Sergison's ambition and independent interest surpassed even the power of a plentiful supply of colonial sinecures.

Nevertheless, the distribution of places to Sussex supporters was sufficiently widespread to attract the attention and to incur the wrath of Newcastle's enemies. It was only the Duke's long tenure in office which prevented re-

[44] June 1, 1746, Add. MSS 32707, foll. 267-68; Poole to Newcastle, June 19, and August 7, 1746, ibid., foll. 334-35 and Add. MSS 32708, foll. 35-36.

[45] April 15, 1747, Add. MSS 32710, foll. 440-41.

[46] Indeed, until 1738 both seats were occupied by members of the Pelham family. Henry Pelham, Senior, an uncle of the southern secretary, resided five miles from Lewes at Stanmer and sat for the town from 1695 to 1700 and again from 1701 to 1702. He was succeeded by his two sons, Henry, Junior (1722-25) and Thomas "Turk" Pelham (1727-38). The other Lewes seat was occupied by the Pelhams of Catsfield and Crowhurst, headed by the grand-uncle of the Duke. Sir Nicholas Pelham represented the town from 1702 to 1705; his son Thomas from 1705 to 1741; and his grandson Thomas from 1741 to 1743.

taliatory action. The purge finally came in 1763, when Newcastle was pushed out of the ministry after forty-six years of continuous service. Lists of those minor officials appointed by the Pelhams were compiled with care and precision by Charles Jenkinson, Bute's Secretary to the Treasury. Jenkinson made a close analysis of each connection. "Collector of Antigua . . . ," read one of his comments, "Pays to a Rider of Sussex 200£ per Annum and to a friend of the Duchess of Newcastle 100£ more. Worth Net 1200£ a year."[47] In the thoroughgoing purge which followed, this official and over fifty others in America and in England were removed from their posts. The income from the colonies which had poured into Sussex since Board's appointment in the 1740's suddenly ceased to flow.

This "Massacre of the Pelhamite Innocents" deeply disturbed the Duke.[48] When Newcastle returned to power in 1765 as a member of the Rockingham ministry, he tried to find new offices for these friends, the "Sussex gentlemen removed from their places."[49] The county had always occupied a special place in the Duke's mind. "Had it been a common house of Commons affair," Richmond wrote to the southern secretary in 1747, "I should only have troubled Mr. Pelham about it, butt as it is a Sussex affair your Grace must decide it."[50] The county had served the Pelhams well in their rise to power. And they, in turn, had amply rewarded their Sussex friends and associates.

[47] "List," circa November, 1762, Add. MSS 38334, foll. 215-16; Barrow, *Trade and Empire*, 126.

[48] The term is from Lewis B. Namier, *England in the Age of the American Revolution*, London, 1930, 403-15.

[49] Memorandum, July, 1756, Add. MSS 33001, foll. 7-9, 13-14, 23-24.

[50] January 2, 1747, Add. MSS 32710, foll. 5-6.

III

The effect of these and other appointments on the American political situation was considerable. By 1750 the governors of New York, New Jersey, and Jamaica were almost completely bereft of authority as a result of the emergence of strong opposition factions within the colonial assemblies; they had neither the energy nor the means to win back the initiative from the representative bodies. Nor was the situation much better in South Carolina, where the bureaucratic structure was on the verge of collapse.[51] The financial and administrative pressures of a long war had combined with the shortsighted patronage policy of the English ministers to shake the fragile edifice of royal government in America to its foundations.

These administrative crises, overshadowed at the time by the threat of a new war with France, were the product of one of the most striking weaknesses of English colonial administration during the first half of the eighteenth century. This was the manifest inability of the home government to enforce parliamentary legislation by means of local laws or to secure the support of the American assemblies for the officials and instructions sent from England. It was the task of the colonial governor to transform the natural allegiance of the inhabitants to the Crown into active collaboration in the ratification of imperial legislation. Success in this endeavor depended upon the ability of the chief executive to form a strong government coalition within the local representative bodies. This could be accomplished either by the promulgation of measures in the mutual interest or by the liberal dispensation of places of profit and advantage to those in dominant social and eco-

[51] Glen to Board of Trade, December 23, 1749, C.O. 5/385, fol. 33.

nomic positions in the colonies. The dependent and inferior status of the American possessions hindered the attempts of the governor to win the support of the inhabitants through favorable legislation. And the paucity of patronage at his disposal, at least in comparison with that available to officials in the mother country, inhibited his efforts to secure the implementation of his instructions by persuasion and bribe.

The difficulties of the governor were increased by the steady attrition of the patronage at his command. Writing to the southern secretary in 1733, Governor Cosby requested permission to dispose of the secretary's post in New Jersey: "This is reckoned one of ye most considerable places belonging to their provinces," Cosby explained,

> & yet brings in no more than £450 a year. . . . I have a very good Caracter of the deputys, therefore have Continued them upon ye Same footing under my Son billy whom I have named untill farther orders from your Grace . . . it will give me a little more power in that province . . . especially at this time, Since I am Sorry to Inform your Grace, that ye example and Spirit of the Boston people begins to Spread amongst these Colonys in a most prodigious manner. . . .[52]

Cosby's application was rejected. Newcastle bestowed this patent place instead on Robert Burnet, his political agent in Sussex. Cosby retained control of the selection of deputies, yet this was meager compensation for his loss of income and prestige. The political demands of an official in the Old World had outweighed those of his subordinate in America.

[52] October 26, 1732, C.O. 5/1093, foll. 254-55 and June 19, 1734, Add. MSS 33688, foll. 278-79. After the cost of the deputies was deducted, the patentee received a profit of £170 sterling per annum.

The difficulties of the governor did not stem entirely from unsympathetic superiors in the mother country. He had to do battle with the local legislature as well. In South Carolina, Governor Glen complained in 1748,

> Almost all the Places of either profit or trust are disposed of by the General Assembly. The Treasurer, the Person that receives and pays away all the Public money raised for His Majesty is named by them and cannot be displaced but by them . . . they appoint the Commissary, the Indian Commissioner, the Comptroller of the Dutys imposed by Law upon Goods imported, The Powder Receiver . . . further . . . much of the executive part of Government and of the Administration is by various Laws lodged in different sets of Commissioners. Thus We have Commissioners of the Market, of the Workhouse, of the Pilots, of the Fortifications, and so on without number.

As Glen concluded, "No wonder if a Governor be not cloathed with Authority, when he is stripped naked of Power. . . ."[53] This was more than a two-sided struggle between governor and assembly. In Glen's own province of South Carolina the southern secretary had the disposal of no fewer than fifteen places, including most of the more valuable ones.[54] There was a three-way tug of war among English politicians, royal governors, and colonial assemblies for the control of American patronage. In this contest, the colonial executive was as frequently allied with his legislature as with the home administrators.[55]

[53] Glen to Bedford, October 10, 1748, C.O. 5/388, foll. 111-21; Glen to Newcastle, February 6, 1744, ibid., foll. 364-65.

[54] "List of Places," February, 1748, C.O. 5/5, foll. 270-72.

[55] Howe to Newcastle, February 4, 1734, C.O. 28/45, foll. 311-12. Bernard Bailyn, *The Origins of American Politics*, New York, 1968, 66-80, provides a general discussion of this problem.

This situation was both an inheritance from the last decades of the seventeenth century and the result of the activities of the southern secretary in the eighteenth. In 1657, because of the royalist sympathies in the important colony of Jamaica, Cromwell had taken the appointment of the provost marshal out of the hands of the local officials. The authority exercised by the Protector as a precautionary measure was employed by the Restoration Stuarts as a reward. The posts of secretary, provost marshal, and naval officer in all of the West Indian and many of the continental colonies were filled by the Stuarts by letters patent under the great seal.[56]

These appointments undercut the position of the governor in two ways. The chief colonial executive lost both the political influence from this patronage and effective administrative control over the appointees. Governor Portland of Jamaica complained to the southern secretary in 1724 that

> There is nothing to reward any body, or encourage any One to distinguish himself in the Service of the publick. The Patent Officers think themselves entirely independent from the Governour . . . and brag of it in private, that their Patents are given to them by the King, in the same manner as the Governours Commission. . . . The Deputies who are here, are generally such Persons as that nothing can be expected from them; All other Posts by wch one ought to keep up ones interest, & keep the People in some Awe, are only feathers. . . .[57]

[56] Parry, "Patent Offices," 200-25.

[57] Portland to Carteret, July 13, 1724, C.O. 137/52, foll. 75-76; Hope to Board of Trade, April 12, 1723, C.O. 37/26, foll. 108-11.

When Portland attempted to suspend the Deputy Provost Marshal for misbehavior, Richard Rigby, the patentee and a friend of Sir Charles Wager, protested vigorously against this interference with "his Freehold & his property."[58] As Rigby had "a very good Interest in the County of Essex and has made use of it, in favor of the ffriends to the Governmt," his complaints had considerable weight.[59] Eventually the Governor restored the Deputy to his position. Paradoxically enough, the extension of the patent office system to the colonies, begun in an attempt to extend the bounds of the central authority, had become one of the main obstacles to the efficient direction of the local administration by the governor and his superiors.

Under Newcastle the patent system was preserved and expanded to include the naval office in the continental colonies.[60] During the 1730's these posts were appropriated one by one by the southern secretary. At first this process was more haphazard and absentminded than purposeful and determined. Upon the death in 1733 of William Hammerton, the long-time Naval Officer of South

[58] Portland to Newcastle, February 8, 1725, C.O. 137/52, foll. 113-16.

[59] Wager to Craggs ?, January 29, 1719, Stowe MSS 246, foll. 216-17. Rigby's son, Richard (1722-88), became the chief man of business for the Duke of Bedford. He was an M.P. (1745-68), a Lord of Trade (1755-60), and Paymaster of the Forces (1768-82).

[60] The Naval Office was originally vested in the person of the governor himself and was intended in part as a way of checking upon the Collectors of the Customs. See Pemberton to Delafaye, November 3, 1733, C.O. 5/899, foll. 48-49; Carkesse to Powys, December 30, 1713, Add. MSS 22617, foll. 145-49; Bellomont to Partridge, April 10, 1700, C.O. 5/931, fol. 32; and Barrow, *Trade and Empire*, 117-19.

Carolina, Newcastle secured a royal warrant appointing William Fox to the position. Rejecting a protest entered by Governor Johnson, who maintained that the governor had always exercised the right of nomination, the southern secretary noted that the proprietors had held ultimate authority in the past, since they had issued the patents of office, and that their prerogative had now passed to the Crown.[61]

There was no such traditional sanction for the appointment in the same year of Benjamin Pemberton as the Naval Officer of Massachusetts Bay. Pemberton was an English merchant who had suffered heavily in trade, "owing to some National reasons between the Crowns of Great Britain and France." In January, 1733, he sought recompense from Sir Robert Walpole in the form of "a promise of some post under the Government, when any became vacant."[62] Pemberton proceeded to engage himself as agent to Herbert Pelham, a distant relation of Newcastle, who was attempting to recover an estate in New England. Then he gave bond to Colonel Shute, the former Governor of the colony, and Mr. Yeamans, an influential merchant, "that a Friend of theirs should enjoy one third part" of the fees of the naval office.[63] Even with all this "interest" behind him, Pemberton felt obliged to justify his nomination on the grounds of past precedent. "It can't,

[61] See the material in C.O. 5/388, foll. 50, 115; C.O. 5/383, foll. 137, 203a; S.P. 36/26, foll. 337, 352; and Add. MSS 33688, foll. 206-207.

[62] Pemberton to Delafaye, September 8, 1732, S.P. 36/28, foll. 102-103; Pemberton to Newcastle, November 1, 1732, and January 23, 1733, ibid., foll. 211-16 and S.P. 36/29, fol. 30; Pemberton to Walpole, January 4, 1733, W.C., no. 1945.

[63] Shirley to Newcastle, January 23, 1742, C.O. 5/900, foll. 29-30; Herbert Pelham to Newcastle, May 13, 1733, S.P. 36/29, fol. 207.

I humbly think, be called an innovation," he argued in a letter to Walpole in March,

> because the Naval Officer in some of the plantations, particularly Barbados, is already appointed by the Crown, neither will it at all interfere with the New England Charter . . . and as to its taking a perquisite from the Governor . . . many circumstances in my case are very sufficient to outweigh any interest of the present Governour. . . .[64]

When Governor Belcher received the royal warrant directing him to appoint Pemberton to the Naval Office, he wrote immediately to Newcastle that "By the Act of 7: & 8: of KW [King William]: 3: The Governour is made intirely accountable for that Office . . . one of the best Perquisities of this Government."[65]

Belcher was completely correct in his interpretation of the statutes; yet rational argument was unlikely to prevail against the patronage demands of Walpole and Newcastle. Pending the outcome of his appeal to the southern secretary, Belcher decided to offer Pemberton the substance of his demand while denying the form. He therefore gave Pemberton a commission as Naval Officer, but one which was valid only during the pleasure of the governor. Belcher argued that "it was his duty to dispute the Kings orders, when they interfered with an act of Parliament, which was above the King."[66] There was something about the politics

[64] March 6, 1733, W.C., no. 1951.

[65] October 4, 1733, C.O. 5/899, foll. 8-12; Belcher to Popple, December 4, 1733, C.O. 5/877, foll. 153-54; Belcher to Newcastle, December 3, 1733, C.O. 5/899, foll. 120-23.

[66] Pemberton to Newcastle, October 8, 1733, Add. MSS 32688, foll. 474-75. Belcher attempted to have the royal warrant transferred to William Fairfax, a personal friend who had influential

of Massachusetts Bay that elevated into a matter of principle what in any other colony would have been considered as a mundane squabble.

By the late 1730's, Newcastle's attitude toward the rights of the governors under his command had begun to change. The arguments from precedent and administrative efficiency which had been raised at the time of Pemberton's initial request seemed no longer to have the same weight with the southern secretary. The demands of his associates and supporters at home were making him think more like a politician and less like an administrator with regard to colonial affairs. In May, 1739, for example, the Duke wrote strongly to Lieutenant-Governor Gooch in Virginia on Lord Albemarle's behalf. Newcastle suggested that Gooch had erred in appointing an adjutant in Virginia without consulting the absentee Governor-in-Chief. The southern secretary recommended that in the future all appointments should be made with a provision for the approbation of the governor. This reprimand elicited a prompt rejoinder from the colonial executive. "I am so

---

connections in England and who had been a classmate of Newcastle at Westminster School. See the material in C.O. 5/899, foll. 19-21, 48-49, and Add. MSS 30306, foll. 60, 96-99, 120-21.

When Shirley replaced Belcher in 1742, he turned Pemberton out of office in favor of his own son, arguing that the Naval Officer's commission had expired on the change of governors. Shirley was then forced to name Pemberton as Clerk to the judges of the Superior Court, a post worth £130 sterling per annum, when he discovered that Newcastle, as well as Walpole, was a supporter of the Naval Officer. In order to prevent his son's removal, which would "lesen Mr. Shirley very much in ye Eyes of ye People," the governor thus had to sacrifice his control of another post. See Mrs. Shirley to Newcastle, July 5, 1741, Add. MSS 32697, foll. 282-83; Pemberton to Newcastle, November 15, 1740, Add. MSS 32695, foll. 411-12; and the material in C.O. 5/900, foll. 25-30.

well acquainted with the Practice of this Government for sixty years past," Gooch wrote to Albemarle in September, 1739,

> that I can Assure Your Lordship there is not one Instance in all that time of a Lt. Governour being Controlled by the Chief Governour in the disposal of any Office of Trust or Profit, whenever such became vacant; tho some of those Chief Governours, as Lord Culpeper and Ld. Effingham, had been in Virginia, knew the Offices, and had ffriends and acquaintance in the Country to gratify: and the Reason, My Lord, is very evident, because the Letters Patents, by which they were constituted, devolve the whole Power of Government upon the Person, who is Commander in Chief of the Place. . . . And if your Lordship will be pleased to recollect, you will find no Power given you by your Commission to Exercise any Act of Government in this Colony, during your Residence elsewhere; . . . it would be subverting the fundamental Principles of Government to take away from the Chief Officiating magistrate the Power of rewarding Merit . . . and in the present case, it would be making a meer Cypher of the Lt. Governour and Council. . . .[67]

This carefully marshaled argument apparently convinced the home authorities of the advisability, if not the legal necessity, of allowing the Lieutenant-Governor and the Council the disposal of certain appointments. The post of adjutant never passed into the control of the Governor-in-Chief or the Secretary of State. Certainly precedent was on the side of the Lieutenant-Governor. Alexander

[67] September 3, 1739, C.O. 5/1337, foll. 208-11; Newcastle to Gooch, May 21, 1739, ibid., foll. 204-205.

Spotswood, his predecessor in the office, had very carefully delineated the respective rights of the Deputy-Governor and the home authorities in the selection of officials in the colony.[68] Likewise, the colonial chief executive had a strong legal position to defend. As Gooch noted, it was stated "by the King's Instructions and the Laws of the Country," that the "Advice and Consent" of the Council had to be obtained before appointments could be made. Any attempt to do otherwise would be "no less than a Revocation of Letters Patent and Instructions, and a Repeal of our Laws."[69] Gooch's only weakness, in fact, was in his own political position. He remained in power on Albemarle's sufferance. The Governor-in-Chief had it within his power at any time to relieve his deputy of his duties and appoint another, more amenable, lieutenant. If Albemarle, backed by the power of the Pelhams, wished to have his way, neither past practice nor the laws of the country would prove an insurmountable obstacle.

This was illustrated in the following year. In January, 1740, Albemarle secured a royal warrant directing the appointment of Head Lynch to the Naval Office of the York River. Only a short time before the Governor had bestowed the place on his son. Now the issue of Albemarle's authority had been joined on a personal as well as on a constitutional level. Soon Attorney-General Blair was writing to Newcastle for his opinion. One half of the Virginia Council favored a representation to the King to decide which man was entitled to the office; the other half wished to execute the royal warrant and to advise the contending

[68] See the correspondence in the *Spotswood Papers*, Virginia Historical Society, *Collections*, I, 6-13, 13-14, 29-33, 66, 69-70, 96-98, 112-15, 163-72; ibid., II, 103-106, 346.

[69] Gooch to Albemarle, September 3, 1739, C.O. 5/1337, foll. 208-11.

parties to settle their differences at law.[70] Blair was not the only one seeking the attention of the southern secretary. The Governor's brother, the Bishop of Norwich, petitioned Newcastle in Gooch's behalf, assailing this "Abridgement of the Authority & Proffit of ye Governour there."[71] Even Horace Walpole wrote to the southern secretary giving his thoughts on the matter. "Your Grace know[s] that I am of opinion," the Auditor-General declared in June, 1741,

> that ye Governour of Virginia, who resides constantly here, and receives a certain proportion of ye Salary & Emoluments, has nothing at all to doe with ye dispersale of ye places that are under ye Civile Government of that Province; but that power is actually lodged in ye person, who has ye Kings warrant resident there. . . .[72]

This was the same argument propounded by Gooch. The only difference was that Walpole had a better grasp of the political realities of the situation. "If your Grace has thought fitt to give other directions," Walpole admitted, "I am not to weak to think, that I . . . can dispute that matter with your Grace and Ld Albemarle." Even two years before Walpole would not have been so submissive. This letter of 1741 was as much an indication of the declining fortunes of the Walpoles as a confirmation of the campaign of aggrandizement upon which the Pelhams had embarked.

[70] May 2, 1741, C.O. 5/1337, foll. 247-48; Gooch to Newcastle, September 15, 1741, ibid., foll. 252-53.

[71] May 5, 1740, S.P. 36/50, fol. 389. In 1746, Gooch was made a baronet as a result of the Bishop's influence with the Pelhams. See Norwich to Newcastle, July 3, August 22, and September 15, 1746, Add. MSS 32707, foll. 392-93 and Add. MSS 32708, foll. 180, 292.

[72] June 24, 1741, Add. MSS 32697, foll. 236-37. Walpole wrote at the request of John Blair, his deputy in Virginia. See Blair to Walpole, March 24, 1741, Add. MSS 32696, foll. 357-58.

Hitherto Newcastle had acted at the instigation of others and for their benefit. Fox, a disappointed officeseeker in South Carolina, and Pemberton, a charity case from Walpole, were specific examples from the Naval Office, but the pattern was generally the same elsewhere as well. Now, pressed by Albemarle and on the point of assuming complete hegemony over the conduct of American affairs, the Duke began to exploit the administrative resources of the colonies for his own political ends. Neither Gooch nor any of his fellow governors could prevail against the power of the Secretary of State. In 1741, the Virginia Governor removed his son in favor of Albemarle's candidate. Two years later, following Lynch's death, the Naval Office of the York River was converted into a patent post and given to John Courand, one of the Undersecretaries of State. When Gooch protested that it was impossible for this post to be served by deputy because of the duties involved, he was silenced by a letter from Newcastle. The Duke instructed Gooch to cease obstructing Courand's efforts to put the office under a deputy, "being persuaded, you will, upon reflection, employ Your best Offices in Mr. Courand's behalf. . . ."[73] This discreet warning was sufficient to prevent any further agitation by the Deputy-Governor for the local control of appointments.

There was another factor at work in this development in addition to the Pelhams' growing patronage requirements. In January, 1742, William Wood, secretary to the Commissioners of the Customs, requested from the Board of Trade the names of all naval officers in America, their places of residence, and a collection of the laws passed in the plantations dealing with trade. This was apparently part of a concerted effort to improve the efficiency of the

[73] September 18, 1744, C.O. 5/1337, foll. 298-99. Additional correspondence on the subject is ibid., foll. 279, 302-303.

bureaucracy concerned with the regulation of commerce. "I Apprehend it my Duty to Acquaint thee," Richard Partridge wrote to the governor of Rhode Island in March, 1743,

> that of late the Crown has appointed Naval Officers in Severall Governments of the Plantations one reason for which I understand is that it is more likely the Acts of Trade and Navigation wo[ul]d then better be put in due Execution than by those who are Appointed in the Colony by the respective Governor's tho' by Act of Parliament the right is in the Govr.[74]

If this was the intention of the new and illegal procedure, it was certainly not the result. The extension of the patent system to the Naval Office only caused a deterioration of service. The deputies sent out to the colonies were more diligent in their duties because of the need to amass sufficient income to make a profit and pay a high rent. But the gain in revenue did not offset the damage caused by the complaints the deputies elicited from colonial assemblies and merchants. Likewise, the increase in the efficiency of trade regulation was gained only at the expense of the governor's ability to influence the settlers and the assembly in the Crown's interest. As Gooch informed Newcastle with regard to the Naval Office on the York River: "being an office of great Trust, it was always committed to men in the best circumstances in the Colony."[75] In the long run this "reform" of the Naval Office did more harm than good.

The implementation of this ill-advised policy took only a short time. In 1744, on the death of the officer for the

[74] March 3, 1743, Kimball, *Rhode Island Correspondence*, I, 226-28; Wood to Hill, January 17, 1742, C.O. 323/11, fol. 29. The board's list is in C.O. 324/12, fol. 283.

[75] December 27, 1744, C.O. 5/1337, foll. 302-303.

upper district of the James River in Virginia, the post was converted into a patent place and bestowed upon Edward Fredcroft, a Sussex supporter of the Pelhams.[76] Two years after this appointment, another place became available with the capture of Cape Breton from the French. This was bestowed on Henry McCulloch, the cousin of the colonial speculator and Stamp Act advocate Henry McCulloh.[77] In the same year, Benjamin Wheatley was issued letters patent for the post in North Carolina. Finally, in 1747, the Naval Office of the South Potomac River in Virginia underwent the same change. By this time the generous patronage policy inaugurated by the Pelhams had built up a momentum of its own. Places were granted where none actually existed. "I am at a loss how to Admit him," Governor Gabriel Johnson of North Carolina protested on receiving Wheatley's patent,

> for there is no such Office here. There is A Naval Officer in the Port of Brunswick, Another in Port Beaufort, in Port Bath, and another in Port Roanooke, But none of these places are mentioned in the Patent. . . .

[76] Gooch's appointee offered to pay £500 in order to keep the post. See Leheup to Stone, September 24, 1746, Add. MSS 32708, fol. 365; Gooch to Albemarle, November 21, 1743, Add. MSS 32701, fol. 267; "List of Sussex Gentlemen," July, 1765, Add. MSS 33001, foll. 7-9, 13-14; Fredcroft to Newcastle, July 14, 1749, and October 16, 1753, Add. MSS 32718, fol. 305 and Add. MSS 32733, foll. 76-77.

[77] Henry McCulloch to Stone, October 29, 1746, Add. MSS 32709, foll. 119-20; John Cannon, "Henry McCulloch and Henry McCulloh," *WMQ*, 3rd ser., xv (1958), 71-73; Jack P. Greene, "A Dress of Horror: Henry McCulloch's Objections to the Stamp Act," *Huntington Library Quarterly*, xxvi (1963), 253-62. Although the two men spelled their names differently, historians have often considered them as a single individual or have attributed the acts of one of the cousins to the other.

Johnson had no wish to dispute Newcastle's authority; he had long before decided to forego any battle with the Assembly or the Crown and to live in the luxury of an "easy" administration regardless of the damage done to the Governor's authority. Rather than contest this encroachment by the home government, Johnson helped to facilitate it. "His Grace was not Apprized," the Governor told Courand,

> that Instead of giving one post he was bestowing four pretty Genteel Employments under one General name, and indeed if posts are given Away thus by the lump, the Crown will have fewer places to bestowe, and his Grace will not have it in his power to Oblige so many friends as he might otherwise do.

Newcastle promptly instructed Johnson to install Wheatley in the first of the places which became vacant and "for the future immediately acquaint me when any of the Offices within your Government shall become void."[78] There could be little doubt by this point that the Duke had embarked upon a calculated and purposeful campaign to place as many American posts as possible at his personal disposal.

This program of aggrandizement was not limited to the formal transformation of offices into patent posts. In 1741, Apsley Brett of Lewes in Sussex was given a royal warrant directing the Governor of South Carolina to appoint him to the Naval Office under the seal of the province. The same means were employed again in 1747 in New Hampshire. This time the beneficiary was the brother of Major General Huske. Huske was a close friend of Richmond and Newcastle, and his brother had already received a number of favors from the southern secretary. Subsequently, the Duke persuaded Governor Trelawney of Jamaica to appoint a relation of Solicitor-General William Murray as Naval

[78] See Add. MSS 32711, foll. 362-68.

Officer of that province. The technicality that this place was incompatible with the younger Murray's commission in the army had to be overlooked by the Governor, as did the soldier's connivance in the illegal trade carried on with the French under flags of truce.[79]

By the end of Newcastle's tenure as Secretary of State, only the Naval Offices of the Lower James River in Virginia, of New York, and of Newfoundland were not under his control. The Virginia place was lost in the rush for the five other posts in the colony. In Newfoundland, the office had been established only in 1743 and was as yet on an uncertain footing; while in New York, Clinton's presence deterred the Duke from making an assault on the Governor's prerogative. As soon as Clinton had left the government, Halifax appropriated the control of the Naval Office in New York to the Board of Trade.[80]

The only colonies which had some immunity from this concerted office-grabbing campaign were those where the governor had a strong interest at home or those protected by corporate and proprietary charters. In 1738, Hardwicke asked Newcastle to use his influence with the proprietors to secure the continuance of Robert Charles in the Naval Office of Pennsylvania. "It is with the greatest concern," John Penn replied to the Duke's request,

[79] Wentworth to Newcastle, March 16, 1741, and June 7, 1747, C.O. 5/10, fol. 118 and C.O. 5/984, foll. 312-16; Richmond to Newcastle, September 18, 1745, Add. MSS 32705, fol. 194; Trelawney to Stone, November 12, 1747, Add. MSS 32713, foll. 432-33.

[80] "Memd of the State of the Naval Offices . . . not fill'd up from Home . . . For Lord Halifax," no date, Add. MSS 33029, foll. 92-93; Byng to Newcastle, February 22, 1743, C.O. 194/24, fol. 213; Board of Trade to Fox, February 11, 1756, C.O. 194/23, foll. 313-14, reports that the Naval Officer in Newfoundland had been killed while attempting to perform his duties.

> that I find it is not in my power in this Case to comply. . . . For while I was in Pennsylvania above two years ago, that post was given to my Bror in Law, who married My own Sister, & I believe he is now in Possession of it.

Despite Hardwicke's injunction "to press Mr Penn as far as You can," the southern secretary was unable to win a reversal of this verdict.[81]

A similar stalemate developed in Rhode Island when Major Leonard Lockman, a friend of Lord Carteret, was named to the Naval Office when his patron came into power with the Pelhams in 1742. The Governor refused to recognize the validity of the royal warrant and Richard Partridge, the Rhode Island agent, lodged an appeal against the nomination at the Council office. Partridge hoped that the high cost of litigation would deter Lockman from pressing the issue.[82] In the event, Carteret's rapid loss of power after 1744 was probably the chief factor in preventing further action; five years later the case was still pending. The story might have been quite different had Lockwood been a friend of the Pelhams rather than an associate of their arch-rival. In his dealings with the Naval Office, Newcastle had expressed few qualms about weakening the position of the colonial chief executive through the establishment of patent posts. It was even less likely that he would hesitate to encroach upon the privileges of a charter government, especially one without a strong proprietary interest in England.

Indeed, it was the situation in the mother country which was the key to the entire matter. The great increase in the

[81] Penn to Newcastle, April 5, 1738, Add. MSS 32691, fol. 111; Hardwicke to Newcastle, April 4, 1738, ibid., fol. 109.

[82] See Kimball, *Rhode Island Correspondence*, I, 226-47; Mr. Pollard's Letter, May 5, 1742, Add. MSS 32699, fol. 207.

number of American positions controlled by the home authorities during the 1740's had been the result of the Pelhams' determination to improve their position in domestic politics. The need to "reform" the system was simply a rationalization and a justification of actions taken for other reasons. Two series of developments combined to permit the implementation of this ruthless and shortsighted policy. After 1743, the Pelhams enjoyed a complete hegemony in the management of colonial affairs. The Board of Trade had been reduced to a position of docile impotence; and Wager, Wilmington, and Walpole were no longer present to act as restraining influences, if only in the interest of their own clients. With these countervailing forces removed, there was no practical obstacle to prevent the trampling of the traditional prerogatives of the colonial chief executives or to uphold the quasi-professional standards of the bureaucracy.

These changes coincided with and contributed to a shift in Newcastle's own attitude. A young conscientious administrator in the 1720's, the Duke slowly gravitated toward a less elevated and enlightened position during the succeeding decade. By the time the Pelhams had achieved a dominant place in the ministry, this process was complete; Newcastle's treatment of the colonies had become completely exploitative. No longer required to defend his policies and appointments to associates with a good grasp of American conditions, the Duke indulged himself in the freedom bestowed by complete power. Nor was it difficult to find an intellectual rationale for this behavior. "Giving sinecures in the colonies as a reward of merit was rather a relief than a burden to this country," a speaker declared in Parliament as late as 1814, "for otherwise, such persons must be rewarded from some other source."[83]

[83] Quoted in Parry, "Patent Offices," 221.

The history of the American colonies during the eighteenth century was sufficient to refute this argument. The growing independence of the colonial assemblies in the 1740's was increased by the creation of new patent posts and the consequent decline in the political strength and authority of the governor. Without large numbers of places at his disposal, the colonial chief executive could not create a viable administration. Governor Clinton warned Newcastle explicitly in this regard, in 1745, following the nomination of a councillor by the southern secretary:

> Mr. Rutherford is but a Stranger in the Country, and his appointment has greatly alarm'd the People, particularly those of the better sort who expect to be advanced to that preferment, as Vacancies happen.[84]

In the home country, those appointed to government posts had an interest in the society they served. In America, however, there was no such automatic identification between the political hierarchy and the gradations of the economic and social order. Only in the case of elected representatives and of the officials appointed by them was there a "natural" identification of state and society. When the southern secretary appointed Englishmen to American posts or deprived a colonial chief executive of his patronage, he weakened the imperial connection. Unable to reward local supporters and associates, the colonial governors never succeeded in harnessing the indigenous political leadership to imperial ends. This need not have been the case.

[84] January 2, 1745, C.O. 5/1094, foll. 378-79. Shy, *Toward Lexington*, 355, details the later history of the Rutherfords while Daniells, "New Hampshire," describes the successful use of favors by a colonial governor.

"Patronage," J. H. Plumb has pointed out, "created, extended, and controlled by the English for the use of Scots was one of the major reasons for the success of the Union. . . ."[85] The contrast with the colonies was startling. Newcastle's patronage policy widened rather than narrowed the distance between England and America and so accelerated the long silent revolution which was changing the nature of the colonial system.

IV

The political exploitation of the colonial administrative system was not a new development. During his long tenure at the Treasury, Walpole had made extensive use of American positions, especially in the customs service, for his domestic needs. Nor had Walpole sought to reform the management of any branch of the American bureaucracy. Year after the colonial customs service operated at a loss. The Pelhams inherited an inefficient and corrupt system when they came into office in 1742; they did not create it.

The failure of the Pelhams consisted in their refusal to correct the abuses they found or to prevent a further deterioration in the standards of administration. Indeed, there was some indication that the process of decline in some departments of the government was accelerated by their accession to office. The virtual collapse of the Salt Office came only after Walpole's departure. By 1750, the situation there was serious enough to warrant the intervention of the Treasury. Fifteen years later, an act of Parliament was required to deal with the collusive frauds which had developed in the collection of the salt duties. At that time the cashier for these taxes was a borough agent

[85] *Growth of Political Stability*, 182.

for Newcastle who had turned his office into a sinecure. The methods employed by the Pelhams to reward their friends were the same in domestic as in colonial administration.[86]

This political utilization of government posts on a widespread basis brought with it an alteration in the responsibilities of certain junior officials. During the first three-quarters of the eighteenth century, one of the two Secretaries of the Treasury became more of a political broker than an administrator. "Ways and Means" Lowndes, who held one of these posts from 1695 to 1724, was primarily a financial expert; John Robinson, who served under Lord North and the younger Pitt, was at once the leading election agent of the ministry and its chief whip in the House of Commons. This transition had been facilitated by the Pelhams. On the death of Henry Pelham in 1754, it was James West, one of the Secretaries of the Treasury, who carefully explained to Newcastle the various political commitments which had been made by the younger Pelham in preparation for the general election.[87]

A somewhat similar development had taken place in the office of the Undersecretary of State. At the beginning of the century, most of these officials were primarily administrators with political connections. By 1751, when Newcastle's associate Andrew Stone resigned from the post, the relationship had been reversed. Stone was an astute politician with administrative abilities. Indeed, during his tenure, there was a distinct possibility that the undersecretary would begin to use colonial patronage in the same fashion

[86] Edward Hughes, *Studies in Administration and Finance . . . 1558-1825*, Manchester, 1934, chap. 7.

[87] Ibid., 314-15; Dora Mae Clark, "The Office of Secretary to the Treasury in the Eighteenth Century," *AHR*, XLII (October, 1936), 22-45.

in which the secretary of the Treasury was soon to exploit domestic positions.

Other appointments made by the Pelhams did not threaten to alter the character of the bureaucracy in such dramatic fashion. They did, however, result in a decline in the standard of service. One nomination stood out in retrospect as particuarly disastrous. This was the selection of Thomas Hill as Secretary of the Board of Trade in 1738. The board's lack of initiative during the following decade stemmed as much from Hill's mismanagement and lack of interest as from Lord Monson's feeble presidency. Within a few years of Hill's appointment, the Duke of Richmond was petitioning Newcastle to elevate Hill to membership on the board itself, as the poet and man of letters was finding the work of the secretary's post too demanding. It was unfortunate that the southern secretary did not oblige. For it was only when John Pownall took over most of Hill's duties in the late 1740's that the standard of service in the secretary's office was restored to the high level which had been consistently maintained during the long tenure of the Popple family.[88]

The primary concern of the Pelhams was not administrative efficiency but political advantage. This scale of priorities determined even those changes in the bureaucracy which eventually redounded to the improvement of the colonial relationship. A prime example was the creation by the Treasury in 1746 of the post of Agent for Nova Scotia, Cape Breton, and Newfoundland. Corbyn Morris, the man for whom the post was devised, initially had closer ties with Sir Robert Walpole than with the Pelhams. In

[88] Richmond to Newcastle, August 30 and October 2, 1743, Add. MSS 32701, foll. 62-65, 143-44; Franklin B. Wickwire, "John Pownall and British Colonial Policy," *WMQ*, 3rd ser., xx (1963), 543-54.

March, 1731, the M.P. for Bishops Castle in Shropshire petitioned the First Lord of the Treasury for a clerk's post for Morris, "an ingenuous industrious young man now of the University [of Cambridge]." As Robert More continued, "My interest here, chiefly depends upon the father of that person . . . the only person for whom I have ever solicited preferment." In 1733, the worried candidate sought a further advancement for the young official. "If I cannot now serve Morris," More explained, "he must go into the country & I shall loose the family wch is my grand support, & sink under Mr. Walcott's opposition."[89] Morris' steady climb up the hierarchy of Treasury clerks was intimately tied to his political indispensability.

By the 1740's, Morris had become a power in his own right. He achieved some fame in 1741 as the author of an influential pamphlet on the organization of the army and militia. In the general election of that year, the young ministerial publicist assumed the management of the Shropshire borough for himself. Using governmental patronage to bolster his own interest, Morris secured the election of Peter Burrell of the South Sea Company and J. Windham Ashe, the patron of Governor Benning Wentworth of New Hampshire. This was a victory of some importance for the ministry. Shropshire was in the center of the Tory stronghold of northwest England, and it required considerable finesse on the part of the Whigs to return 8 of the 12 members from the county. In addition to Morris, Henry A. Herbert, the future Lord Powis, was active in the region and was acknowledged as the head of the "Shropshire Whigs."[90]

[89] See More to Walpole, various dates, W.C., nos. 1830, 1505a, 2003, 2355.

[90] J. R. Western, *The English Militia in the Eighteenth Century*, London, 1965, 112-15; W.C., nos. 2962, 2994, 3079, 3293, 3294.

Herbert's key position in Shropshire politics gave him an influential voice in the distribution of patronage. "Mr Herbert was most intimate with Sir Robert and never had been refused any favour he asked," Egmont noted in 1737.[91] The Pelhams were equally solicitous of the interest of the northern politician. One of Herbert's relatives secured a reversionary grant of the secretary's post in Jamaica in 1747; another became Chief Justice of Nevis in 1754.[92] When Corbyn Morris sought yet another promotion within the administration in 1745, he turned to Herbert for support. By August, Herbert had struck a bargain with the First Lord of the Treasury. As the Shropshire man informed Newcastle, Pelham had advised Morris that the first step in his appointment was to be charged by the southern secretary with

> ye Correspondence, & Applications from Nova Scotia, Cape Breton, & Newfoundland;—And to be recommended by his Grace to the Treasury, for an Appointment proportionate to the Service. After which the Office would be established by the Crown.[93]

The crucial importance of having the southern department and the Treasury in the hands of the same family or faction was readily apparent. By September, 1745, Morris received a warrant constituting him agent for these three undeveloped and unpopulated colonies. Upon further application to Newcastle, the bureaucrat was appointed Secretary of Nova Scotia in January, 1746.[94]

[91] Egmont, *Diary*, II, 352.

[92] Memorandum, March 21, 1754, Add. MSS 32995, fol. 110; Herbert to Newcastle, April 6, 1747, Add. MSS 32710, fol. 218.

[93] Herbert to Newcastle, August 13, 1745, Add. MSS 32705, fol. 39; Morris to Herbert, August 12, 1745, Add. MSS 32705, fol. 41; Newcastle to Treasury Lords, no date, ibid., foll. 43-45.

[94] Morris to Newcastle, December 6 and 23, 1745, C.O. 194/24,

There was some gain in administrative efficiency from these appointments. Certainly the well being of the three frontier provinces was furthered by making their welfare identical with a private interest within the bureaucratic structure. Yet it was not clear that this region was valuable enough to justify such treatment, or that the job performed by Morris could not have been assumed by the Board of Trade. Morris' appointment was less an administrative necessity than a political expedient. When the status of the three colonies was changed in 1751, Morris was given another employment, this time as Secretary of the Customs and Salt Duties in Scotland. Here was proof, if any was needed, that the decline in colonial administration and in the management of the Salt Office proceeded from the same political source. It was not accidental that in the 1760's parliamentary legislation was required both to reform the revenue departments at home and to rationalize the government of the American colonies.

There was a certain paradox in the decline in the standards of colonial administration during Newcastle's twenty-four years in the southern department. With the control of the colonies in the hands of a man with considerable personal prestige and with direct access to the King, there existed a definite opportunity to strengthen the Anglo-American connection. This favorable administrative situation was neutralized by the peripheral nature of colonial affairs during the first half of the eighteenth century. The outcome of a colonial dispute could not topple a ministry; it could not even jeopardize the prestige of an individual minister. Important English interests were at stake in

---

fol. 310 and S.P. 36/78, fol. 35. John W. Wilkes, *A Whig In Power: the Political Career of Henry Pelham*, Northwestern, 1964, 134, views this appointment as an attempt at governmental efficiency but this was certainly not the prime motive.

America only in military and commercial matters. Only here was full accountability accepted; for only in these areas was the domestic advancement of the southern secretary contingent on the outcome of events in America. The neglect of ordinary colonial business needed no profound explanation. It was inherent in the situation.

It was the periodic intervention into the internal affairs of the American colonies by those at the apex of the English political nation which was abnormal. In this regard there was a definite parallel between the activities of the Earl of Halifax during his first years as a colonial administrator during the 1750's and the efforts of Newcastle and of Horace Walpole a generation before. Early in their political lives, when they had few other responsibilities and had been imbued with burning ambition, Walpole and Newcastle had both taken a keen interest in America and both had become involved in at least one turbulent controversy. From 1717 to 1725, the Auditor-General of the Plantation Revenues waged a bitter fight with the New York Assembly over the prerogatives of his office. A quarter of a century later there was nothing left of this victory. Walpole confessed to Newcastle in 1754 that

> As to other monys raised annually by the assemblys for publick Services I have no Cognisance of them, they having long since taken ye Receipt, examination & audit of them out of the hands of ye officers of ye Crown into their own management, altho my office was originally established with a view to have from time to time an account of all ye monys raised and expended there, & upon what funds, & for what purposes. . . .[95]

[95] June 14, 1754, Add. MSS 32735, foll. 485-89.

Newcastle's own experience had been similar. His close attention to colonial affairs had flagged after the dispute with the Assembly of Massachusetts Bay and after his own success as a politician no longer depended on his record as a colonial administrator. "The letter I have just own'd the Receipt of," the Governor of Barbados complained to Newcastle in 1746, "is the very first from Your Grace during an Administration of more than four years . . . [and is only] to acquaint me of my removal from this Government." A year before, Governor Clinton of New York had written to the southern secretary of a similar breakdown in communication, "which I impute to your Graces Engagement in matters of higher Importance."[96] Colonial administration had come to run itself, subject only to the demands of domestic patronage.

Indeed, it was this distribution of offices which came to constitute the core of Newcastle's colonial "policy" during his last ten years in the southern department. The domestic political advantage of his family, and later of his "party," provided him with a set of criteria by which he could judge every request for preferment and every substantive issue which arose in America. The prime consideration in the Duke's mind was not the intrinsic merit of the measure, its impact on the viability of the imperial system, but which individuals it would help and which it would hurt. Within narrow limits these standards were rigorous ones. If an appointment or policy would serve the political interest of the Pelhams, the southern secretary would do his best to arrange it. "About Employments," he wrote to Henry Pelham on Lord Monson's death in 1748,

[96] Clinton to Newcastle, January 2, 1745, C.O. 5/1094, foll. 378-79; Robinson to Newcastle, December 24, 1746, C.O. 28/47, foll. 256-58.

> I always *think* with my Friends, and in Everything else, as far as I can. In short I do my best, as I have often said, & am hurt to the last Degree, when That *Best* is not approved.[97]

As Horace Walpole was quick to point out at the time, the welfare of Newcastle's friends was not completely congruent with that of the imperial administrative system. "Had your Grace been at leisure to take under your protection, & give proper encouragement to those that Govern'd well there," Walpole observed in 1746, "it would have been no discredit to Your Grace; & might have been of use to those colonys."[98]

Walpole was a friendly, if persistent, critic. Viewed from the perspective of the English nation, a much more vigorous condemnation of the Duke would not have been out of place. As southern secretary for a quarter of a century, Newcastle failed to make a single positive contribution to the functioning of the colonial system. Not one administrative measure, not a solitary piece of legislation, was connected with his name. His was an era devoid of achievement and vision, a period of culpable mismanagement and negligence which led directly to many of the intractable problems of the next generation. The policies of administrative efficiency and colonial responsibility proposed by Grenville and Townshend were neither new nor radical; the great majority had been suggested, in one form or another, by the Board of Trade in the years between 1696 and 1721.

That these same measures aroused the strong hostility of the colonists of the 1760's and 1770's was only to be expected given the lax administrative practices and the

[97] August 9, 1748, Add. MSS 32716, foll. 26-27.

[98] July 16, 1746, Add. MSS 32707, foll. 421-22.

weak political control of the intervening period. If the English statesmen of the revolutionary generation must bear the responsibility for not coming to terms with the newly self-confident representative assemblies in the colonies, then the politicians of the Walpole and Pelham eras must accept the blame for limiting so drastically and so tragically the options open to their successors. By 1763, perhaps even by 1754, the American colonies as inferior and subordinate possessions had already been lost. Only the terms of the tarnished legacy were left to be decided.

This much was clear even to Newcastle when the threat of war with France in America added a new dimension to the colonial situation. "We hear," the Duke wrote to Horace Walpole in 1754,

> poor Adml Knowles is dead. I wish, I knew, who were the Two best Men, in all England, for New York & Jamaica; And I would recommend them immediately against all Competitors. For We will have the best Men We can find.[99]

In one sense Newcastle had always had "the best Men." Previously the criteria for appointment had been financial need, personal influence, and political interest; now they were administrative expertise and military ability. When the colonies were far away and unimportant, one set of standards could apply; when Europe had to be won in America, a new perspective was necessary.

Always the superb tactician, Newcastle was preparing to respond to the altered situation. In so doing, the Duke exhibited his greatest weakness as well as his main strength. As Waldegrave perceived at the time, Newcastle was a politician, not a statesman. He could negotiate an agree-

[99] May 14, 1754, Add. MSS 32735, foll. 268-72. The report of the death of Governor Knowles of Jamaica was erroneous.

ment, drive a bargain, maneuver an appointment, or extricate himself from a difficult situation with consummate ease. But he was unable to plan far enough ahead to avoid a crisis situation. Nor could he appreciate that the interest of the nation was not necessarily synonymous with that of the Pelhams. Preoccupied with means rather than ends, with personal advancement rather than public service, Newcastle failed to use his considerable abilities in a manner which would win the esteem either of his own or of future generations.[100]

[100] The attempt of Philip Haffenden to revise the long-standing historical consensus with regard to the deterioration of the colonial administrative system during the Newcastle era is not very successful. If Haffenden demonstrates that some of the more extreme criticisms of the Duke are without foundation, he does not show that Newcastle made a single positive contribution to the welfare of the colonies or to the strength of the imperial connection. The achievements of Bladen and of Halifax, both of whom had much less power than the Duke, were much more impressive. See Philip Haffenden, "Colonial Appointments and Patronage under the Duke of Newcastle, 1724-1739," *EHR*, LXXVII (July, 1963), 417-35.

CHAPTER 6

The Consolidation of Power
1742-1754

THE rewarding of old friends was the first consideration of the Pelhams upon taking office. Subsequently, the creation of a strong ministry through the attraction of new supporters was to become the overriding concern. The possibilities opened up by Walpole's departure had to be exploited by the prompt consolidation of an administration weakened by four years of internal strife. The creation of a stable parliamentary majority from among the ranks of the Whigs demanded the highest priority. Dissident factions had to be assimilated into the government without alienating the members of the fragile coalition bequeathed by Walpole. The election of 1741 had yielded only a scant majority of eighteen to the "old corps"; this margin would have to be increased substantially if the new ministry wished to govern effectively.[1]

It was evident from the outset that this problem would be resolved neither with speed nor with ease. After a year of ministerial instability Benjamin Keene noted that

> Terror . . . does not come from without . . . but from within, From the difficulty of agreement of so many Persons as at present compose this administration, whose Swords are pretty near of the same Length.[2]

[1] Owen, *Rise of the Pelhams*, 6-7. Before the election of 1741, Walpole's majority had fallen to 42 in a full house; the election of 1747 gave the Pelhams a majority of 125.

[2] Keene to de Castres, May 10, 1743, Add. MSS 43441, foll. 12-13.

"Decisions are difficult," the former Ambassador continued, "when power is not settled."

This danger was not lost on the Pelhams. In the aftermath of Walpole's resignation, Lord Carteret had become the northern Secretary of State and the single most influential member of the new ministry. As the leader of the "new Whigs," Carteret provided the ministry with a comfortable majority in the House of Commons.[3] Even more important in establishing the predominant authority of the northern secretary was his great influence with George II; he was, without doubt, the King's minister. Only the cohesion of the Pelhams, their long experience in the chief offices of state, and their parliamentary strength enabled them to struggle toward a position of parity. "It will be impossible for Me, in these Circumstances, to go on, with Credit, and Security to Myself, or with Advantage to My Friends," Newcastle told Hardwicke in August, 1742,

> if The World don't see, and understand, that You, My Brother, and I, are One; Not in Thought only, but in Action; Not in Action barely, but in the first Conception, or Digestion, of Things. This will give Us real Weight; This will add Strength to Us, in the closet, and in the Ministry.[4]

The first turning point in the four-year-long struggle between the Pelhams and Carteret came in July, 1743, with the death of Lord Wilmington, the First Lord of the Treasury. Passing over the Earl of Bath, the close associate of the northern secretary, the King placed the control of the Treasury in the hands of Henry Pelham, the Chan-

[3] In 1746, there were about 50 "new Whigs" who had been brought into the government by Carteret and Bath and who continued to support the administration after Carteret's resignation. See Owen, *Rise of the Pelhams*, 307.

[4] August 3, 1742, Add. MSS 32699, foll. 347-49.

cellor of the Exchequer. Once again Walpole's two offices were held by a single person; once again the immense patronage of the Treasury was in the gift of a member of the House of Commons. The way was now open not only for the emergence of the Pelhams as the chief ministers, but also for the eclipse of Newcastle by Henry Pelham. "My brother," the Duke complained bitterly to Hardwicke in November, 1743,

> has been long brought to think, by Lord Orford, that he is the only person fit to succeed him, and that he has a credit with the King upon that foot, and this leads him into Lord Orford's old method, of being the first person, upon all occasions. This is not mere form, for I do apprehend that my brother does think that his superior interest in the Closet, and situation in the House of Commons, gives him great advantages over everyone else. They are indeed great advantages, but may be counterbalanced, especially if it is considered over *whom* those advantages are given.[5]

If the major theme of the decade following Walpole's fall was the Pelhams' consolidation of their power, then a minor chord was Newcastle's growing jealousy of his brother's success.

I

The uneasy alliance between Carteret and the Pelhams continued for a year after Wilmington's death. "There are great Divisions among the present ministry," Henry Lascelles informed a fellow opponent of the Sugar Bill in January, 1744,

[5] Quoted in Barnes, "Pelham and Newcastle," 71. Barnes argues convincingly that the Duke refused to acknowledge his brother's predominance until 1748.

> Lord Carteret is said to be in high favour and wants to carry all before him, and that he has treated the Duke of Newcastle as insolently as if he had been a footman. Mr. Pelham is a Man of Spirit, and they say he will not submit to the favourite and that there is now a tryal of skill which of them shall be the primier. Would to God they would divide also upon the Bill, but that is too good a thing to expect.[6]

It was only in November that the First Lord of the Treasury mustered enough strength to secure the resignation of the northern secretary. Carteret's disdain for the other members of the ministry and the imminent collapse of his elaborate system of European alliances had made his position increasingly untenable. Under severe pressure from the overwhelming majority of his servants, George II finally acquiesced in Carteret's removal, elevating him to the peerage as Lord Granville.

To safeguard their position in Parliament, the Pelhams took into the government those Whigs who had been excluded at the time of Walpole's resignation. The appointment of the Duke of Bedford as First Lord of the Admiralty and of the Earl of Chesterfield as the Lord Lieutenant of Ireland won the support of one important faction. A similar distribution of minor places satisfied the Whig group, headed by Lord Cobham and consisting primarily of the Grenville family and William Pitt. George Grenville was given a seat on the Admiralty board and George Lyttleton a place on the Treasury bench. Finally, Sir John Phillips and John Pitt were named Commissioners of Trade in place of Benjamin Keene and Sir Charles Gilmour.

[6] Quoted in Penson, *Colonial Agents*, 283-84; Newcastle to Pelham, June 10, 1744, Add. MSS 32703, foll. 108-10.

This reversal of the ministerial changes of 1742—the substitution of "new allies" for "new Whigs"—was sufficient to guarantee the predominance of the Pelhams and the "old corps" in Parliament. It was not sufficient, however, to undermine the position of Lord Granville at Court. Angry that he had been forced to part with his favorite minister, the King withheld full support for the new administration and actively encouraged Granville to amass sufficient support in the House of Commons to form a ministry of his own. The Pelhams found that they had assumed the responsibilities of office but lacked the power required to fulfill them.[7]

At the end of 1745, the triumvirate of Pelham, Newcastle, and Hardwicke undertook to put an end to this period of instability and uncertainty by entering into a closer alliance with the Cobhamites, a move that was certain to have farreaching repercussions at Court. The conclusion of this union committed the Pelhams to securing a ministerial post for William Pitt, who was personally repugnant to the King, and to acquiescing in the demand of the Cobhamites for "the total Alteration of the foreign system" to diminish involvement on the continent and "to increase Our Navy and to act, as Principles, at Sea, in the war against France and Spain."[8]

It was not an easy matter for the Pelhams to agree to this shift in military strategy and to begin to contest Bourbon ascendancy through maritime warfare rather than continental diplomacy. As much as Newcastle disagreed with Granville, he was at one with the former secretary with

[7] Owen, *Rise of the Pelhams*, 244-47, 274, 307.

[8] Newcastle to Chesterfield, November 20, 1745, Add. MSS, 32705, foll. 318-36; Owen, *Rise of the Pelhams*, 285-93.

regard to the need to fight at least a defensive war in Europe. "If France and Spain," the Duke warned Chesterfield at the time of the rebellion in Scotland,

> had nothing to deal with but England, they might easily keep the Rebellion on foot, for Years, if not destroy us quite; and by delivering them from Expenses on the Continent, wee should force them to re-establish their marine; of which wee should hereafter feel the bad effects.[9]

In retrospect it was clear that the Pelhams had always been more partial to the system of continental military alliances pioneered by William III than to the unilateral policy of colonial warfare espoused by Pitt and his friends. Newcastle's action in overruling Walpole and sending a military force to the West Indies in 1740 was seen almost immediately by the Pelhams themselves as an undesirable aberration. "It looked last year," Hardwicke declared to Newcastle in August, 1741,

> as if the old world was to be fought for in the new; but the Tables are turn'd & I fear that now America must be fought for in Europe. Whatever Success we may have in the former, I doubt it will always *finally* follow the Fate of ye latter. . . .[10]

Now, for the second time within a decade, the exigencies of the domestic political situation had committed the Pelhams to an active military posture in the western hemi-

[9] November 20, 1745, Add. MSS 32705, foll. 318-36.

[10] August 17, 1741, Add. MSS 32697, foll. 424-27. The Pelhams' earlier commitment to an American war is described ibid., foll. 215-33, and in Richard Pares, "American versus Continental Warfare, 1739-1763," *EHR*, LI (1936), 429-65.

sphere. The colonists themselves were partially responsible for this sudden shift in emphasis. With the assistance of the royal navy, troops from the New England colonies under the command of William Shirley and William Pepperell had captured the French stronghold of Cape Breton in the summer of 1745. This remarkable feat of arms aroused great excitement in England because of its striking contrast to the dismal military reports from the continent. The pressure of public opinion combined with the proddings of the Cobhamites to turn the attention of the ministry firmly in the direction of North America. "My Lord Duke thinks it extremely material to provide for the Safety of Louisburg," Andrew Stone informed Hardwicke in October, 1745,

> but is, at the same time, very apprehensive, that if all the Force is taken away from Georgia, South Carolina, & c there can be little Doubt, but an attempt will be made by the Spaniards from St. Augustine, or the Havana, who, it is to be feared, might, in that Case overrun all Our Northern Colonies, without resistance.[11]

Whatever the implications of the new military situation in America, the effect of the alliance which it permitted with Lord Cobham and his followers in England was to assure the hegemony of the Pelhams. When George II refused once again, in February, 1746, to give the government his unqualified support, the Pelhams and their associates resigned from office. Within a fortnight they were back in power. With few personal followers and unable to use the votes of the Tories because of the rebellion in Scotland, Granville had been unable to create an effective

[11] October 31, 1745, Add. MSS 35408, foll. 194-95.

party in the Commons and to fashion an alternative administration. The King had no choice but to recall the Pelhams.[12]

The cost of this victory was a firm commitment to the military and diplomatic defense of Cape Breton. "All mankind must see," Newcastle proclaimed to Chesterfield in April, 1746, "that it is idle to think of peace, without restoring Cape Breton; & when no Man dares, at present, to think of giving it up."[13] The war had to be continued. Moreover, the new members of the ministerial coalition now joined with Bedford, the First Lord of the Admiralty and a longtime advocate of a maritime campaign, to force the consideration of an English expedition against Canada designed to consolidate and to expand the gains of the colonists. "I wish our new Friends had not espoused this," Hardwicke confided to Newcastle early in April, but in the end the Pelhams were forced to acquiesce in order to retain the parliamentary support of William Pitt. With rebellion still raging in Scotland and with the French threatening to overrun Flanders, the home administration dispatched letters to the colonial governors on April 9, 1746, directing them to raise troops for an attempt on French Canada.[14]

This expedition proved abortive. Although there was, as Governor Shirley reported, "a Spirit . . . in the Colonies

[12] Newcastle to Chesterfield, February 18, 1746, Add. MSS 32706, fol. 164; Pelham to Newcastle, January 17, 1746, S.P. 36/80, foll. 315-16; Chesterfield to Newcastle, February 27, 1746, Add. MSS 32706, foll. 221-24. The battle of Culloden was fought in April, 1746.

[13] April 6, 1746, Add. MSS 32707, foll. 21-28.

[14] Hardwicke to Newcastle, April 2, 1746, ibid., foll. 5-6. When the King refused to accept Pitt as Secretary for War, the Pelhams installed him as Paymaster of the Forces and sought to oblige him in matters of policy.

for pushing that Success [of Cape Breton] as far as Canada . . . ," no help was forthcoming from England.[15] Adverse winds, insuperable logistic difficulties, and the changing political situation in Europe prevented the sailing of the English troops in time for a descent on Canada before the winter. At first, General St. Clair was instructed to sail for New England in the autumn to prepare for an attack in the early spring. Then pressure from the King and the Duke of Cumberland to use the assembled troops in Flanders or in raids upon the French coastline undermined this alternative arrangement. Only the hard-pressed southern secretary wished to uphold the bargain with Bedford and the Cobhamites. "In my Way of Thinking," Newcastle argued in a letter to Henry Pelham in August, 1746, "Flanders will be better supported by the Subsisting of this Expedition, than by Sending Six Regiments thither. . . ."[16]

Newcastle's sudden conversion to a maritime strategy was dictated less by personal conviction than by political expediency. The Duke now feared that his new friends would withdraw from the government, thus making it difficult to continue a war which he was determined to see to a successful conclusion. The reluctance of Pelham and Hardwicke to commit English resources in America was one more factor which had led to the cancellation of the proposed Canadian expedition. Overruled on matters of policy by his colleagues, Newcastle fell back on patronage to compensate his allies. Already two of the Grenvilles had been named to the Board of Trade and the Admiralty. Now a third brother, Henry, was appointed to the lucrative gov-

[15] Shirley to Newcastle, October 29, 1745, C.O. 5/900, foll. 255-68, received January 25, 1746.

[16] August 26, 1746, Add. MSS 32708, foll. 150-51. Other relevant correspondence is ibid., foll. 138-39, 162, 182-83.

ernment of Barbados. Shortly thereafter, the poet James Thomson was named Surveyor-General of the Leeward Islands. This was a favor for George Lyttelton, a junior Lord of the Treasury and a close friend of William Pitt.[17]

It was symptomatic of Newcastle's attitude to the colonies that throughout the controversy over the Canadian expedition he had been guided primarily by the changing political situation in England. The Duke's support of the project vacillated from one extreme to another as his personal interest demanded. Twenty years as the chief colonial administrator had not given him any sympathy for the legitimate demands of the colonists. Even the southern secretary's advocacy of war in 1739 had proceeded primarily from domestic considerations—the appeasement of the merchant interest, the safeguarding of his ministerial position, the assertion of England's power—rather than from a genuine concern for the security and prosperity of the colonies. Pitt and Bedford were the real zealots for America in the government. To postpone the expedition for another year, the Admiralty chief told Stone in November, 1746, would

> not only give the Enemy an opportunity of throwing Succours of all kinds, into their favourite Colony, but might also damp the Ardour of our American Colonies, who had almost exhausted themselves by the extraordinary Efforts they had made . . . in order to gain that point which they justly looked upon as their

[17] Lyttelton to George Grenville, September 21, 1747, William James Smith, ed., *The Grenville Papers*, London, 1852, I, 68-70; Lyttelton to Newcastle, April 24, 1746, Add. MSS 32707, fol. 92; Henry Grenville to Stone ?, December 26, 1746, Add. MSS 32709, fol. 379; Henry Grenville to Newcastle, April 16, 1747, C.O. 28/49, foll. 15-16; Owen, *Rise of the Pelhams*, 300-302.

> only Security, I mean the entire Expulsion of the French out of the Northern Continent of America.[18]

As long as Newcastle remained in the southern department, there would be little pressure to engage in an American campaign. The colonies had served the Duke well, but they rated low on his list of priorities.

II

The possibility for colonial expansion came only when Newcastle lost the stranglehold on the formulation of American policy which he had held for nearly a decade. By 1748, Newcastle had found Chesterfield, Granville's replacement in the northern department, as troublesome as his old adversary. When Chesterfield resigned in protest against Newcastle's interference in the affairs of his province, the Duke took the opportunity to improve his own position. "The Duke of Bedford," a friend reported to the Earl of Orrery in February, 1748, "has taken the southern province as secretary, which is generally thought the most profitable; his Grace of Newcastle having quitted that for the Northern, in which the greatest scene of business lies."[19]

For the first time in a quarter of a century, the formal control of American affairs was not in Newcastle's hands. Equally significant was the fact that a capable and ambitious politician with a distinct set of policies was now the chief colonial administrator. The Duke of Richmond warned Newcastle of this at the time of Bedford's appointment:

> My only objection against your new Colleague, is, that if you do not agree together, you can not gett rid of him so easyly as of the last . . . [but] since your only

[18] November 20, 1746, Add. MSS 32713, foll. 426-27. In order to secure peace in 1748, the Pelhams were forced to return Cape Breton to the French.

[19] Birch to Orrery, February 20, 1748, Boyle, ed., *Orrery Papers*, II, 19-21.

view was to prove to the world that you did not mean to be sole Secretary, you certainly have pitch'd upon the most propper man in England.[20]

As Richmond had discerned, Bedford wanted power and authority, not merely a lucrative place. He differed from the Pelhams on the question of military strategy. Moreover, Bedford saw clearly what Newcastle had realized during his own struggle with Walpole: that the predominance of a leading minister could be countered only by the creation of a unified and powerful faction within the ranks of the administration.

The death of Lord Monson, the President of the Board of Trade, presented the new southern secretary with an opportunity to expand his personal power by bringing Lord Halifax into the ministry in his place. Newcastle's first thought, on the other hand, was to replace Monson with Lord Edgecombe. This would create a vacancy as Chancellor of the Duchy of Lancaster for the Pelhams' brother-in-law, the Duke of Leeds. "His Rank, His Estate, His Neighbourhood, all point him out," the northern secretary reminded Henry Pelham from Hanover, "I beg You would be so good as to talk this Matter over with the Duke of Bedford. . . ."[21] Pelham agreed that the chancellor's post would be "the properest place" for their impecunious relation, but he was less certain that Edgecombe could be induced to give it up. "Besides," he noted, "Lord Edgecombe will be as much a Cypher att the board as Tanley [Lord Monson]."[22]

[20] February 17, 1748, Add. MSS 32714, foll. 235-36; Richmond to Newcastle, December 11, 1744, Add. MSS 32703, foll. 404-405.

[21] July 31, 1748, Add. MSS 32715, foll. 490-93; Pelham to Newcastle, August 2 and 9, 1748, Add. MSS 32716, foll. 1-4, 28-31.

[22] August 9, 1748, Add. MSS 32716, foll. 28-31.

Bedford shared the doubts of the younger Pelham. In a carefully worded letter to Newcastle in August, 1748, the southern secretary sought to win the support of his colleagues for his own plan:

> I think both your Graces and Mr. Pelham's idea is . . . that it would be highly improper, considering the present Situation of things, to have a nonefficient Man at the head of the Board. . . . If Lord Halifax could be prevailed upon to exchange from what he now has to the Board of Trade, (for which I should think him perfectly well qualified) the Duke of Leeds might succeed him as Chief Justice in Eyre.

As Bedford concluded, this plan would be "a means of getting the Duke of Leeds into an employment suitable for him, and at the same time putting an efficient Man at the head of the Board of Trade."[23]

To Newcastle, this seemed "the best scheme of All."[24] He did not pause to consider that this appointment was more in Bedford's interest than his own. It might aid the declining fortunes of the Duke of Leeds, but it would also augment the power of the new southern secretary within his own department. More important, it would put yet another politician with a commitment to an expansionist colonial policy in a position to influence the course of events in America. These possibilities had been in Bedford's mind all along. He told Halifax that there were two reasons why he had pressed for his appointment:

> the one was, that I look upon it, as *a Post of business and usefull business & a good qualification for better*

[23] August 11, 1748, ibid., foll. 38-39.

[24] Newcastle to Bedford, August 21, 1748, Add. MSS 32716, fol. 96. Both Halifax and Leeds were relations of Newcastle; Halifax to Newcastle, June 18, 1746, Add. MSS 32707, foll. 328-29.

> *& greater things*; and the other, (which I own has a little the Air of selfishness) was my desire to have a Person of Yr Lordship's weight and consequence, and for whom I have so true a regard, at the head of a Board, with wch in my present situation as Secy of State for ye Southern department, I must have so close & frequent a correspondence.[25]

The nomination of the capable Halifax as First Lord of Trade was only the culmination of series of appointments which had already transformed the character of the advisory body. By the middle of the 1740's, a seat on the board had become a stepping stone for young and ambitious politicians or a temporary resting place for men of considerable influence and ability. The lesser men who had bulked large in the selections of the previous decades retired gracefully from the scene. Mr. Charleton, one of Newcastle's political agents in Nottingham, wrote to his patron in 1750, "I should wish something more out of the Eye of the world & the envy of it, than the Board of Trade."[26]

As in the decline of the advisory body forty years before, the crucial variable affecting the quality of the board's membership was less the importance of the colonies to England than the changing political situation within the mother country. Determined to avoid Walpole's mistake of creating a strong opposition party, Henry Pelham was careful to bring men of ability and influence into the ministry. Walpole had broken down the amorphous Whig

[25] September 3, 1748, Add. MSS 32716, foll. 337-38, and Halifax's reply, ibid., fol. 339.

[26] Charleton to Newcastle, March 24, 1750, Add. MSS 32720, fol. 158; Pelham to Newcastle, July 26, 1741, Add. MSS 32697, fol. 355. Cayley to Newcastle, June 1, 1754, Add. MSS 32735, foll. 355-56, mentions the great number of competitors for a vacancy on the board.

party of the early part of the eighteenth century into clearly defined groups of "ins" and "outs"; now his protégé was attempting to erase this sharp cleavage and to re-establish a sense of unity and common purpose within the ranks of the Hanoverians.[27] Beyond this, Pelham had begun to sense the potential importance of the colonies to England. As he declared to his brother in October, 1748, with regard to Walter Plumer and Baptist Leveson-Gower, the two ailing members of the Board of Trade, "If they go, we must consider to recommend those that will supply their places well."[28]

The appointment of Thomas Robinson and Charles Townshend to the board in the following year raised the caliber of the personnel of the advisory body to a level unparalleled since the first decade of its existence.[29] Robinson was shortly to become a secretary of state, the first commissioner to do so since Joseph Addison thirty years before; while Townshend eventually became the Chancellor of the Exchequer and the author of the American duties of 1767. Even before the nomination of these men and of Halifax, the activity of the board had increased markedly. When Lord Monson was absent from the board

[27] Wilkes, *Henry Pelham*, 59-61.

[28] October 4, 1748, Add. MSS 32717, foll. 23-26.

[29] Arthur H. Bayse, *The Lords Commissioners of Trade and Plantations . . . 1748-1782*, New Haven, 1925, 57. This Thomas Robinson was the diplomatist, the first Baron Grantham, not the deposed Governor of Barbados.

For Townshend's appointment see H.M.C., *Eleventh Report*, pt. IV, 366, and Add. MSS 32717, foll. 153, 245-46, 318-20. Newcastle sought one of these vacancies for his friend William Baker, the merchant, but Pelham objected on the grounds that Baker had only recently come into Parliament and that there were more deserving candidates. Three years later, Baker received the provisioning contract for the troops in Nova Scotia, Add. MSS 33029, foll. 78-82.

because of illness after April, 1748, twenty-eight letters were dispatched to American governors within nine months, more than the total of the two preceding years.[30] The initiative in this activity was taken by Pitt, Dupplin, Grenville, and Leveson-Gower, precisely those members appointed by the Pelhams in an attempt to bolster their parliamentary position.[31] The selection of Halifax in 1748 only accelerated the board's activist policy. Where the Pelhams' original quest for power had caused a decline in the standards of colonial administration, their attempt to preserve their dominant position had produced a reformist movement within the plantation office.[32]

The first success of Bedford, Halifax, and the new Board of Trade was the transformation of the colony of Nova Scotia from a military to a civilian outpost. This alteration had been sought for years by the bureaucracy of the plantation office. As far back as 1729, Martin Bladen had proposed a civilian establishment in order to draw off settlers from the recalcitrant colony of Massachusetts Bay. By the middle of the following decade, merchant groups and speculators thought they had finally succeeded in this quest. The English merchant and philanthropist Thomas Coram wrote to a friend in New England in 1737 that

> We were in Expectation of seeing . . . this Somer . . . the Settling Nova Scotia with good Protestant Fam-

[30] Bayse, *Lords of Trade*, 30; Newcastle to Board of Trade, February 7, 1747, C.O. 323/11, fol. 132.

[31] Leveson-Gower joined the board in May, 1745, while James Grenville replaced the deceased Martin Bladen in February, 1746; Lord Dupplin and Francis Fane were named at the end of 1746.

[32] Baugh, *British Naval Administration*, 503-505, describes how the entry of Bedford, Sandwich, and Anson into the Admiralty in December, 1744, produced a similar revitalization. Discipline and the selection of officers was improved, although more far-reaching reforms were largely frustrated.

> elies British and Foreigners under a Civil Government not military nor Arbitrary. . . . The Chiefest Difficulty . . . is breaking the Regiment there (w'ch in reality is not half a Regiment tho paid for a Whole and the Chiefe Officers remain in England w'th very high pay). . . .[33]

As Coram pointed out, it was the "Kings great affection for Military Forces" and especially for Governor Phillips of Nova Scotia which had inhibited the settlement of the region for decades. In 1719, Phillips had been prevailed upon by the ministry to give up an English regiment for one in Nova Scotia and for control of the government there, and was "assured that I should Enjoy both as long as I lived."[34] Thirty years later, at the age of ninety, Phillips was still in control. What had been intended as a temporary financial expedient by the Sunderland government had become a tiresome and restrictive burden to its successors.

By 1745, it had become apparent that the continuance of Phillips in his command constituted a positive danger, for the success of the Cape Breton expedition had increased the strategic importance of the northernmost English possession in America. This, at least, was the argument used by William Shirley, Jr. within a few months of the capture of the French fortress. In a letter to Andrew Stone, the younger Shirley maintained that the defense of the region was a responsibility "which Mr. Phillips on account of his

[33] Coram to Benjamin Coleman, July 9, 1737, MHS, *Proceedings*, LVI, 36-37; Coram to Coleman, March 2, 1737, ibid., LVI, 33-34.

[34] Phillips to Newcastle, March 19, 1749, Add. MSS 32718, foll. 179-80; Newcastle to Phillips, March 15, 1731, C.O. 324/36, p. 266.

great Age cannot be suppos'd capable of undertaking."[35] The younger Shirley suggested that his father be named in place of the old general. William Vaughan, the former Lieutenant-Governor of New Hampshire and a participant in the Louisburg expedition, also petitioned Newcastle for the post.[36] This agitation was to no avail. George II would not consent to the removal of Phillips, because of the General's services in the revolution of 1688. Likewise, Shirley's proposal to pay the salary to the Governor while assuming his command was turned down, probably because of the King's unwillingness to relinquish control of military appointments.[37] The best that Shirley could receive from Newcastle was "a repeated Assurance that his Majesty design'd to bestow on me the Government of Nova Scotia" on Phillips' death.[38]

What Newcastle and Bladen had not been able to achieve for a generation, Bedford won within a year of his appointment as southern secretary. In April, 1749, General Edward Cornwallis was appointed as the first civilian governor of Nova Scotia, and plans were made to settle the colony. Under urging from Bedford and Halifax, Phillips had agreed that the "Public Service" required the appointment of a new governor; his only condition for resigning was that the regiment remain in his hands.[39] This was a

[35] W. Shirley, Jr. to Stone, March 9, 1745, C.O. 5/900, fol. 165; Shirley to Newcastle, September 27, 1745, ibid., 236-39.

[36] See the letters in C.O. 5/753, foll. 136, 157-58, 167-68.

[37] Shirley to Newcastle, August, 1747, C.O. 5/901, foll. 145-47.

[38] Shirley to Newcastle, March 28, 1750, Add. MSS 32720, foll. 166-67.

[39] Phillips to Newcastle, April 19, 1749, Add. MSS 32718, foll. 179-80; Bedford to Board of Trade, April 28, 1749, S.P. 44/129, p. 518; Bayse, *Lords of Trade*, 41-45.

Earlier the Duke of Richmond had urged Newcastle to secure a change in the status of the colony in order to aid a speculative

small price for Bedford to pay. The presence of a chief executive with a military background in the colony would bolster its defenses and perhaps deter a French attack. Moreover, the establishment of a civilian government provided the opportunity to dispense patronage to deserving friends and supporters. Cornwallis was an old political ally of the new southern secretary. And the Governor's appointees as Secretary and Receiver of the King's rents were personal acquaintances of Bedford's Undersecretary, Richard Neville Aldworth.[40] On the death of General Phillips in 1750, Bedford secured the transfer of his regiment to Cornwallis. Newcastle's previous assurances to Shirley meant little when the control of the southern department was in Bedford's hands.[41]

It was not surprising that the new southern secretary took such a keen interest in the affairs of Nova Scotia. Bedford had been the prime mover within the administration in the abortive Canadian expedition of 1746. His position as First Lord of the Admiralty had given him a share in the credit for the taking of Cape Breton. In the aftermath of this victory, he had secured the command of the Louisburg garrison for his subordinate, the naval commander Sir Peter Warren, in preference to Newcastle's correspondent, General William Pepperrell. And when Warren asked to resign his place for reasons of health, Bedford secured the post for Charles Knowles, another

---

scheme in which he was involved with the New England merchants Waldo and Reeves. See Add. MSS 32705, foll. 20-21 and Add. MSS 32707, foll. 348-49.

[40] Davidson to Aldworth, October 19, 1749, P.R.O. 30/50/39, foll. 29-31; Halifax to Newcastle, December 8, 1752, Add. MSS 32730, fol. 367.

[41] See Shirley to Newcastle, March 28 and April 10, 1750, Add. MSS 32720, foll. 166-67 and 199-200.

naval captain. Newcastle's only appointment in this region was the nomination of Lieutenant-Colonel Hopson to succeed Knowles in the winter of 1747.[42]

Whatever minor claims Newcastle might make on Nova Scotia patronage, Bedford retained the initiative in the frontier colony. It was his intervention, strongly supported by Halifax at the Board of Trade and the Duke of Cumberland at Court, that won the reluctant agreement of Henry Pelham for Treasury support for the new civilian colony. Like Walpole before him, Pelham was unwilling to commit English resources in America.[43] Perhaps he remembered Walpole's difficulties with Georgia. The subsidization of the colony on the southeastern frontier had constituted an increasing drain on the home exchequer and had helped to bring on the financially debilitating war with Spain. And now Cornwallis' activities in Nova Scotia were having much the same result as Oglethorpe's earlier agitation in Georgia. Within a year of the new Governor's arrival in the colony, British and French troops were skirmishing near the boundary line separating Nova Scotia and Acadia and were soon entrenched on opposite sides of a narrow creek.[44]

Neither Newcastle nor Pelham relished the idea of an American war, but the presence of Bedford and Halifax

[42] See the extensive correspondence on these appointments in C.O. 5/13, foll. 53-54, 58, 71-74, 81; Add. MSS 32709, foll. 98-99, 194-95; Add. MSS 32715, foll. 196-98, 200-201.

[43] Lord John Russell, ed., *Correspondence of John, Fourth Duke of Bedford*, London, 1842-46, I, 563, 572; Clark, *Rise of the Treasury*, 55, 84.

[44] The expansionist-minded Board of Trade had instructed Cornwallis to settle colonists on the St. John River. It was here that the first armed conflict took place in 1750. See Max Savelle, *The Diplomatic History of the Canadian Boundary*, New Haven, 1940, 21-42.

in key administrative positions gave the expansionists a definite advantage. Perhaps this was no more than the Pelhams deserved. It had been Newcastle's agitation from within the Walpole ministry which had played a large role in the outbreak of the war with Spain and in the subsequent disintegration of the administration. Now the Pelhams were being subjected to similar pressure from Bedford and Halifax. Like the Walpoles before them, the Pelham brothers were being forcibly converted to a strong American policy. As Newcastle wrote to Bedford in June, 1750, the maintenance of the colonial boundaries was an affair of the highest importance

> on which may depend, (as Governor Cornwallis very rightly observes,) not only the Fate of Nova Scotia, but of all the Northern Colonies; which are of so infinite Importance to Great Britain.[45]

What Newcastle did not realize at this time was that the fate of the Pelham ministry likewise had come to hinge on developments in America. If a peaceful accommodation of the boundary disputes with France was not achieved, the coming of a new war would undermine the parliamentary position of those in power just as it had a decade before. By the middle of the eighteenth century, the techniques of patronage and of parliamentary management had been brought to such a degree of perfection that the domestic political position of a ministry was nearly im-

[45] June 9, 1750, Add. MSS 32721, foll. 87-88. Patrice Louis-René Higonnet, "The Origins of the Seven Years War," *JMH*, XL (March, 1968), 57-90, presents a convincing argument that the major statesmen of France and Britain neither planned nor welcomed the recourse to arms in 1754 and that the war was precipitated by the provocative actions of their subordinates at home and especially in the colonies.

pregnable. Only royal wrath or the twin scourges of death and war were sufficient to topple a ministry. In 1754, death was to strike down Henry Pelham at the height of his career while leaving his older brother to fight an American war. Newcastle's inability to maintain his brother's dominant position in the government in the years after 1754 stemmed not only from his own shortcomings as a statesman, but also from military and diplomatic developments beyond his control. When the Duke gave control of the southern department to the expansionist faction in the ministry in 1748, he had unwittingly set in motion a series of events which would eventually undermine his own leadership of the ministry.

III

The threat posed by Bedford and Halifax to the interests of the Pelhams was not limited to the realm of diplomatic strategy. A conflict between the two groups of ministers arose as well with regard to the internal administration of the colonies. The points at issue here were neither as obvious nor as clearly defined as was the case in military affairs. In a number of American colonies, the governor and a strong faction in the assembly had fallen out over a matter of local importance. These disputes among colonial politicians had been referred to London for resolution by the home authorities. There they sparked off a conflict between the various factions within the ministry. Bedford, Halifax, and the new Board of Trade were arrayed on one side; the Pelhams and their associates on the other.

The struggle which developed in England at mid-century was not a clearcut one between "reformers" and "traditionalists." The terms in which American politics were conducted were both too nebulous and too unfamiliar to most Englishmen to obtain such an easy definition. What was at issue in London were tendencies rather than programs, patronage as much as policy. Most of the officials in America had been appointed by past ministries, and their performance in office would now be judged by Bedford and Halifax.

The first attacks were directed against those governors appointed by Wilmington and Walpole. "I understand by my Correspondents at Home," Gabriel Johnson of North Carolina told Bedford,

> that my Enemies have taken the Liberty to represent me as a Jacobite at all the Offices. . . . For the last Seven Years before I came abroad I lived almost constantly with the late Lord President Wilmington, and have the Honour to be known for many years by the Earl of Bath, Lord Anson [and] The Bishop of Worcester.[46]

By this time, however, Wilmington had been dead for six years, while Bath was in opposition. Moreover, Newcastle and the Earl of Powis were pressing Bedford to remove Johnson in favor of George Whitmore, a Shropshire Whig and a longtime place-hunter.[47]

A second incident involved James Glen of South Carolina, Wilmington's son-in-law. Upon the wreck of a Spanish flotilla on the Carolina coast, Glen had urged the governors of the neighboring colonies to lay an embargo upon the recovered goods in reprisal for prizes taken by Spain since the peace of Aix-la-Chapelle. This unilateral action drew a stinging reprimand from Bedford. "I must inform you," the southern secretary warned Glen early in 1751, that

[46] May 10, 1749, C.O. 5/13, foll. 164-65.

[47] Memo, June 7, 1748, Add. MSS 32715, foll. 168-72; Earl of Powis to Newcastle, June 7, 1748, ibid., fol. 174; Memo, no date, Add. MSS 32995, fol. 16.

> it is highly probable, His Majesty will no longer suffer you to remain in your Government, as that Person can by no means be proper for such a Post, who shall be indiscreet enough, to say no worse, to advise a measure which may, nay must, throw the Nations, now so happily united, again into Confusion.[48]

If a showdown with France was to come in America, Bedford wanted Spain to remain neutral.

Of greater significance than this concern with diplomatic affairs was Bedford's interest in internal colonial developments. After a careful investigation into the background of Charles Price, the man proposed by Governor Trelawney of Jamaica to serve during his leave of absence, Bedford informed the King that Price was not a proper person to be trusted with a commission as Lieutenant-Governor.[49] A few years later the southern secretary mounted an even more direct attack on the conduct of the Governor. Trelawney had banned a solicitor, Andrew Arcedeckne, from practicing law in any court presided over by himself. When this suspension came to Bedford's attention, it was quickly and decisively struck down. "It by no means appears, from the Papers that have been laid before me," Bedford advised his subordinate,

> that this Gentleman's Behavior deserv'd so rough a Censure & Punishment. . . . it is certainly right in his Majesty's Governors to exact . . . Respect for those under their Command . . . but it is as certain that they

[48] March 12, 1751, C.O. 324/38, pp. 199-201; Glen to Bedford, July 26, 1748, C.O. 5/389, fol. 64.

[49] Trelawney to Bedford, July 7, 1748, C.O. 137/58, foll. 106-109, and Bedford's remarks on the back of the letter; Trelawney to Bedford, May 25, 1749, ibid., foll. 139-40.

> should at least with equal Caution, avoid giving Grounds for any just Complaints against them.[50]

Not since Newcastle's first years in office had a southern secretary taken such a strong interest in the day to day conduct of the colonial governors.

The chief executives who had been appointed by the Duke during his long tenure in the southern department were no more immune from Bedford's scrutiny than were the nominees of Walpole and Wilmington. In 1749, Bedford secured a royal warrant restoring Benjamin Pemberton to the Naval Office of Massachusetts Bay, a clear repudiation of Newcastle's client, Governor William Shirley.[51] Governor Clinton in New York was even more vulnerable than Shirley to a stringent review of his performance in office. There had been a severe erosion of the prerogatives of the Crown and of the authority of the Governor during his administration; indeed, Clinton himself had advised Newcastle in 1748 that he wished to remain in New York until he had settled "His Majty Government in this Province upon the Same foot it was upon, in the time of my Predecessors."[52]

Despite Bedford's active surveillance of their administrations, none of these five governors was immediately removed from office.[53] They still had sufficient interest in

[50] December 20, 1750, C.O. 324/38, p. 187; Report of Attorney-General Ryder, December 12, 1750, C.O. 137/59, foll. 62-68; Trelawney to Bedford, March 10, 1751, ibid., foll. 84-85.

[51] Ryder to Bedford, February 18, 1749, S.P. 36/110, foll. 78-80; Warrant, August 18, 1749, C.O. 324/37, p. 515.

[52] September 30, 1748, Add. MSS 32716, foll. 399-402; Clinton to Bedford, October 17, 1749, C.O. 5/1096, foll. 177-79; "State of Affairs in New York," no date, C.O. 5/1095, foll. 20-27.

[53] Trelawney, however, resigned his government to Admiral Knowles in 1752, Clinton was replaced in the following year, and Shirley was removed in 1756. A letter of recall was prepared for

England to protect them from anything less than a major catastrophe. The distribution of power within the ministry with regard to colonial affairs resembled that of the mid-1730's, when no single official or faction held absolute power. Bedford and Halifax could harass the incumbent officials and deny them further favors, but they could not displace them; similarly, the Pelhams could protect their friends from dismissal, but they could no longer guarantee an easy administration.

The appearance of Bedford and Halifax in key positions of colonial administrative authority in 1748 had brought to an abrupt end the informal system of imperial control which had emerged during the Newcastle era. The bureaucrats in London and the officials in America who had previously served as buffers between the colonists and the home authorities suddenly found their performance in office judged by more strict and more rational standards. Within the space of a very few years, there was an almost complete alteration in the perspective from which colonial problems were viewed. Accompanying this more critical outlook was the willingness to propose a range of solutions which had been neglected for more than a generation.

The new sense of urgency and purpose which had come to characterize the discussions of the bureaucrats within the southern department was revealed by the fierce debate over the situation in New Jersey. The circumstances in the colony itself were partly responsible for this. The political battle which broke out following the death of Governor Morris in 1746 exhibited aspects of a social revolution as well as the more common attributes of factionalism within the ranks of the governing elite. The engrossment of the

---

Glen in 1754, as part of the ministry's election preparations, but was not used; both Glen and Johnson had died in office by the mid-1750's.

land of the province by a few proprietors constituted the basis of the dispute, and the conflict was accentuated by the stranglehold on the government achieved by the large landowners through their control of the Council. The Assembly was unable to secure the ratification of legislation designed to curb the abuses. Denied a political solution, the small landowners and tenants resorted to force. Riots against property and authority occurred without redress.

There was a distinct possibility of a complete breakdown of the administrative system. Governor Belcher reported on his arrival in August, 1747, that he found

> the Province, in much Disorder, from great Numbers, of Seditious People, in several parts of it, trampling upon the Laws, breaking the Kings Goals, rescuing Prisoners, in the most autrosious Manner.[54]

The Governor's experiences in Massachusetts Bay had taught him the dangers involved in turning over the solution of colonial problems to those in London. Belcher therefore called upon the Assembly to restore order. Only when this plea had failed did he heed the advice of the large landholders on the Council and seek assistance from home. In April, 1748, Belcher apprised the southern secretary of the Assembly's refusal to aid in "Suppressing this Wicked Spirit of Sedition, and Rebellion, which Animates Such Numbers of Audacious Villains, In Many Parts of the Province."[55]

The receipt of Belcher's letter prompted the Board of Trade to immediate action. The disturbances in New Jersey had previously come to the attention of the advisory body, but they had been ignored because of the board's preoccu-

[54] Belcher to Newcastle, August 27, 1747, C.O. 5/985, nos. 81-82; Belcher to Bedford, June 24, 1748, ibid., no. 86.

[55] Belcher to Bedford, April 22, 1749, ibid., no. 275; Council petition, December 22, 1748, ibid., no. 132.

pation with the settlement of Nova Scotia and with the drafting of legislation to regulate the emission of paper currency in the colonies. The situation had now become sufficiently serious for the advisory body to suggest that the matter be considered by the "great board," which included the major officers of state in addition to the regular commissioners of trade.[56]

The meeting of the "great board" on July 12, 1749, to discuss the riots in New Jersey was one of the few such deliberations during the entire eighteenth century. Immediately upon its conclusion after four hours of discussion, the five senior ministers retired to hold a private conference of their own. In this session Hardwicke, Newcastle, and Henry Pelham supported Belcher's handling of the disturbances, while Bedford and Sandwich reflected the sentiments of Halifax in adopting a much more critical position. It was only the personal influence of Hardwicke, supported by the authority of the Pelhams, which saved the Governor from immediate recall. As the Lord Chancellor wrote subsequently to Belcher,

> The disorders and confusions in New Jersey, carried almost to the height of revolution, and the difficulties which they have brought upon your administration there, have given me a great deal of concern, principally on the public account, but partly on account of the share I had in recommending you (though then a stranger to me) to that government. . . .

[56] Bayse, *Lords of Trade*, 45-48. The chief ministers were *ex officio* members of the board but had ceased to attend its meetings after the first few years of its existence. This was the only meeting of the "great board" between 1749 and 1782. At the time of the salary dispute in Massachusetts Bay in 1729 and 1730, the Privy Council committee for plantation affairs had requested the presence of a few board members at its meetings, thus uniting the two bodies under a different aegis.

> For my own part, I have always maintained that, however you might possibly be mistaken in some points, yet I was persuaded you had acted with integrity, according to your judgement. . . .[57]

The aftermath of the meeting of the "great board" was something of an anti-climax. Unable to agree among themselves, the chief ministers referred the matter to the Board of Trade for a report. This document, released in July, 1749, placed most of the blame on the Assembly. Belcher's conduct did not escape criticism, but the strongest censure was reserved for the representative body and the traditional structure of government and administration:

> It seems necessary to establish as a fundamental Principal, that as long as the Governor is so absolutely dependent upon the Assembly as he is at present, Order and Good Government cannot be re-established. . . .[58]

The urgency of the board's statement was unique, but its content was not. The suggestion that colonial governors be placed on the home establishment had been made in 1726 on the occasion of Shute's dispute with the Assembly of Massachusetts Bay. The new Board of Trade was simply traversing the same ground as its predecessor of twenty years before. Indeed, Newcastle may have thought it was all a bad dream. Jonathan Belcher, the Massachusetts native sent out to quell the agitation in his own colony, was now the beleaguered Governor of New Jersey. The points at issue were as similar as the cast of characters. In both

[57] August 31, 1751, quoted in Yorke, *Life of Yorke*, II, 27-29; Belcher to Hardwicke, October 9, 1749, Add. MSS 35909, foll. 112-13.

[58] Board of Trade to Bedford, July 28, 1749, C.O. 5/982, foll. 244-47.

cases the authority of the governor and the prerogatives of the Crown were endangered by the intransigence of the lower house of the legislature.

If there was a difference between the two controversies, it was in the nature and seriousness of the colonial dispute. Officials in America and in England drew a parallel between the rioting in New Jersey and Bacon's rebellion in Virginia in the last quarter of the seventeenth century. This was very different from the struggle between the home authorities and the Assembly of Massachusetts Bay. There the contest had been conducted within constitutional forms; the violence had been verbal, not physical. In Bacon's Virginia, Leisler's New York, and Belcher's New Jersey, the political framework had become too rigid and unyielding to accommodate the legitimate demands of an important section of the local population. The battle had therefore been taken out of the constituted institutions and into the streets and fields. It was no longer a question of interpreting legal documents, as in Massachusetts Bay; rather, the choice lay between bowing to the demands of the extra-legal agitators or subjugating them by the application of overwhelming force.

Belcher advocated the first of these alternatives; Halifax, backed by the landowners and Council of New Jersey, strongly favored the second. The Governor's plan was quick, simple, and inexpensive. Belcher suggested that a commission composed of the chief justices or leading officials of the neighboring provinces should be appointed to hear the complaints of the interested parties and to propose a just and impartial solution. Once the underlying difficulties had been solved, Belcher thought the legitimacy of the government would automatically reestablish itself.

The plans advanced by the Board of Trade reversed the order of priorities. The authority of the Crown was to be guaranteed by appropriate action; when this had been accomplished, a solution could be sought for the land problem. The board's report canvassed three alternative courses of action. The dispatch of a military force from England, the Virginia precedent, was rejected as too severe and too expensive. Quite apart from the Pelhams' favorable attitude toward Belcher, it was obvious to the board that the First Lord of the Treasury would not tolerate a costly military operation. In order to achieve the same end at much less cost, the board proposed the transfer of the four independent companies in New York to New Jersey and the payment of the Governor's salary from home.

Even this cost-conscious alternative labored under the disadvantage of being too expensive. The drain on the English exchequer from the payment of Belcher's salary was as unpalatable to the Treasury in 1750 as it had been in 1730, when the Governor had been sent back to Massachusetts Bay with firm instructions to extract a permanent stipend from the local legislature. Now the board had no real alternative but to fall back on the proposal of Robert Hunter Morris, the council's agent and the son of the late governor. Reversing his father's position, Morris suggested that the governments of New York and New Jersey be reunited under a single chief executive. With financial backing and military power from his New York post, the governor would be in a position to enforce order in New Jersey and to uphold the authority of the Crown.[59]

For all its apparent logic, this was not a particularly convincing argument. As Belcher himself pointed out, the Governor of New York had been singularly unsuccessful in having his way in his own colony despite the military

[59] Report, July 28, 1749, ibid., 246-47; Belcher to Hardwicke, November 25, 1749, Add. MSS 35909, foll. 114-17; Bayse, *Lords of Trade*, 45-48.

force at his command. Even Clinton, son of one Earl and uncle to another, had very little weight or prestige with the Assembly. It was obvious to Belcher that this should

> Show the Case to be common, in the plantations . . . That Governours can neither draw, nor drive Assemblies, or people, from their Obstinate wayes of Thinking, into reasonable Measures. . . .[60]

This fact should have been apparent to the Board of Trade as well. But the inherited beliefs of those at home died hard and slow. For four years Halifax attempted to secure the reunification of New York and New Jersey under a single governor and the appointment of "a proper Person of Weight."[61] At the same time, he sought to undermine Belcher's already tenuous position in the colony. In August, 1751, the Governor complained bitterly to Hardwicke and to Bedford that the Board of Trade had rejected his nominees for Council while recommending the men suggested by Morris. "Their Lordships proceeding, in this manner," Belcher declared to the southern secretary,

> is not only an infraction, upon the Original Constitution, of this Government; but also upon His Majesty's Royal Orders, to me, for the filling of Vacancies, in the Council. . . .[62]

The Governor was mistaken in the interpretation of the powers conveyed by his instructions, but there was no ques-

[60] Belcher to Hardwicke, November 25, 1749, Add. MSS 35909, foll. 114-17.

[61] This was Newcastle's description of Sir Danvers Osborne, the brother-in-law of Lord Halifax, who was sent out as Governor of New York in 1753, only to commit suicide shortly after his arrival in the colony. See Katz, *Newcastle's New York*, 36.

[62] Belcher to Bedford, August 10, 1751, C.O. 5/986, no. 192; Partridge to Hardwicke, August 24, 1751, Add. MSS 35909, foll. 142-43.

tion that Halifax was having his revenge for his inability to institute his program of reform. With Pelhamites installed in the chief executives' posts in New York and New Jersey, there was little prospect for dramatic action. The divisions within the ministry had combined once again with the limitations imposed by financial considerations to defeat the attempt of the Board of Trade to alter the character of the colonial system and to exhibit its determination to enforce the authority of the home government in America.

IV

By the end of 1750, Halifax had become sufficiently frustrated by his lack of effective power as First Lord of Trade that he was threatening to resign.[63] By this time as well, the political alliance which had brought him to the board was also on the verge of collapse. After an initial period of agreement, Newcastle found Bedford's presence in the secretaries' office as irritating as that of his predecessor. Political and administrative friction was exacerbated by personal animosity. Chesterfield, who had first-hand knowledge of the situation, had perceived these difficulties as far back as 1749:

> One *Grace* [Newcastle] is too jealous not to suspect his best friend, and the other *Grace* [Bedford] too obstinate to forgive or forget the least injury. Lord Sandwich, who governs the latter and detests the former, who in return abhors him, takes care to keep this fire alive, so that he may blow it into a flame whenever it may serve his purpose to do so. . . .[64]

[63] Halifax to Newcastle, November 28, 1750, Add. MSS 32722, foll. 343-50.

[64] Chesterfield to Dayrolles, April 25, 1749, Dobrée, ed., *Chesterfield Letters* IV, 1332-34.

By September, 1750, Newcastle was urging Henry Pelham to exclude Bedford from the ministry at the first opportunity.

The obvious solution to both of these problems was to increase the power of the First Lord of Trade by giving him control of the southern department. The troublesome Bedford would then be out of the government and Halifax would have a free hand in America. Despite its attractions, this alternative was unacceptable to Newcastle. "As to Halifax," the Duke advised his brother,

> I love Him, & esteem Him & think He has very Efficient Talents; but He is ye last Man in ye Kingdom (except Sandwich) that I should think of for Secretary of State. . . . He is so conceited of His parts that He would not be there one Month, without thinking He knew as much, or more of the Business than any one Man. . . .[65]

Newcastle hoped to win his brother's approval of the ineffectual Earl of Holderness as southern secretary and to compensate the energetic Halifax by bringing him into the cabinet.

This expedient was poorly conceived. As Henry Pelham pointed out to his brother, the First Lord of Trade would still be required to "take his orders from the Secretary of State of the Province; and that I take to be Hallifax's objection."[66] Because of Newcastle's unwillingness to share the secretaries' office with a capable colleague, the Pelhams found themselves in a quandary. If Halifax were to be kept in the government by the expansion of the powers of his office, Holderness would have to acquiesce in this limitation of his authority and to accept a loss of face. More

[65] September 2, 1750, Add. MSS 32722, foll. 300-17.

[66] September 9, 1750, ibid., 343-50.

important, the King would have to be persuaded to admit the First Lord of Trade into the cabinet.

The death of the Prince of Wales in March, 1751, precipitated a showdown between the Pelhams and the faction led by Bedford and Sandwich and backed by the Duke of Cumberland. "It appeared to me," Bubb Dodington wrote in his diary at the time,

> that, if the Pelham party did not, instantly, drive out the Bedford interest . . . the Bedford party would become the strongest, having the King's favourite, and now, only son at their head; that he would, by their interest, small as it might be, and by the military interest, force the regency, and then, where are the Pelhams?[67]

Previously the threat posed by Bedford and Sandwich to the hegemony of the Pelhams had been a limited one. Changes in policy and in personnel had begun in the Admiralty and in the southern department, but these had not shaken the strength of the leading ministers. Now, however, Henry Pelham began to look with greater interest on the latest scheme of his suspicious brother. By April, it was widely rumored that Holderness was to replace Bedford and some of the powers of his office given to Halifax.[68]

For a quarter of a century such a diminution in the authority of the Secretary of State had been completely unacceptable to Newcastle because of the loss in colonial patronage which it would have entailed. Now, securely ensconced in the northern department, the Duke was able to take a more detached view of the situation. The urgent need to remove Bedford justified this tampering with the

[67] Dodington, *Diary*, 100. [68] Ibid., 113, 123.

traditional system, especially as Newcastle's personal interest would no longer be affected by the change. The consideration that this alteration would aid in the creation of a more rational and efficient administrative system hardly entered into the picture at all. At best it was an effective rationalization for actions taken for more selfish motives.

The real intentions of the Pelhams were obvious to all concerned. Indeed, the radical character of changes called forth a series of bitter protests. "It is fit You should know it, that you may conduct your Scheme Accordingly," Hardwicke warned Newcastle in August, 1751, that

> the D. of B[edford], in his valedictory Speech to the K. (among other Complaints) told His M. that everything relating to His Service was so concerted, as to serve Your Grace's Convenience, & encrease Your Power . . . That H.M. would find that, as soon as He was out of the Secretary's office, one considerable part of it, America, was to be lopped off, & thrown into the hands of the first Commissr of Trade . . . [that] the chief Offices of the State were to be mangled, engrossing all power to Them & their Creatures.[69]

The Pelhams' manipulation was so evident that even Newcastle was conscious of the liberties he had taken and of his delicate position with regard to the King. A year later the effects of this action were still being felt. "The Duke of Newcastle begs you would . . . write to him, the Same

[69] August 13, 1751, Add. MSS 32725, foll. 59-60. See also the satirical letter composed by Horace Walpole the younger on this occasion and addressed from Holderness to Newcastle, January 30, 1752, Add. MSS 35335, foll. 62-64.

again," the Duchess informed her brother, the Duke of Leeds, in July, 1752,

> only leaving out, those two lines, that are mark'd under them: it will then be, Inst what we woud wish to shew to the K. but as it is, he knows what interpretation would be put upon, those two lines, viz. that *some people* had taken too much upon them & pretended to the disposal of things, and *that*, he fears woud hurt, any body he wishes to serve. . . .[70]

These fears were not without foundation. When the Pelhams had presented to the King their scheme to aid Halifax, George II had declined to increase the size of the cabinet council by the addition of the First Lord of Trade. It was only the intervention of Lord Granville, himself a former southern secretary and now President of the Council, which provided a way out of this impasse. "Ye publick End," Granville suggested,

> may be answer'd by ye Commissioners of Trade being suffer'd to act up to the Letter of their Commission, by presenting to the Council the names of proper People to be Employ'd as Governors, Deputy Governors, Secretarys & by taking Cognizance of the Government of the Colonies. . . .[71]

A reliance on traditional forms would clothe the transaction with the appearance of continuity and legitimacy.

Such scholarly exegesis did not conceal the fact that a significant change had taken place in the locus of the power over colonial patronage. Recommendations to those positions in America formerly in the hands of the southern

[70] July 1, 1752, Add. MSS 28051, fol. 354.
[71] "Ld H______x," August 6, 1751, Add. MSS 32725, fol. 17.

secretary were now vested in the Board of Trade. More important, the division of authority between the Secretary of State and the Board of Trade had been resolved in favor of the latter. After half a century of agitation, the advisory body had won extensive executive powers and had regained a formal monopoly of information about developments in the colonies. The American governors were instructed to disregard the directions contained in Secretary of State Nottingham's circular letter of 1702 and for the future to "transmit all Accounts of their Proceedings, and Matters, relative to their Government, to the Lords Commissioners for Trade and Plantations only. . . ."[72]

If this directive constituted a first step in vesting complete power over American affairs in the hands of the Board of Trade, it was by no means completely successful. The authority of the First Lord of Trade was limited, just as that of the southern secretary had always been, by his own weight within the administration. Halifax acknowledged his dependence on his colleagues in explicit terms in a memorandum sent to Newcastle in August, 1751:

> In order to prevent the Possibility of the Board's recommending any Person to whom his Majesty or his Ministers may have objections, it [should] be understood that the Earl of Halifax on his part engages that no Such Recommendation shall be made, till after he has consulted with his Majesty's Ministers on the Subject.[73]

[72] Memorandum by Holderness, January 22, 1752, Add. MSS 33029, foll. 88-90; Newcastle's Memorandum, "Laid before the King & approved by His Majty," no date, Add. MSS 33030, foll. 285-86; Halifax to Newcastle, January 5, 1752, Add. MSS 32726, foll. 20-23; Holderness to Board of Trade, March 30, 1752, C.O. 324/38, pp. 306-11; Grenville to Holderness, October 20, 1752, C.O. 28/49, foll. 282-83.

[73] "Ld Halifax's paper," December 17, 1751, Add. MSS 32994,

In the last analysis, the final decision with regard to a major colonial appointment would continue to reside in the hands of the leading ministers. Bureaucratic forms could disguise the real source of power and could on occasion divert its flow from its accustomed channel; but they could never completely stem the tide. The authority of the senior members of the administration found its own level regardless of the structural obstacles placed in its path. Halifax had gained the right to formulate alternative policies for the consideration of his colleagues, but it was the latter as always who would have the power to decide among them.

This fact was obvious from the very beginning of the board's assumption of the full powers outlined in its original commission. One major appointment, that of Charles Knowles to the government of Jamaica, was managed by Holderness before the order in council came into effect in March, 1752.[74] Even then, the influence of the other officials over colonial nominations was still strong. The appointment of Arthur Dobbs to the government of North Carolina was the result of the intervention of Andrew Stone, now the tutor to the future King George III, and Lord Hertford, a gentleman of the bedchamber.[75]

Even with his augmented power, Halifax was not able to prevent the subordination of colonial interests to the requirements of domestic politics. The ministry won the support of George Selwyn, the M.P. for Gloucester, in the general election of 1754 by means of a huge grant of land

---

foll. 286-87; Halifax to Newcastle, August 25, 1751, Add. MSS 32725, foll. 81-89; "Method practiced for naming to Governments in America," no date but circa 1765, Add. MSS 33001, fol. 34.

[74] Trelawney to Holderness, November 6, 1751, C.O. 137/59, foll. 159-60; also the material in Add. MSS 32724, foll. 408-10, and Add. MSS 32726, foll. 163, 503-504.

[75] Dobbs to Newcastle, November 27, 1752, Add. MSS 32730, fol. 301; Clarke, *Arthur Dobbs*, 95-103.

in North Carolina.[76] Henry Pelham negotiated an even more important arrangement with Thomas Pitt. In return for his assistance to the government interest at Camelford, Oakhamption, and Old Sarum, Pitt was to be named Governor of South Carolina and the salary of the post increased to £2,400 sterling per annum; by the time of Pelham's death, this scheme had progressed to the point where Halifax had prepared a letter of recall to the incumbent Governor Glen. It was only Pitt's last-minute decision to accept a gift of one thousand pounds a year from the ministry which preserved Glen in office.[77]

The acquiescence of Halifax in this abortive scheme was not hard to understand. He had his own friends to oblige and his own demands to make on the ministry. Richard Cumberland, Halifax's secretary, was named Crown Agent for Nova Scotia and later Provost Marshal of South Carolina.[78] More important, the First Lord of Trade was still attempting to win entry to the cabinet council or, if this continued to be denied, a substantial increase in his salary.[79]

It was not surprising, therefore, that Halifax continued to permit the political exploitation of American patronage. A particularly striking instance occurred in 1754, when

[76] Memorandum, March 16, 1754, Add. MSS 32994, foll. 96-101; Sellers, "Henry McCulloh," 544.

[77] "Minutes," March 23, 1754, Add. MSS 32995, foll. 120-21; Dupplin Memorandum, no date, Add. MSS 33030, foll. 346-47; Thomas Pitt to Newcastle, November 7, 1754, Add. MSS 32737, foll. 302-303.

[78] Richard Cumberland, *Memoirs*, London, 1807, I, 205; Richard Brown, *The South Carolina Regulators*, Cambridge, Mass., 1963, 69-73.

[79] This agitation eventually resulted in the creation of a separate office of secretary of state for the plantations. See Pelham to Newcastle, September 29, 1752, Add. MSS 32729, foll. 400-409, and the memoranda in Add. MSS 32726, foll. 338-39; Add. MSS 33029, foll. 104-105; and Add. MSS 33030, foll. 295-96.

Lord Chancellor Hardwicke intervened to secure the appointment of Captain John Reynolds as the first royal Governor of Georgia. When Reynolds first petitioned for the post in January, 1753, Halifax had sought to counter Hardwicke's recommendation by reminding the naval man that "there were Five or Six had Applied for it, and that his Majesty's Service must be regarded in Appointing such who should appear to be best quallified, all Circumstances being considered. . . ."[80]

The outcome of this second major venture by the Lord Chancellor into the disposal of American patronage was more embarrassing than his support for Jonathan Belcher during the crisis in New Jersey. Reynolds proved to be a completely incompetent governor. Within a few months of his arrival in Georgia, he had alienated the Assembly and mismanaged the patronage at his disposal. He bestowed no fewer than seven offices on his private secretary.[81] After two years in the colony, Reynolds was recalled from Georgia for a hearing before the Board of Trade. At the same time, a new chief executive was dispatched to the province. Halifax informed Hardwicke in July, 1756, that the dismissal of Reynolds was inevitable, given "the present declining and disorder'd State of the Province of Georgia."[82] The significance of this episode was not in the method of the Governor's appointment, which conformed so precisely to the traditional pattern, but in the speed with which he was recalled. His rapid removal was virtually without precedent in the history of colonial admin-

[80] Reynolds to Hardwicke, January 18, 1753, Add. MSS 35909, foll. 170-71, and other correspondence between the two men, ibid., foll. 105-106, 174-75, 202-203.

[81] W. W. Abbot, *The Royal Governors of Georgia, 1754-1775*, Chapel Hill, 1959, 45.

[82] July 20, 1756, Add. MSS 35909, fol. 239; Reynolds to Hardwicke, July 28, 1758, ibid., foll. 283-87.

istration and testified to the new vigilance and the new power of the Board of Trade.

Less novel but no less important were the standards governing the distribution of patronage which were enunciated by Halifax and his subordinates. The assumptions of the new administrators first became clear in the discussions surrounding the appointment of George Thomas as Governor of the Leeward Islands in 1753. Halifax had contested Thomas's fitness for the post because of his ownership of a considerable estate in the islands. The First Lord of Trade argued that Thomas's personal interests would cause him to favor the local planters and merchants at the expense of the Crown.[83]

Halifax's position was not without its merits, but his logic was not completely convincing. A governor without a stake in American society might be more inclined to heed his instructions, but he would also have less power to implement imperial policies. Deprived of a "natural" place in the social and economic hierarchy of the community, the governor would have to depend entirely on the formal authority and perquisites of his political position. If, as Harrington had claimed long before, political power rested ultimately on economic power, the authority of the governor would be severely compromised by his divorce from local society. This loss would have to be offset by a corresponding increase in the power of the home government in the colonies.

The financial cost of such an arrangement would be high, much greater in fact than the Treasury or Parliament had ever given any indication they would be willing to pay. Yet the policy of the Board of Trade was moving in this direction. The decision in 1754 to pay the salary of Gover-

[83] Thomas to Newcastle, November 21 and 24, 1752, Add. MSS 32730, foll. 275-76, 289-90.

nor Dobbs of North Carolina by a warrant on the home Treasury was more than testimony to the influence of the new Governor at the Privy Council committee; it was also a logical step in the implementation of the policy adumbrated by Halifax.[84] So also was the board's action in using Treasury funds to underwrite the civil establishment of the new royal colony of Georgia. Under the plan proposed by the board and accepted by the ministry, none of the major offices in the new government would be dependent on the local legislature for support.[85]

This was a significant departure from past practice. When the Carolinas had been taken under the control of the Crown in 1729, there had been no such comprehensive funding of the establishment from English funds. Indeed, at that time even the proposal that £1,000 sterling be taken from the Crown's quit rents for the support of the governor had come under severe attack in Parliament.[86] A quarter of a century later, the ministry was gradually coming to accept the view that the efficient government of the colonies was worth the expenditure of English resources. At this point, it was not clear that Parliament could be brought to accept this reasoning. There would certainly be demands in the House of Commons for a careful scrutiny of American expenditures. And it was equally probable that the English legislators would soon insist that the colonists be taxed to defray the cost of administration. Even before the

[84] Clarke, *Arthur Dobbs*, 103; Leonard W. Labaree, *Royal Government in America*, New York, 1958, 333; Greene, *Quest for Power*, 142-43.

[85] Abbot, *Royal Governors*, 9-10; Dickerson, *American Colonial Government*, 194-95; Reese, *Colonial Georgia*, 38, takes a different view.

[86] Newman, ed., *Knatchbull Diary*, 101-102, 145-47; Greene, *Quest for Power*, 139-42.

great war for empire, there were pressures threatening to disrupt the traditional fiscal system of imperial administration.

Such a result would be welcomed by Halifax and his associates. For two generations, the Board of Trade had sought to involve Parliament more closely in the management of the colonies. But in its haste to undo the cumulative effect of sixty years of relative neglect, the advisory body failed to consider some of the other implications of its newly implemented policy. In Georgia, for example, the sending out of officials from England and their payment from home severely inhibited the growth of a strong government party within local Assembly. Royal officials, together with the Scottish merchants who appeared in the colony in the wake of economic prosperity, came to constitute the hard core of the Governor's supporters.[87] It was not surprising that most of these men followed their chief executive into exile in 1775. They had never really been integrated into the society in which they lived.

Georgia was perhaps an extreme case. In the other colonies the distinction between English imperial officials and American colonists, between rulers and ruled, was never as great. Still, the thrust of the new policy was to widen this gap. Under Halifax, the board continued for administrative reasons the patronage policy which the Pelhams and their predecessors had developed and exploited for political ends. Even where it might easily have done so, the board refused to consider an alternative course of action. In 1750, for example, Peter Wraxall had used a connection with Richard Neville Aldworth, the Undersecretary of State to the Duke of Bedford, to secure a royal warrant appointing him to the office of Town Clerk and Indian Agent at

[87] Abbot, *Royal Governors*, 23.

Albany in New York.[88] On Wraxall's return to the colony, Governor Clinton refused to accept this encroachment on the traditional authority of his office and declined to honor the sign manual. By the time Wraxall's appeal reached the Board of Trade, the situation was such that the commissioners had almost complete freedom of action. Clinton had not challenged their appointee but that of the deposed Bedford. There was therefore no possibility of a personal political conflict; nor was the question of the Crown's prerogative necessarily involved. The board could have reaffirmed the general right of the home authorities to override the nominations of a colonial chief executive while allowing Clinton to keep the disposal of this particular post because of past precedent. But the main concern of Halifax, backed by Fane and Dupplin, was to insure the centralization of American patronage. The board therefore recommended that Wraxall be confirmed in his offices and that Clinton be reprimanded for acting "in a manner inconsistent with his Duty to the Crown."[89]

During Halifax's tenure at the head of the board, not one of the offices which had passed from the control of any governor into the hands of the southern secretary during the previous century was returned to the colonial chief executive. Indeed, by 1760, the board had also appropriated the right of appointment to the Naval Offices of New York and the Bermuda Islands from the local governors.[90]

[88] Wraxall to Aldworth, July 20, 1751, C.O. 1096, foll. 365-66. See also the correspondence between Wraxall and Andrew Stone in Add. MSS 32714, foll. 69, 185-86, 377-78. A detailed financial history of the office of Provost Marshal in Jamaica, which Aldworth secured for himself, is in P.R.O. 30/50/63.

[89] Report, November 7, 1752, C.O. 5/1087, foll. 242-52.

[90] Compare the "List of Places in the West Indies in ye Disposal

Two offices which Newcastle had missed in his political exploitation of the administrative resources of America, Halifax had now acquired in the name of efficient central control. Whatever the motive, the result was much the same. The ability of a governor to win the support of the population through the disposal of patronage was severely limited just at the time that the home government was demanding the strict implementation of the royal instructions and the acts of trade and navigation.

Although a precise definition of the contest escaped them, Halifax and the other members of the new Board of Trade found themselves at the center of a struggle between two distinct types of colonial administration, each justified in the last analysis by its own theory of empire. The first system was based on the primacy of the colonial assembly; it sought, in fact if not always in theory, to involve the settlers in their own governance. Laws and instructions, governors and generals might be sent out from England, but the predominant political authority was manifest in the legislation enacted and enforced by the colonists themselves. Whatever controversies might surround the ultimate origin or subsequent development of this type of imperial rule in America, it possessed the stamp of legitimacy by the middle of the eighteenth century. Officials in London recognized clearly, if unenthusiastically, that one of the defining features of the colonial system which they had inherited was the devolution of political and administrative responsibilities into the hands of the governed.[91]

---

of a Secy of State," circa February, 1748, C.O. 5/5, pt. II, foll. 273-75, 288-91, with a similar tabulation for 1761 printed in Bayse, *Lords of Trade*, appendix B.

[91] See Richard Koebner, *Empire*, New York, 1965, 87-90, for

In opposition to the reality which confronted them in America, these administrators posited another conception of empire, equally logical, equally coherent, but based ultimately upon different psychological and philosophical principles. In their view the basic institution of colonial administration was not the local assembly but the imperial bureaucracy. And it was this component of the old colonial system which they attempted to strengthen. The administrative machinery established in Georgia expressed the essence of their ideas. The colonies were the possessions of England; they were to be administered by those sent out and instructed from London, by bureaucrats financially and politically immune from the control of those they ruled.

Succeeding generations of Englishmen would distill each of these imperial traditions into its pristine form: colonies of white settlers would eventually form self-governing dominions, while territories of colored peoples would be paternalistically administered by dedicated civil servants. No such easy definitions obtained in 1750; the English colonial experience in America contained both a tradition of bureaucratic control and one of political self-rule. If the latter was in the ascendency at mid-century, its foundations were weak and its future in doubt. The proponents of a system of strong central supervision of the American possessions now occupied key posts in the colonial bureaucracy and were seeking parliamentary sanction for administrative measures which would embody their own theory of empire.

---

an analysis of the new ideas of empire which were appearing in the colonies by the middle of the eighteenth century.

CHAPTER 7

The Legacy of the Past

THE changes which were made in the colonial system between 1748 and 1754 were more the result of external pressures—financial, military, and political—than of the intellectual stimulus to reform provided by the Board of Trade. Indeed, the very concept of reform, of purposeful progressive change, was largely foreign to men of the time. A certain veneration for the past, for the traditional ways of doing things, pervaded the consciousness of Englishmen of the first half of the eighteenth century. That a given procedure had been followed in the past was sufficient to justify its continuance for the future. Secretary of State Stanhope clearly articulated these assumptions in a letter to the Board of Trade in 1717:

> As to the . . . Governor's pretension of appointing himself, or naming a Clerk to the Assembly, it appears not to have been the practice for many years, and seems to be overruled by prescription.[1]

By mid-century this unthinking reliance on past precedent had hardened into a positive antipathy to change. Lord Egmont commented on the occasion of the third reading of the Jew Bill of 1753 that the measure was prompted by "nothing but a wanton spirit of innovation, with changing the old laws of England, and setting up for every novel institution (the very disease of the times)."[2]

[1] April 12, 1717, S.P. 44/119, pp. 37-38.

[2] Quoted in Thomas W. Perry, *Public Opinion, Propaganda, and Politics in Eighteenth Century England: A Study of the Jew Bill of 1753*, Cambridge, Mass., 1962, 185.

It was the prospect of a new war with France which shook the English political nation out of its accustomed lethargy and brought about a refreshing review of traditional practices. "If, at this critical conjuncture . . . ," Halifax argued in a letter to Newcastle on the death of Governor Albemarle of Virginia in December, 1754,

> late Precedents should be suffer'd to prevail, and that Employment which ought to be so busy and is so important an one should be continued a Sinecure, I leave your Grace to judge what uneasiness it would create, and how little Serious the World would think us in the present Measure of embarking Troops for the Defence of Virginia. . . .[3]

Even at this late date, the Pelhams and their associates found it difficult to divest themselves of the legacy of the past. While admitting that the government in Virginia had long been filled "in a wrong way," Hardwicke recommended Lord Cholmondoley for the post "if it falls to be disposed of in a Court Way . . . by reason of the opening it will make either for Egmont or Legge." "I am Sorry there is so much difficulty," Newcastle replied to the Lord Chancellor, "in finding out any thing, that can cleverly answer our two great and necessary Objects, viz, the doing something for Mr. Legge, and my Ld Egmont." For his own part Hardwicke was confident that the Duke would find a way out: "I don't pretend to know how, but your Grace, who has great Dexterity in turning & shaping those things, may be able to chalk it out."[4]

The scale of priorities underlying this exchange between

[3] December 28, 1754, Add. MSS 32737, foll. 505-506.

[4] December 29, 1754, ibid., foll. 516-17; "A List of Employments," December 28, 1754, ibid., 514-15; Hardwicke to Newcastle, December 26, 1754, ibid., 485-86.

Hardwicke and Newcastle appeared slightly anachronistic in view of the crisis confronting the English nation in 1754. And yet it was not surprising that matters appeared in this light to those in London. In 1719, Alexander Spotswood had complained of having given up his chances of preferment in the army "to go to be buried in obscurity in America," and such notions continued to have their adherents in the mother country.[5] It would take the impact of a major war to create a new perspective and to bring forth a more responsible and rational approach to the problems of colonial administration.

I

Much of the hesitation of the past stemmed from the fact that the society which had evolved in America by 1750 was considerably different from what had been expected at the beginning of the century. "From the Healthfullness of the Climates on this Continent and the Surprizing Growth of its Inhabitants within the last Century," William Shirley predicted to Newcastle in 1745,

> it may be expected that in one or two more Centuries there will be such an addition from hence to the Subjects of the Crown of great Britaine, as may make 'em vye for Numbers with the Subjects of france, and lay a foundation for a Superiority of British power upon the continent of Europe. . . .

It was one thing to have colonies which produced wealth in the form of precious metals or staple goods, and quite another to have settlements which rivaled the mother country in population, natural resources, and economic power. The Massachusetts Governor reminded his patron that

[5] Spotswood to Board of Trade, August 18, 1719, VHS, *Collections*, II, 328-35.

> This is a Remarkable Difference between the other acquisitions in America belonging to the Several Crowns in Europe and this Continent, that the others diminish the Mother Country's Inhabitants, as Jamaica, Barbadoes, and the other Southern Collonies belonging to Great Britain have done; and the Spanish West Indies have done even to the exhausting of Old Spain.[6]

Shirley's comments reflected the growth of a feeling of distinctiveness in the continental colonies. The appearance of this sentiment was the result both of the emergence of a coherent colonial culture and of increasing external pressure. The passage in the 1730's and 1740's of parliamentary legislation favoring the West Indies aroused considerable discontent on the American mainland. "The Act [of 1746] against pressing in the Sugar Islands," Admiral Knowles informed his superiors at the Admiralty, had

> fill'd the Minds of the Common People ashore as well as Sailors in all the Northern Collonies (but more expecially in New England) with not only a Hatred for the King's Service but [also] a Spirit of Rebellion each Claiming a Right to the same Indulgence as the Sugar Collonies and declaring they will maintain themselves in it.[7]

The new idea of "empire" which was slowly being articulated in British North America was only vaguely sensed by those at home. Franklin's tentative conception in 1751 of a "greater England" embracing both mother country and colonies achieved little recognition in London.[8] Yet even in the capital there was a new awareness. Since 1739,

[6] October 29, 1745, C.O. 5/900, foll. 255-68.
[7] January, 1748, quoted in Baugh, *Naval Administration*, 221.
[8] Koebner, *Empire*, 89.

English military strategy in the western hemisphere had been founded on the assumption that "grate numbers of men must be raised on the Continent of America. . . ."[9] The success of the New England forces against the supposedly impregnable fortress of Cape Breton provided a definite index of this military potential. The new respect accorded to the Americans in the aftermath of this victory was paralleled by the realization in Europe of the intimate connection between the affairs of the two continents. In 1746, Bedford hoped to outfit an expedition in England in the late spring for a summer descent upon Canada. This was little more than the time needed to deploy troops on the fields of Flanders. Bedford's strategic assumptions were shared by others. "The King believes . . . ," the French foreign minister wrote a few years later, "that it is possessions in America that will in the future form the balance of power in Europe. . . ."[10]

This consciousness of the immediacy of colonial problems and of the potential power of the American settlers effected a significant shift in the outlook of the colonial bureaucracy in London. The complaints of the governors were seen in a new light. From the time of Edward Randolph at the end of the seventeenth century, successive waves of officials had gone to America determined to implement imperial policy. Almost to a man they had found their idealistic plans crushed by the intransigence of the inhabitants and the indifference of those in England. "Upon my first beginning to do business here," Governor Gabriel Johnson

[9] Newcastle's phrase as recorded by Admiral Norris in his journal for November 22, 1739. See also the entry for December 6, 1739, Add. MSS 28132, foll. 80-82, 92.

[10] Quoted in Max Savelle, "The American Balance of Power and European Diplomacy, 1713-1778," in Richard B. Morris, ed., *The Era of the American Revolution* . . . , New York, 1939, 160-61.

of North Carolina wrote to Lord Wilmington after three years in office,

> I imagined like most young beginners, that with a little assistance from home, I should be able to make a mighty change in the face of affairs, but a little experience of the people, and reflection on the situation of things at home has absolutely cur'd me of this mistake. I now confine my care intirely, to do nothing, which upon a fair hearing . . . can be reasonably blamed, and leave the rest to time, and a new sett of inhabitants. . . .[11]

Moderate men quickly became aware of the futility of the struggle; only zealots like Randolph persisted in their fight for the abstract principles conceived in London. It was less tiresome and more profitable to cooperate with the local assemblies.

When new ideas began to flow out of England in the 1740's, there was no one in America prepared to implement them. Upon hearing of a "proposal for Establishing by Act of Parliament dutys upon Stamp papers and Parchment in all the British and American Colonys," Governor Clinton cautioned his patron against such a move. "The people in North America," he told Newcastle in December, 1744,

> are quite Strangers to any Duty but such as they raise themselves and was Such a Scheim to take place without their Knowledge It might prove a dangerous consequence to his Majesty's interest. . . .[12]

[11] February 10, 1737, H.M.C., *Eleventh Report*, pt. IV, 262-63.

[12] December 13, 1744, C.O. 5/1094, foll. 374-75. This was probably the plan suggested by William Keith in December, 1742, Add. MSS 33028, foll. 376-77.

Some years before, Governor Morris of New Jersey had felt obliged to issue a similar warning. As Morris wrote to the southern secretary in 1739,

> It has been suggested by Brigadier Hunter . . . that if his Majestee would appoint & fix what sume he thought propper for the sallaries of each of his governors . . . & by an act of a British Parliament oblige the severrall generall assemblys . . . it would put an end to the constant wranglings between governours and assemblies. . . .

"Yet I dare not adventure to say the expedient is advisable . . . ," Morris continued, "I'm afraid the remedy suggested may prove either Impracticable or worse than the present distemper complained of. . . ."[13] The continued neglect of colonial problems by those in England had broken the spirit of the officials in America.

It was only when parliamentary intervention became a distinct possibility that the colonial bureaucracy began to regain its morale. In 1744, when British merchants petitioned the House of Commons to prevent the emission of colonial bills of credit, the Board of Trade drafted a bill which not only outlawed paper money but also gave to royal instructions all the force of acts of Parliament. This proposal, rejected on its first reading, was greeted with dismay by colonial agents and proprietors alike. "If this passes into a Law," wrote one member of the Penn family,

> It at one Stroke deprives us of all our Rights & Privileges—the King's Instructions will have the force of Laws, and must consequently render our lives Liber-

[13] Morris to Newcastle and to the Board of Trade, October 4 and 10, 1739, NJHS, *Collections*, v, 58-63.

> tys & Estates to his pleasure—We are no longer Freemen but Slaves. . . .[14]

The fears of the Penns were premature; there were still great constitutional obstacles to parliamentary action on sensitive colonial matters. Moreover, the political security enjoyed by the Pelhams was the result, in large measure, of their instinct for avoiding controversy of any sort. Any measure, however laudable or necessary, which would imperil the ministerial coalition was rejected out of hand. When Richard Jackson analyzed the domestic political situation for the benefit of Benjamin Franklin in 1758, he was careful to point out that

> The principal Ministers in this Country wish to carry their great points with as little Struggle and Opposition as possible [and] . . . they are not easily engaged to permit Contests in Parliament on other Points that People of Weight will interest themselves in. . . .[15]

In 1747, and again in 1751, bills designed to ease the naturalization of aliens were lost as a result of the unwillingness of the government to push them through Parliament. And in November, 1753, the Pelhams were forced to secure the repeal of a similar bill for the naturalization of resident Jews, after backing its passage less than six months before. On this occasion Newcastle and Henry

[14] Quoted in Kemmerer, *Path to Freedom*, 175n. The board's initiative may have been the result of the presence of Carteret in the government, for the board's proposal was very similar to the view expressed by Carteret, then Lord Granville, to Benjamin Franklin in 1759. Granville claimed that the King's Instructions were the "law of the land" in the colonies, a position of doubtful constitutional validity. See above, chap. 1, note 63. No other senior minister held such an extreme view during this period.

[15] "Private Sentiments and Advice on Pennsylvania Affairs," circa April 24, 1758, Labaree, ed., *Franklin Papers*, VIII, 26.

Pelham feared that the clamor which had been raised by the Tories and the opposition Whigs would diminish their majority in the coming election and would lead to the recurrence of mob violence in London.[16] "*The Opinion of the Bulk of Mankind without Doors*," Jackson concluded, "is the only Restraint that any Man ought reasonably to rely on for securing what a Ministry . . . [might] wish to deprive him of."

The same considerations which inhibited the passage of contentious domestic legislation operated with regard to American affairs. In March, 1750, Thomas Sherlock, the new Bishop of London, sent Hardwicke and Newcastle a memorandum describing the "distressed" state of the Church of England in the colonies. "The Church there is without any Government or Inspection," the Bishop explained, "& it is absolutely necessary to put an End to this State, which will soon be a State of Confusion."[17] Backed by the Society for the Propagation of the Gospel, the prelate hoped to settle two bishops in the plantations and to give them the ecclesiastical jurisdiction vested in his own office.

Newcastle was greatly disturbed by this proposal. "I have always thought it of such Importance," he replied to the Bishop, "that It required the most mature Consideration." He asked the prelate to delay presenting the matter to the King in Council until "His Majesty's principal Serv-

[16] Perry, *Jew Bill of 1753*, 171-77; George Rudé, *The Crowd in History: A Study of Popular Disturbances in France and England, 1730-1848*, New York, 1964, 51-52.

[17] Bishop of London to Hardwicke, March 4, 1750, Add. MSS 35909, foll. 117-18; "The State . . . ," no date, Add. MSS 33029, foll. 63-64; Bishop of London to Newcastle, March 23, 1750, Add. MSS 32720, fol. 156. See, in general, Arthur Lyon Cross, *The Anglican Episcopate and the American Colonies*, New York, 1902, chap. 5.

ants have had a meeting with You, upon it."[18] Newcastle's caution was understandable; the question was politically explosive. Whatever the religious requirements of the Church of England in the plantations, this measure threatened to disrupt Parliament and the country by splitting high from low Anglicans and both of these groups from the Dissenting interest. "Reasons of State," Horace Walpole explained to Sherlock, demanded that the issue be dropped at once.[19] "I never approve of such Starts," Newcastle complained to Hardwicke when the prelate defied the expressed wishes of the ministry and raised the question of the American establishment at the general meeting of the Society for the Propagation of the Gospel,

> But they will often appear in Shapes, where We don't expect Them, When there is not sufficient Authority to prevent any Attempts of this Nature.[20]

The opposition of the ministry to the initiative of the Bishop of London, and to the legislation regarding naturalization, had little to do with the intrinsic merit of these measures. It was the government's position in Parliament and in the country which was the crucial desideratum in each instance. In the past the opposition had proposed controversial legislation, such as sanctions against colonial infringements of mercantilist principles, in order to distress the administration. Richard Partridge explained to the Governor of Rhode Island, following a debate in 1740 concerning the regulation of colonial currency, that

> it [i]s believed that the chief aim of some of them in it, was more with a view to puzle and perplex the

[18] March 24, 1750, ibid., foll. 160-61.
[19] May 29, 1750, Add. MSS 32721, foll. 60-68.
[20] June 1, 1750, ibid., 17-18.

> Ministry and Spirit up the Plantations against them than any thing else. . . .[21]

Whatever the motives of the proponents of new and unusual legislation, the government was not prepared to risk parliamentary action unless it could be assured in advance of overwhelming support.

By the 1750's, however, the ministry had little room for maneuver. The expenses incurred in the long struggle with France and Spain made it more difficult than ever to spare funds for colonial purposes. At the same time, the settling of Nova Scotia and the subsidization of the administrative costs of the new royal province of Georgia increased the drain on the English exchequer. The annual cost of the military establishment of four thousand men in the western hemisphere in 1754 was nearly £100,000, a significant increase over the expenditures during the preceding years of war.[22] It was becoming increasingly evident to those in the administration that the populous and prosperous colonies on the North American continent would have to be brought to support the costs of their own government and to provide for their own defense. "Ye settlement of Nova Scotia has already cost great sums," Horace Walpole warned Newcastle in 1754,

> wch I must own are very necessary and must in time of war be continued, because ye Loss of that Province would mean ye Loss of all our Northern Colonys; but this expense, necessary as it is, goes down but heavily

[21] Partridge to Wanton, April/May, 1740, Kimball, *Rhode Island Correspondence*, I, 152-55; Partridge to Green, March 25, 1745, ibid., I, 310-11.

[22] Shy, *Toward Lexington*, 34-35, gives £95,000 as the annual cost in the years immediately prior to 1754; in 1743, the total expenditure was £73,800: "State of Annual Expenses," 1743, C.O. 5/5, foll. 236-37.

> with ye Country-Gentlemen, and should any new extraordinary supplys be demanded, for keeping up forces raised by ye assembly to prevent encroachments threatened by ye French upon ye Boundarys of such Colonys as are well settled, & in a flourishing condition; & who enjoy their property, with ye same freedom & privileges as English men doe, I am afraid ye Landed Gentlemen of this country will be terribly alarmed. . . .[23]

On the eve of a new war with France, the Pelhams were faced with a dilemma. There was a distinct danger that colonial appropriations would become an issue in domestic politics and endanger the position of the ministry in Parliament. Yet it was not obvious that this contingency could be avoided. If the Pelhams sought to force the colonial assemblies to defray the cost of administration and defense, there was a similar possibility of a split within the home legislature. Either alternative was dangerous, and it would not be possible much longer to avoid choosing between the two. "This country encreases in wealth every year," Henry Pelham warned his brother in 1752,

> but there is such a load of debt, and such heavy taxes already laid upon the people, that nothing but an absolute necessity can justifie our engaging in a new War. And that necessity must be very apparent to enable us to carry it on.[24]

[23] June 14, 1754, Add. MSS 32735, foll. 485-90. Between 1749 and 1752, the home government had spent £336,700 on the settlement and the military defense of Nova Scotia. "Of late years great sums have been drawn from England for American Services," Hardwicke reminded Newcastle in August, 1754, "which has been much complained of here. . . ." See Add. MSS 32736, foll. 340-43.

[24] October 19, 1752, Add. MSS 32730, foll. 142-45.

Pelham's analysis applied with equal force to the colonial situation. The need would have to be very obvious before the ministry would be prepared to ask Parliament to enjoin the colonial assemblies to lay taxes to defray the costs of empire.

II

Until the urgency of the English financial situation forced a re-examination of the colonial administrative system, there was only a limited number of alternatives open to those who wished to alter the character of the Anglo-American relationship. During the first fifty years of the eighteenth century, the mercantilists on the Board of Trade had to work within the limitations imposed by the weakness of the economic resources of the country and by the unwillingness of the ministry to take remedial political action.

There was a definite pattern to the various expedients proposed by the Board of Trade during this period. Whenever there was an armed threat from France or Spain in America, the specialists in the plantation office proposed a union of the colonists under a military commander-in-chief. The first such proposal was advanced by John Locke after his appointment to the Board of Trade in 1696.[25] Locke's scheme was subsequently resurrected in 1721, when the Board of Trade called for the nomination of a military governor-general of the continental colonies in order to prepare for a possible war against Spain.[26] The more serious danger posed by the Spanish after 1737 called forth

[25] The Secretary of the Board of Trade sent a copy of Locke's plan to Townshend, thus establishing a direct link between this scheme and the board's proposal of 1721. See Popple to Townshend, July 22, 1720, H.M.C., *Eleventh Report*, pt. IV, 296.

[26] The board's report is in Callahan, ed., *New York Documents*, V, 593-630.

another such plan, this time from Martin Bladen. Bladen's scheme was more comprehensive than the preceding proposals, with a provision for a bicameral legislature composed of representatives from the colonies as well as the more traditional feature of a governor-general appointed by the Crown.

Despite the new feature of a "Plantation Parliament" designed to prevent violations of the acts of trade and navigation and to bring the charter and proprietary colonies more closely under the supervision of the Crown, Bladen's plan followed in the tradition of the earlier suggestions for the military defense of the continental colonies. As such, it commanded a wider respect than the ordinary administrative proposals advanced by the Board of Trade for the more efficient management of the colonies. Yet the two types of plans were intimately related, as Bladen himself noted in the text of this latest blueprint for a colonial union:

> those, who have had apportunitys of considering the true State, and Interest of our Plantations, have always wished, that they might be put under one Uniform Direction, and that the Crown would appoint a Captain General for the Government of all the British Colonies on the Continent of North America.

The threat of war merely provided a pretext for Bladen and his fellow reformers. "In such a Circumstance of time," the Colonel continued, "I am perswaded the Parliament, if no other way could be found, would easily be induced to provide a Salary, upon the Military Establishment, for so usefull an Officer."

The danger of war with Spain had provided the Commissioner of Trade with a lever by which to extract parliamentary support for the reconstitution of the system of colonial administration. If this expedient failed, Bladen was prepared to bypass the home legislature in his continuing effort to obtain "an Authority over these Independent Colonys. . . ." Given the urgency of the situation, Bladen argued that his plan could be implemented "by virtue of the Prerogative still inherent in the Crown, even without the Assistance of Parliament."[27]

It was this reliance on the royal prerogative which the Earl of Halifax utilized in 1752 as part of his own plan for the better internal management of the colonies and for their defense in the impending American war against France. Initially the scheme proposed by the First Lord of Trade embraced only the reunion of New York and New Jersey under a single governor and the strengthening of the royal prerogative in those provinces. The threat of war persuaded Halifax to broaden his plan. His personal choice for the joint governorship was Lord Barrington. And Barrington would accept the appointment, Halifax explained to Newcastle in March, 1752, only on the condition "of his being first in Command, whenever he shall be order'd on his Majesty's Business in North America. . . ."[28] Under the guise of improving the royal government of New York and New Jersey, Halifax had revived Bladen's plan to use the prerogative of the Crown to invest a single man with authority over all the mainland colonies. There was a definite continuity of policy stretching from Locke through Bladen to Halifax across half a century of English colonial history. In 1752, as in 1739 and 1697, the threat of war in America called forth different versions of the

[27] Greene, "Bladen's Blueprint," 523-25 and passim.

[28] Halifax to Newcastle, March 2, 1752, Add. MSS 32726, fol. 207; "Lord Barrington's Paper," March 6, 1752, ibid., 229-30; Alison Gilbert Olsen, "The British Government and Colonial Union, 1754," *WMQ*, 3rd ser., XVII (January, 1960), 22-34.

same plan to install, by royal order, a governor-general over all the American continent.

The expedient adopted by imperial reformers and planners in moments of crisis was of little political value during the intervening eras of peace. In these periods a different administrative strategy was employed by those who were dissatisfied with the government's ability to manage the colonies in the interest of the mother country. In 1726, and again in 1729, midway between his participation in the formulation of the Board of Trade report of 1721 advocating the appointment of a governor-general and his own enunciation of a similar plan in 1739, Martin Bladen advised Townshend and Newcastle that keeping the colonies separate was now in the national interest. This policy, Bladen argued, would prevent "any dangerous Union" among them.[29]

There was an inner consistency to Bladen's seemingly contradictory statements. On those occasions when the Commissioner of Trade could reasonably expect national backing for his designs, he urged the creation of a strongly unified government in America. In the intervening periods of ministerial indifference, Bladen realized that a concentration of power in the colonies would only make the task of the Board of Trade more difficult. At such times, a strategy of "divide and rule" was the most intelligent policy. Given the financial and political limitations on its ability to affect developments in America, the board had to insure that authority in America remained diffuse and fragmented.

The pragmatic character of Bladen's campaign emerged clearly once Walpole and the Pelhams had rejected his

[29] Greene, "Bladen's Blueprint," 517-18; [Martin Bladen], "For the Settling of Carolina," September 27, 1729, C.O. 5/4, foll. 159-63.

comprehensive scheme to establish a "Plantation Parliament" presided over by a military governor-general. By 1740, Bladen was supporting the division of the joint governorship over New Hampshire and Massachusetts Bay, just as he had acquiesced in the decision two years earlier to separate the chief executive's post in New Jersey from that in New York. In each case, Bladen and the Board of Trade argued that the change would benefit both the inhabitants of the smaller colony and the imperial administrative system. There would be fewer political disputes if the colonies were separated; this of itself would enhance the authority of the Crown. In the case of New Hampshire, moreover, there would be the additional advantage that the power of Massachusetts Bay in the affairs of New England would be curtailed significantly. As Bladen told Newcastle in 1740, the division of the two colonies would be

> agreable to the Interest of the Crown for New Hampshire is immediately under the Kings Direction, but the Massachusetts Bay is a kind of Common Wealth, where the King is hardly Stadholder; and yet upon Occasions New Hampshire has been Sacrificed by her Governours, to the Interest of the Massachusetts Bay.[30]

Just as there was a policy of military centralization designed to unify the colonies under a governor-general appointed by the King, so also there was an administrative scheme which had as its goal the elimination of archaic and competing sources of power in America and the establishment of a strong board of trade charged with the overall supervision of colonial affairs. Proponents of the latter policy had attempted unsuccessfully during the first dec-

[30] October 8, 1740, C.O. 5/899, foll. 524-26.

ades of the eighteenth century to secure the abrogation of the proprietary and corporate charters by act of Parliament. Their failure, and the renewed danger of war, brought about an uneasy and ill-conceived synthesis of the two lines of strategy in the Board of Trade's report of 1721. The abortive plan proposed by the board would have created a military governor-general at the same time that it abolished charter colonies and elevated the First Lord of Trade to cabinet status. The consequent bifurcation of power and authority between the traditional colonial chief executives and the new governor-general and between the latter and his powerful civilian superior in London would have created as many problems as it would have solved.

It would have produced bitter ideological and political controversies as well. Whatever its immediate rationale, the policy of military centralization advanced by Locke, Bladen, and Halifax shared some of the underlying assumptions of the administrative framework established by James II in the shortlived Dominion of New England. The appointment of a military governor by the King would create jurisdictional disputes with civilian officials and local assemblies; moreover, it would infringe on some of the rights granted by the various colonial charters. Bladen might argue that "this Act of the Crown would operate *per Incrementum* not *per Ablationem*," but this was to evade the realities of the political situation.[31] For all its apparent simplicity, the nomination of a governor-general would raise as many constitutional questions as the proposed abrogation of the royal charters by parliamentary decree. Given the unwillingness of the ministry to confront such delicate legal questions during the first half of the eighteenth century, the peacetime expedient of "divide and rule" propounded by the administrators at the Board

[31] Greene, "Bladen's Blueprint," 526.

of Trade attained a certain primacy despite the periodic challenge of a wartime strategy of military centralization.

In 1754, the options were still open. But now the problems of defense and of efficient colonial administration were complicated by acute financial stringency at home and a thinly-veiled resentment against the exemption of the colonists from an increasing tax burden. "Should this country," Horace Walpole inquired of Newcastle in the spring of that year, "by Parliamentary supply undertake ye defense of those colonys upon all emergencys of encroachments upon them by land; would not the procedure be of bad consequence?"[32] The alternative was to devise a method of financing the defense of a colony against external attack which would avoid a drain on the home Treasury and the resort to coercive legislation, both of which were certain to encounter opposition in Parliament. Within a few days, Walpole thought he had the answer. "Our whole continent in America should look upon this as a Common cause . . . ," he told Newcastle, and "a plan of Union . . . formed between ye Royale, Proprietary, & Charter Governments, under ye protection, & with ye approbation of ye Crown of Gr: Britain."[33]

Within two months of the ministry's request in June, 1754, the Board of Trade had devised a scheme for a general union of the North American colonies. The speed of this endeavor testified not only to the efficiency of the board but also to the reliance on past plans and to the limited extent of the suggested alterations. The cabinet council had already rejected a proposal from Halifax which called for parliamentary legislation to establish a general fund for all revenues collected in America. Unable to muster minis-

[32] June 14, 1754, Add. MSS 32735, foll. 485-90.

[33] June 22, 1754, ibid., foll. 539-41; H. Walpole to Newcastle, June 26, 1754, ibid., foll. 566-68.

terial support for a battle in the House of Commons on this issue, Halifax explained to Newcastle that the Board of Trade had "endeavoured as much as possible to adapt the Plan to the Constitution of the Colonies. . . ."[34] A military governor-general was to be sent out, and commissioners from each of the colonies were to meet to adopt a scheme for the building and funding of a series of defensive forts. In the urgency of the moment, the board did not consider the implications of these changes for the internal administration and government of an individual province.[35]

News of the French victory over the Virginian forces on the Ohio gave increased urgency to the discussions taking place in London. " 'Tis monstrous that People will not help themselves . . . ," Hardwicke complained to Newcastle on hearing of the colonial defeat.[36] The Duke was even more pessimistic than the Lord Chancellor: "Tho' We may have Ten Times the Number of People in Our Colonies," he protested to Granville, "They don't seem to be able to defend Themselves, even with the Assistance of Our Money. . . ."[37] The Duke summed up the situation in a letter to Hardwicke:

> Every body is full of North America, and our Defeat there. . . . Something must be resolv'd and *that Something* must be (if possible) Effectual.[38]

At this critical juncture, the ministry drew back from the proposed plan of a union for mutual defense. There was a

[34] August 15, 1754, Add. MSS 32736, foll. 243-46; Newcastle to H. Walpole, June 29, 1754, Add. MSS 32735, foll. 597-98; Olsen, "Colonial Union," 25-26.

[35] "Plan," August, 1754, Add. MSS 32736, foll. 247-52.

[36] September 7, 1754, ibid., foll. 436-37.

[37] September 5, 1754, ibid., foll. 432-33.

[38] September 21, 1754, ibid., foll. 554-56.

sudden realization of the potential drawbacks of such action. Newcastle himself noted in a memorandum prepared prior to a discussion with the Speaker of the House of Commons

> the ill Consequence to be apprehended from uniting too closely the Northern Colonies with Each other; An independency upon this Country being to be apprehended from Such an Union.[39]

Newcastle's doubts could only have been reinforced by the opinions of Charles Townshend of the Board of Trade. "The Plan," Townshend told Newcastle, "begins a great work in a wrong manner; whatever is done, can only be done by an act of Parliament, concerted with great candor & conducted with great prudence & knowledge. . . ."[40] Townshend argued that the emergency plan prepared by the board was not feasible. Even if the commissioners sent from the individual colonies could overcome their local prejudices and agree upon a plan of union, the provincial assemblies would not vote a supply of money to complete the project. As Townshend pointed out,

> the provinces have been for many years engaged in a settled design of drawing to themselves the ancient and established prerogatives wisely preserved in the Crown . . . by their annual Bills of Supply, in which they have appointed all the Officers of the Crown by name to be employed in the Exchequer, Substituted warrants for drawing out public money in the place of the Governor's & in one word dispossest the Crown of

[39] "Conference with the Speaker," September 9, 1754, Add. MSS 32995, foll. 309-10; Newcastle to Murray, September 10, 1754, Add. MSS 32736, foll. 472-73.

[40] Townshend to Newcastle, September 13, 1754, Add. MSS 32736, foll. 508-509.

almost every degree of executive power ever lodged in it. . . .

The tone and content of Townshend's memorandum reflected the experiences of the Board of Trade during the previous six years. The imprint of Governor Glen's letters from South Carolina, describing in graphic detail the financial and administrative aggrandizement undertaken by the Assembly, was readily discernible here. So also were the important issues raised by the great debate which had transpired at the board at the time of the land crisis in New Jersey. Townshend's own proposal was at once a response to the problems of the immediate past and a prescription for the ideal imperial relationship of the future. This "great work" would be accomplished, the Commissioner of Trade argued, only by an act of Parliament which would provide for financial stability as well as political unity. His model was the bill proposed in 1710 for the creation of a permanent Crown revenue in New York by means of a duty on imports and exports.[41] Here, then, was the origin of the scheme which Townshend, as Chancellor of the Exchequer, was to implement thirteen years later.

In 1754, this plan for the establishment of a civil list financed by a tax on trade was coupled with a proposal for a colonial union. As such it represented both a restatement and an extension of the policies of centralization advocated in the past. Townshend's conception resembled earlier formulations in its emphasis on central control and direction; but it differed radically in its constitutional reliance on parliamentary legislation rather than on the royal pre-

[41] "Drht of a Bill prepared in 1710 by the Attorney General & the Sollictor General," no date, Add. MSS 33028, foll. 22-32. An extended passage from one of Glen's letters appears in the text, above; see chap. 5, note 53. The New Jersey situation is described above, chap. 6, sec. III.

rogative. It was precisely at this point and upon this issue that the views of the old colonial administrators parted from those of the men who were to assume the burden of empire in the aftermath of the Seven Years' War. Even in September, 1754, Newcastle thought that the dangers proceeding from a union of the colonies outweighed the advantages. His experience had given him no indication how such a strong American organization could be ruled from home; he could only fall back on the traditional administrative solution of "divide and rule." Hardwicke likewise showed traces of the old constitutional and bureaucratic mentality. When asked to comment on the Board of Trade's plan, he suggested that the results of the commissioners' meeting should be sent directly to England for study and approval and then returned to the individual colonies for their approbation. Hardwicke noted, however, that the draft composed in London could ultimately be "alter'd, or perhaps disagreed to by the Assemblies." "As they are Legislative Bodies," he concluded, "I see no help for it."[42]

[42] Hardwicke to Newcastle, August 25, 1754, Add. MSS 32736, foll. 340-43. Benjamin Franklin to Issac Norris, March 19, 1759, Labaree, *Franklin Papers*, VIII, 291-97, indicates that Franklin thought Hardwicke was a "prerogative Man" who believed that the colonists had too many privileges. This may have been the case, but Hardwicke's view in this regard was much more favorable to the Americans than that of Lord Granville. An assessment of the Lord Chancellor's position in the spectrum of English constitutional thought is presented from a somewhat broader perspective by Herbert Butterfield, "Some Reflections on the Early Years of George III's Reign," *JBS*, no. 4 (May, 1965), 78-101.

Lewis Namier, *England in the Age of the American Revolution*, London, 2nd ed., 1963, 61-62, notes the dramatic change in the composition of the English political elite in the ten years between 1760 and 1770 as the generation born in the 1680's and 1690's rapidly retired from the scene.

This was not only the voice of a lawyer, but also that of a generation. Those who had been born at the time of the glorious revolution and who had grown up amid the uncertainties of the Hanoverian succession had a more limited conception of the omnipotence of Parliament than those who received their political education at the hands of those skillful legislative magicians, Sir Robert Walpole and Henry Pelham. Halifax and Townshend did not fear that an attack against the powers of the colonial legislatures would raise constitutional questions that would endanger the position of Parliament at home.[43] They were prepared to move ahead to regulate all aspects of colonial life by legislation from England. No longer would the ministry's fear of a parliamentary battle protect those in America from central control.

Newcastle and the men of his generation were never able to make this jump. Until the end of his days, the Duke resisted the idea that Parliament was omnipotent and could impose its will upon those in America without qualification. His notes for a parliamentary speech in February, 1766, were adequate testimony to the persistence of past dogma. "Colonies not the Object of Taxation," read one note; "I am much against Taxation," declared another. Finally, the former southern secretary stressed the importance of representative government and the difference in status between a conquered country and the American colonies:

> Wales never taxed, tile they were represented—Calias, & Berwick, Guernsy-Jersey, Isle of Man, never taxed . . . Ireland conquered—Act of Parliament to

[43] Townshend to Newcastle, November 7, 1754, Add. MSS 32737, foll. 57-58; Henry Fox to Newcastle, October 6, 1754, ibid., foll. 45-46; "Lord Dupplin's Paper," no date but 1754-55, Add. MSS 33030, foll. 344-45.

> bind Ireland—Yet no Act can bind in point of Taxes, or Subsidy. . . .[44]

By this stage, these ideas seemed out of place. They had been replaced by those of a generation of men who would neither be as cautious nor as legalistic in their dealings with the colonists in America. In 1753, Charles Townshend drafted instructions for Sir Danvers Osborne, the new Governor of New York, which directed the Assembly to make permanent provision for the salaries of the chief executive and his subordinates in the colony. This directive was coupled with another which vested the disposition of the military funds of the province in the Governor and Council and relegated the Assembly to a strictly inferior position.[45] As the agent for Massachusetts informed the Secretary of the province in 1755,

> it was intended, by some persons of consequence, that the colonies should be governed like Ireland, keeping a body of standing forces, with a military chest . . . [and with] the abridgement of their legislative powers. . . .[46]

The analogy with Ireland, used negatively by Newcastle for purposes of contrast, was appropriated by his successors as a description of the ideal colonial relationship.

The English political nation had come to the point at

[44] Notes in Newcastle's handwriting, February 3, 1766, Add. MSS 33001, fol. 83. The Duke's opinion of the constitutional and political relationship between England and the "conquered" province of Ireland can be discerned in Newcastle to Dorset, December 28, 1753, Add. MSS 32733, foll. 582-91.

[45] Sir Lewis Namier and John Brooke, *Charles Townshend*, London, 1964, 37; Katz, *Newcastle's New York*, 188n.

[46] William Bolland to Josiah Williard, March 5, 1758, quoted in Barrow, *Trade and Empire*, 175.

which it would have to undertake a fundamental reassessment of its own constitutional nature if it wished to govern the American colonies more closely in its own interest. When England had been ruled by a monarch with pretensions to absolute power, the legal position of the colonies had been easily defined. Between 1689 and 1754, with power divided between King and Parliament and limited by the "rights" of the individual and the "liberties" of corporate bodies, the state of the colonial relationship was more ambiguous. This uncertainty permitted the development of autonomous assemblies in America just as the weakness of the first Hanoverians promoted the establishment of parliamentary supremacy in England. Until that supremacy was attained, until the long struggle between Crown and Commons was transcended by a redefinition of the sovereign power as the "King-in-parliament," it was impossible to articulate clearly the constitutional status of the American colonies and to conceive a coherent policy on that basis.

It was not accidental that the colonies enjoyed a period of "salutary neglect." For the two or three generations while the implications of the events of 1688 were being worked out in England, politicians fell back on the calculus of individual self-interest as the basis of their colonial policy. In lieu of a single national political purpose, there was no feasible alternative. The failure of the Walpoles and the Pelhams to secure parliamentary legislation over all aspects of colonial life or to enforce royal instructions with vigor and purpose was inherent in the situation. It was the constitutional struggle between the monarch and the legislature in the mother country which constituted the basic parameter defining the nature of the Anglo-American relationship during the first half of the eighteenth century.

III

Within this basic pattern of colonial administration inherited from the last decade of the seventeenth century, there were three important changes which occurred during the following fifty years. The first was the gradual decline in the influence of the proprietary faction in English domestic politics. This development was closely related to the second trend: the growing influence of Parliament in the management of colonial affairs. There was an inner logic to these simultaneous developments. The proprietary interest had been the creation of the Restoration Stuarts; with the revolution of 1688 and the Hanoverian succession, it was bound to suffer the same fate as its progenitors. The initial decline of the Board of Trade, a creation of the strong-willed William III, also symbolized the transfer of authority from King to Parliament. The increased importance of the southern secretary after 1702 and of the Privy Council committee for plantation affairs after 1714 simply dramatized the shift in the locus of power from the monarch to the legislature.

The turning point in this concurrent process came in 1729 with the surrender of the royal charter of Carolina by the proprietors and the purchase of the colony with parliamentary funds. After this point, the proprietors exercised only a minimal influence on the determination of colonial policy. This vacuum was slowly filled by Parliament which, beginning with the Molasses Act of 1733, gradually began to exert its authority over the management of American affairs. At mid-century, when the new Board of Trade attempted to subject the colonies to greater central control, it turned to Parliament for legislation rather than to the King for additional royal instructions to his governors. This was a far cry from 1696, when the board had been created by

William III in an effort to keep the control of the plantations out of the hands of the legislature.

In part, this shift from the supremacy of the monarch to the hegemony of parliament was the result of the third development in colonial policy: the increasing politicization of the bureaucracy. By means of a judicious allocation of places of profit both in England and in America, the Whig ministries solidified their control of the government during the reigns of George I and George II.[47] Backed by a strong and stable coalition in the House of Commons, Sir Robert Walpole and Henry Pelham were able to counteract the influence of the King and to draw more power into the hands of the politicians. This appropriation of administrative resources for political—and indirectly for constitutional—ends affected the character of the colonial bureaucracy as well as other departments of administrative system. The result in every case was a decline in expertise and in the standards of service. The English nation paid a high price for this increase in the power of the representative body.

The damage suffered by the administrative system was especially acute in America. The growing centralization of patronage power in the hands of officials in England undermined the authority of the colonial chief executive, the King's representative in the plantations. Over the years, the governors lost their ability to manage the colonial assemblies in the interest of the home government. In the last analysis, this loss of power stemmed from the growing divergence between the social, economic, and political interests of the American colonies and those of the mother country. But this inevitable development was accelerated by the neglect of colonial problems by those in London and

[47] Plumb, *Growth of Political Stability*, 112-26, notes a similar development in a slightly earlier period.

by the shortsighted and selfish patronage policies pursued by politicians such as Newcastle.

During the generation when the Duke served as southern secretary, colonial policy was determined by the blind interaction of private interests; no concerted attempt was made to administer the political life of the colonies in a purposeful way or to insure the implementation of the economic precepts enbodied in mercantilist dogma and in the acts of trade and navigation. It was only in the 1750's, when the twin pressures of military defense and financial necessity forced a newly self-conscious parliament and a new generation of political leaders to re-evaluate the nature of the colonial system, that any steps were taken to overcome the "natural" dichotomy between the English state and American society. By that time, however, much of the damage had already been done.

Bibliography

Index

Bibliography

UNPUBLISHED SOURCES

British Museum and Public Record Office: There are approximately 120 volumes of the Original Correspondence of the Secretary of State which relate to colonial affairs between 1720 and 1754. These are contained in the Colonial Office series in the Public Record Office and are arranged by colony. This organization facilitates the study of developments in any one colony, but makes it difficult to recreate the complex situation which confronted the administrators in London at any one time. A similar collection of documents, consisting of correspondence between officials in the colonies and the Board of Trade, is also contained in the C.O. series. This material often duplicates that found in the files of the secretary of state, but it does provide fuller information on the policies and activities of the Board of Trade. The letter books of the secretaries of state (State Papers 44/97-148) are valuable for determining the division of administrative business between the northern and southern secretaries and for tracing the prime interests of these officials. The final three volumes are the letter books of the undersecretaries of state. The Domestic State Papers (S.P. 35/48-75 and S.P. 36/1-110) contain miscellaneous papers received by the secretaries of state between 1720 and 1754 and some of their letters. There is little material which relates directly to the colonies in these volumes, except in so far as military or diplomatic affairs are concerned. Additional material of interest was found in the papers of three individuals which are deposited in the Public Record Office: Granville Papers (P.R.O. 30/29/11) Letters of John, 1st Earl Gower, 1741-51; Egremont Papers (P.R.O. 30/47/18 and 30/47/28-29); Aldworth Papers (P.R.O. 30/50/39 and 30/50/63-68) Letters of Richard Neville Aldworth, Undersecretary of State to the Duke of Bedford.

The Newcastle Papers in the British Museum contain a wealth of information pertaining to the political history of England and Scotland during the middle decades of the eighteenth century. There is little material from before 1754 which deals explicitly with the colonies, although there are three volumes of American Papers (Additional Manuscripts 33028-30). Other colonial documents, as well as a great number of requests for patronage, are scattered throughout the fifty volumes of the General and Home Correspondence which cover the period up until the outbreak of the Seven Years' War (Add. MSS 32686-32937). A thorough examination of this material, in conjunction with the data supplied by the Colonial Office Papers in the Public Record Office, made it possible to relate developments in America with the Duke of Newcastle's political fortunes in Parliament and in the English boroughs.

Newcastle's Personal Papers (Add. MSS 33054-55) describe his patronage activities in Sussex, as do the materials in Add. MSS 33059B and 33058. The financial difficulties of the elder Pelham are displayed in a number of volumes of detailed accounts (Add. MSS 33157-67 and 33320-23). Finally, there is his General Correspondence (Add. MSS 32991-99) and his letters to the Duchess of Newcastle (Add. MSS 33073-74); these materials offer an index to Newcastle's changing political interests and objectives.

The papers of Lord Hardwicke and his sons (Add. MSS 35353-35637 and 35910-16) supplement those of Newcastle, but they are not very full for the period before 1754. One volume of legal papers relates directly to the American colonies and another to the West Indies (Add. MSS 35909, 35916). The Carteret-Granville Papers (Add. MSS 22511-45) consist almost entirely of official documents and are of little value. The same can be said of the papers of Lord Holderness, the southern secretary from 1751 to 1754 (Egerton MSS 3425-90). The papers of Spencer Compton, the Earl of Wilmington, contain only a few items relating to America (Add. MSS 45733), while those of George, 4th Viscount Townshend, deal primarily with the period after 1754 (Add. MSS 50010-15). A few bits of information pertaining to domestic politics were found in the papers of the Duke of Leeds, Newcastle's brother-in-law (Add. MSS 28051-52), the Essex papers (Add. MSS 27732-35), and the Egmont papers (Add. MSS 46964-81). The Craggs Papers (Stowe MSS 246, 247, 251) are concerned with an earlier period.

There are a number of smaller collections in the British Museum which have a considerable amount of material relating to the American colonies. The papers of Benjamin Keene, the English ambassador to Spain in the 1730's, are in Add. MSS 43441-43. Naval affairs and the American expeditions of the years 1740 to 1742 are detailed exhaustively in the papers of Sir John Norris, an admiral of the fleet (Add. MSS 28130-58). The "Journal" kept by Norris is of particular interest for its discussion of cabinet debates and of factional alignments within the ministry. The Fairfax manuscripts (Add. MSS 30306) describe the affairs of William Fairfax in Virginia, provide information on the American customs service, and refer to some of the activities of the Carter family of Virginia. Finally, the papers of Samuel Martin, Jr., the Secretary to the Treasury in the 1750's, contain letters and documents relating to the family's estates in the West Indies.

Some additional items of interest are:

Board of Trade, Observations on the Colonies, 1740. Add. MSS 30372.
Board of Trade Papers. Add. MSS 14034-35.
Customs Establishment, 1744. Add. MSS 8131.
Customs Material. Add. MSS 8133c.
Customs Revenue. Add. MSS 36731-32.
Henry McCulloch: "Essay on Trade in America, 1756," handwritten, 116 octavo pages. Add. MSS 22514.
Naval Office: Barbados. Add. MSS 22617.
"Official Appointments in North America and West Indies." circa 1780, 36 folio pages, Add. MSS 22129.
Plantation Duties. Add. MSS 10119.

Cambridge University Library: The Cholmondeley (Houghton) Manuscripts consist primarily of the letters and papers of Sir Robert Walpole. The correspondence (nos. 661-3346) is comprised mostly of letters written to Walpole, but the several volumes of papers provide a considerable amount of information about the activities and programs of the famous minister. Volumes 42, 68, and 84 of the Walpole papers are concerned with the customs service, parliamentary matters, and plantation affairs, and were of particular value in this study.

PRINTED SOURCES

Belcher Papers. Massachusetts Historical Society, *Collections*, 6th ser., vols. VI and VII. Charles Card Smith, ed. Boston, 1893-4.

Bedford. *Correspondence of John, Fourth Duke of Bedford*, Lord John Russell, ed. 3 v. London, 1842-6.

Board of Trade. *Journal of the Commissioners for Trade and Plantations from . . . 1704 to . . . 1782, preserved in the Public Record Office.* 14 v. London, 1920-8.

Byrd. *The Writings of Colonel William Byrd.* J. S. Bassett, ed. New York, 1901.

———. *Another Secret Diary of William Byrd of Westover, 1739-1741.* M. H. Woodfin, ed., Richmond, Virginia, 1942.

Carter. *The Letters of Robert Carter.* Louis B. Wright, ed. Chapel Hill, 1940.

Chesterfield. *The Letters of Philip Dormer Stanhope, 4th Earl of Chesterfield.* Bonamy Dobrée, ed. 6 v. London, 1932.

Cibber, Theophilus, *et al. The Lives of the Poets of Great Britain and Scotland.* 5 v. London, 1753.

Cokayne, G.E., *The Complete Baronetage.* 5 v. Exeter, 1899-1906.

Colden. "The Letters and Papers of Calwallader Colden," New York Historical Society, *Collections*, vols. I, L-LVI, and LXVII-LXVIII. New York, 1918-37.

Coram. "Letters of Thomas Coram," Massachusetts Historical Society, *Proceedings*, LVI (1922-3), 15-56.

Cumberland, Richard. *Memoirs of Richard Cumberland.* 2 v. London, 1807.

Dictionary of National Biography. Sidney Lee, ed. 22 v. New York, 1909.

Dodington. *The Diary of the Late George Bubb Dodington . . . 1749 to . . . 1761*. Henry P. Wyndham, ed. Salisbury, 1784.

Dummer, Jeremiah, *A Defence of the New Englanl Charters*. London, 1721.

Egmont. *Diary of Viscount Percival, afterwards First Earl of Egmont*. R.A. Roberts, ed. 3 v. (Historical Manuscripts Commission, *Sixteenth Report*). London, 1920-33.

Franklin. *The Papers of Benjamin Franklin*. Leonard W. Labaree, ed. New Haven, 1959- .

Grant, W.L., and James Munro, eds., *Acts of the Privy Council of England: Colonial Series*. 5 v. Hereford, 1908-12.

Grenville Papers. William James Smith, ed. 4 v. London, 1852.

Hervey. *Some Materials toward the memoirs of the reign of King George II by John, Lord Hervey*. Romney Sedgwick, ed. 3 v. London, 1931.

———. *Lord Hervey and His Friends, 1726-38*. Earl of Ilchester, ed. London, 1950.

Hutcheson, Archibald, *A Collection of Advertisements Letters and Papers* . . . . London, 1722.

Hutchinson, Thomas, *The History of the Colony and Province of Massachusetts Bay*. Lawrence Shaw Mayo, ed. 3 v. Cambridge, Mass., 1936.

Kimball, Gertrude S., ed., *The Correspondence of the Colonial Governors of Rhode Island, 1723-1775*. 2 v. Providence, 1902.

Knatchbull. *The Parliamentary Diary of Sir Edward Knatchbull, 1722-1730*. A. N. Newman, ed. Camden Society, 3rd ser., vol. XCIV. London, 1963.

Marchmont. *A Selection from the Papers of the Earls of Marchmont*. George H. Rose, ed. 3 v. London, 1831.

Morris. "The Papers of Lewis Morris, governor of the province of New Jersey, from 1738 to 1746," New Jersey Historical Society, *Collections*, vol. V. William Adee Whithead, ed. New York, 1852.

Morris, Robert Hunter, "Diary of Robert Hunter Morris," *Pennsylvania Magazine of History and Biography*, LXIV (1940), 177-217 and 356-407.

O'Callahan, Edmund B., ed. *Documents relative to the colonial history of the state of New York.* 15 v. Albany, 1853-87.

Orrery Papers. E. C. Boyle, ed. 2 v. London, 1903.

Parliamentary history of England . . . 1066 to . . . 1803. William Cobbet, ed. 36 v. London, 1806-20.

Pownall, Thomas, *The Administration of the Colonies.* London, 1764.

Smith, William, *The History of the Province of New York . . . With a continuation from . . . 1732 to . . . 1814.* Albany, 1814.

Spotswood. "Letters of Alexander Spotswood," Virginia Historical Society, *Collections*, n.s., I and II. Richmond, 1882.

Stock, Leo Francis, *Proceedings and Debates of the British Parliaments respecting North America.* 5 v. Washington, D.C., 1924-41.

Talcott Papers, Connecticut Historical Society, *Collections*, vols. IV and V. Hartford, 1892.

Trevor MSS. Historical Manuscripts Commission, *Fourteenth Report*, Pt. IX.

Waldegrave, James, *Memoirs from 1754 to 1758.* London, 1821.

Walpole, Horace. *The Letters of Horace Walpole.* Mrs. Paget Toynbee, ed. 16 v. Oxford, 1903-1905.

———. *Memoirs of the Reign of King George the Second.* Lord Holland, ed. 2 v. London, 1846.

Wentworth Papers, 1705-1739. James Joel Cartwright, ed. London, 1883.

Wilmington MSS. Historical Manuscripts Commission, *Eleventh Report*, Pt. IV.

Yorke, Philip C., *The Life and Correspondence of Philip Yorke, Earl of Hardwicke, Lord High Chancellor of Great Britain.* 3 v. Cambridge, Eng., 1913.

Bibliography

Secondary Works

Abbot, William Wright, *The Royal Governors of Georgia, 1754-1775*. Chapel Hill, N.C., 1959.

Albion, Robert G., *Forests and Sea Power: The Timber Problem of the Royal Navy, 1652-1862*. Cambridge, Mass., 1926.

Andrews, Charles M., *The Colonial Period of American History, IV: England's Commercial and Colonial Policy*. New Haven, 1938.

Bailyn, Bernard, *The Origins of American Politics*. New York, 1968.

Bargar, B. D., "Lord Dartmouth's Patronage, 1772-1775," *William and Mary Quarterly*, 3rd. ser., xv (1958), 191-200.

Barker, Charles Albro, *The Background of the Revolution in Maryland*. New Haven, 1940.

Barnes, Donald G., "Henry Pelham and the Duke of Newcastle," *Journal of British Studies*, No. 2 (May, 1962), 62-77.

———, "The Duke of Newcastle, Ecclesiastical Minister, 1724-1754," *Pacific Historical Review*, III (June, 1934), 164-91.

Barrow, Thomas C., *Trade and Empire; The British Customs Service in Colonial America, 1660-1775*. Cambridge, Mass., 1967.

Baugh, Daniel A., *British Naval Administration in the Age of Walpole*. Princeton, 1965.

Bayse, Arthur H., *The Lords Commissioners of Trade and Plantations . . . 1748-1782*. New Haven, 1925.

Beattie, John M., *The English Court in the Reign of George I*. Cambridge, Eng., 1967.

Brown, Richard M., *The South Carolina Regulators*. Cambridge, Mass., 1963.

Buffington, Arthur H., "The Canada Expedition of 1746 . . . ," *American Historical Review*, XLV (1940), 552-80.

Burns, James J., *The Colonial Agents of New England*. Washington, D.C., 1935.

Burns, John F., *Controversies between Royal Governors and their Assemblies* . . . Boston, privately printed, 1923.

Butterfield, Herbert, "Some Reflections on the Early Years of George III's Reign," *Journal of British Studies*, No. 4 (May, 1965), 78-101.

Cannon, John, "Henry McCulloch and Henry McCulloh," *William and Mary Quarterly* 3rd ser., xv (January, 1958), 71-73.

Clark, Dora Mae, "The Office of Secretary to the Treasury in the Eighteenth Century," *American Historical Review*, XLII (October, 1956), 22-45.

———, *The Rise of the British Treasury: Colonial Administration in the Eighteenth Century*. New Haven, 1960.

Clarke, Desmond, *Arthur Dobbs, Esquire, 1689-1765*. London, 1957.

Clive, John and Bernard Bailyn, "England's Cultural Provinces: Scotland and America," *William and Mary Quarterly*, 3rd ser., XI (April, 1954), 200-13.

Coxe, William, *Memoirs of the Administration of the Right Honourable Henry Pelham* . . . . 2 v., London, 1829.

———, *Memoirs of the Life and Administration of Sir Robert Walpole* . . . . 3 v. London, 1800.

———, *Memoirs of Horatio, Lord Walpole*. 2 v. 2nd ed. London, 1808.

Cramp, Margaret, "The Parliamentary Representation of Five Sussex Boroughs . . . 1754-1768." Unpub. M.A. thesis. Manchester Univ., 1953.

Craton, Michael, *A History of the Bahamas*. London, rev. ed., 1968.

Cross, Arthur Lyon, *The Anglican Episcopate and the American Colonies*. New York, 1902.

Daniell, Jere F., "Politics in New Hampshire under Governor Benning Wentworth, 1741-1767," *William and Mary Quarterly*, 3rd ser., XXIII (January, 1966), 76-105.

Dickerson, Oliver M., *American Colonial Government, 1696-1765* . . . . Cleveland, Ohio, 1912.

Dodson, Leonidas, *Alexander Spotswood, Governor of Colonial Virginia, 1710-1722*. Philadelphia, 1932.

Donnan, Elizabeth, "An Eighteenth Century English Merchant: Micajah Perry," *Journal of Economic and Business History*, IV (November, 1931), 70-98.

Dunn, Richard S., "The Trustees of Georgia and the House of Commons, 1732-1752," *William and Mary Quarterly*, 3rd ser., XI (October, 1954), 551-65.

Ellis, Kenneth, *The Post Office in the Eighteenth Century; A Study in Administrative History*. London, 1958.

Ettinger, Amos A., *James E. Oglethorpe: Imperial Idealist*. Oxford, 1936.

Finer, Herman, "State Activity before Adam Smith," *Public Administration*, X (April, 1932), 157-78.

Finer, S. E. "Patronage and the Public Service," *Public Administration*, XXX (November, 1952), 329-36.

Foord, Archibald S., *His Majesty's Opposition, 1714-1830*. Oxford, 1964.

———, "The Waning of 'The Influence of the Crown,'" *English Historical Review*, LXII (October, 1947), 484-507.

Greene, Jack P., "A Dress of Horror: Henry McCulloch's Objections to the Stamp Act," *Huntington Library Quarterly*, XXVI (1963), 253-62.

———, "Martin Bladen's Blueprint for a Colonial Union," *William and Mary Quarterly*, 3rd ser., XVII (October, 1960), 516-30.

———, *The Quest for Power: The Lower Houses of Assembly in the Southern Royal Colonies, 1689-1776*. Chapel Hill, 1963.

Haffenden, Philip, "Colonial Appointments and Patronage under the Duke of Newcastle, 1724-1739," *English Historical Review*, LXXVII (July, 1963), 417-35.

Hall, Michael G., "Some Letters of Benedict Leonard Calvert," *William and Mary Quarterly*, 3rd ser., XVIII (July, 1960), 358-70.

Higonnet, Patrice Louis-René, "The Origins of the Seven

Years' War," *Journal of Modern History*, XL (March, 1968), 57-90.

Hughes, Edward, *Studies in Administration and Finance . . . 1558-1825*. Manchester, 1934.

Jacobsen, Gertrude A., *William Blathwayt: A Late Seventeenth Century English Administrator*. New Haven, 1932.

James, Francis J., "The Irish Lobby in the Early Eighteenth Century," *English Historical Review*, LXXXI (July, 1966), 543-47.

James, G. F., "Josiah Burchett, Secretary to the Lords Commissioners of the Admiralty, 1695-1742," *Mariners Mirror*, XXIII (1937), 477-99.

Jesse, John H., *George Selwyn and His Contemporaries*. 3 v. London, 1882.

Judd, Gerrit P., IV, *Members of Parliament, 1734-1832*. New Haven, 1955.

Kammen, Michael G., *A Rope of Sand: The Colonial Agents, British Politics and the American Revolution*. Ithaca, 1968.

Katz, Stanley Nider, *Newcastle's New York: Anglo-American Politics, 1732-1753*. Cambridge, Mass., 1968.

Kemmerer, Donald L., *Path to Freedom; The Struggle for Self-Government in Colonial New Jersey, 1703-1776*. Princeton, 1940.

Keys, Alice M., *Cadwallader Colden: A Representative Eighteenth Century Official*. New York, 1906.

Knorr, Klaus B., *British Colonial Theories, 1570-1850*. Toronto, 1944.

Koebner, Richard, *Empire*. New York, 1965.

Labaree, Leonard W., *Royal Government in America*. New York, 1958.

Laslett, Peter, "John Locke, the Great Recoinage, and the Origins of the Board of Trade: 1695-1698," *William and Mary Quarterly*, 3rd ser., XIV (July, 1957), 370-402.

Leder, Lawrence H., *Robert Livingston, 1654-1728, and the Politics of Colonial New York*. Chapel Hill, 1961.

Lilly, Edward P., *The Colonial Agents of New York and New Jersey*. Washington, D.C., 1936.

Lucas, Reginald, *George II and His Ministers*. London, 1910.

Malone, Joseph J., *Pine Trees and Politics; the Naval Stores and Forest Policy in Colonial New England, 1691-1775*. London, 1964.

McAnear, Beverly, "An American in London, 1735-1736," *Pennsylvania Magazine of History and Biography*, LXIV (April, 1940), 164-218.

McAnear, Beverly, *The Income of the Colonial Governors of British North America*. New York, 1967.

McLachlan, Jean O., *Trade and Peace with Old Spain, 1667-1750*. Cambridge, Eng., 1940.

Metcalf, George, *Royal Government and Political Conflict in Jamaica, 1729-1783*. London, 1965.

Morgan, Edmund S. and Helen M., *The Stamp Act Crisis; Prologue to Revolution*. rev. ed., New York, 1963.

Namier, Lewis B., *England in the Age of the American Revolution*. London, 1930.

———, *The Structure of Politics at the Accession of George III*. 2 v. London, 1929.

——— and John Brooke, *The House of Commons, 1754-1790*. 3 v. London, 1963.

————, *Charles Townshend*. London, 1964.

Nulle, Stebelton H., "The Duke of Newcastle and the Election of 1727," *Journal of Modern History*, IX (March, 1937), 1-22.

———, *Thomas Pelham-Holles, Duke of Newcastle: His Early Political Career, 1693-1724*. Philadelphia, 1931.

O'Callahan, Edmund B., *Voyage of George Clarke, Esq. to America* . . . . Albany, N.Y., 1867.

Olson, Alison Gilbert, "William Penn, Parliament, and Proprietary Government." *William and Mary Quarterly*, 3rd ser., XVIII (April, 1961), 176-95.

———, "The British Government and Colonial Union, 1754," *William and Mary Quarterly*, 3rd ser., XVII (January, 1960), 22-34.

Owen, John B., *The Rise of the Pelhams*. London, 1957.

Pares, Richard, "A London West India Merchant House,

1740-1769," in Pares, ed., *Essays Presented to Sir Lewis Namier*. London, 1956.

———, "American versus Continental Warfare, 1739-1763," *English Historical Review*, LI (1936), 429-65.

———, *War and Trade in the West Indies, 1739-1763*. Oxford, 1936.

Parry, J. H., "The Patent Offices in the British West Indies," *English Historical Review*, LXIX (1954), 200-25.

Penson, Lillian M., *The Colonial Agents of the British West Indies*. London, 1924.

———, "The London West Indies Interest in the Eighteenth Century," *English Historical Review*, XXXVI (July, 1921), 373-92.

Perry, Thomas W., *Public Opinion, Propaganda, and Politics in Eighteenth-Century England: A Study of the Jew Bill of 1753*. Cambridge, Mass., 1962.

Pitman, Frank W., *The Development of the British West Indies, 1700-1763*. New Haven, 1912.

Plumb, J. H., *Sir Robert Walpole*. 2 v. Boston, 1961.

———, *The Growth of Political Stability in England, 1675-1725*. London, 1967.

Price, Jacob M., "Party, Purpose and Pattern: Sir Lewis Namier and His Critics," *Journal of British Studies*, No. 1 (November, 1961), 71-93.

Raper, Charles L., *North Carolina: A Study in English Colonial Government*. New York, 1904.

Realey, Charles B., *The Early Opposition to Sir Robert Walpole, 1720-1727*. Lawrence, Kansas, 1932.

Reese, Trevor R., *Colonial Georgia: A Study in British Imperial Policy in the Eighteenth Century*. Athens, Ga., 1963.

———, "Georgia in Anglo-Spanish Diplomacy, 1736-1739," *William and Mary Quarterly*, 3rd ser., XV (April, 1958), 168-90.

Riley, Patrick W. J., *The English Ministers and Scotland, 1707-1727*. London, 1964.

Robbins, Caroline, "Absolute Liberty: The Life and Thought of William Popple, 1638-1708," *William and Mary Quarterly*, XXIV (April, 1967), 190-223.

Robinson, Blackwell P., *The Five Royal Governors of North Carolina.* Raleigh, 1963.

Root, Winfred T., *The Relations of Pennsylvania with the British Government, 1696-1765.* New York, 1912.

Rudé, George, *The Crowd in History: A Study of Popular Disturbances in France and England, 1730-1848.* New York, 1964.

Savelle, Max, "The American Balance of Power and European Diplomacy, 1713-78," in Richard B. Morris, ed., *The Era of the American Revolution: Studies Inscribed to Evarts Boutell Green,* 140-69. New York, 1939.

———, *The Diplomatic History of the Canadian Boundary, 1749-1763.* New Haven, 1940.

Schutz, John A., *William Shirley, King's Governor of Massachusetts.* Chapel Hill, 1961.

Sellers, Charles G., Jr., "Private Profits and British Colonial Policy, The Speculations of Henry McCulloh," *William and Mary Quarterly,* 3rd ser., VIII (October, 1951), 535-51.

Sheridan, Richard B., "The Molasses Act and the Market Strategy of the British Sugar Planters," *Journal of Economic History,* XVII (1957), 62-83.

Shy, John, *Toward Lexington: The Role of the British Army in the Coming of the American Revolution.* Princeton, 1965.

Southwick, Albert B., "The Molasses Act—Source of Precedents," *William and Mary Quarterly,* 3rd ser., VIII (July, 1951), 389-405.

Spencer, Henry Russell, *Constitutional Conflict in Provincial Massachusetts . . . .* Columbus, 1905.

Spurdle, Frederick G., *Early West Indian Government . . . .* Palmerston North, New Zealand, privately printed, n.d.

Steele, I. K., *Politics of Colonial Policy: The Board of Trade in Colonial Administration, 1696-1720.* Oxford, 1968.

Stevens, David Harrison, *Party Politics and English Journalism, 1702-1742.* Menasha, 1916.

Sykes, Norman, "The Duke of Newcastle as Ecclesiastical Minister," *English Historical Review,* LVII (January, 1942), 59-84.

Tanner, Edwin, "Colonial Agencies in England during the Eighteenth Century," *Political Science Quarterly*, XVI (March, 1901), 24-49.

Temperley, Harold W.V., "The Causes of the War of Jenkins' Ear, 1739," *Transactions* of the Royal Historical Society, 3rd ser., III (1909), 197-236.

Thomson, Mark A., *The Secretaries of State, 1681-1782*. Oxford, 1932.

Wake, Joan, *The Brudenells of Deane*. rev. ed., London, 1954.

Ward, W. R., "Some Eighteenth-Century Civil Servants, The English Revenue Commissioners, 1754-98," *English Historical Review*, (January, 1955), 25-54.

Watson, J. Steven, "Arthur Onslow and Party Politics," in H. R. Trevor Roper, ed., *Essays in British History presented to Sir Keith Feiling*, 139-171. London, 1964.

Webb, Stephen Saunders, "The Strange Career of Francis Nicholson," *William and Mary Quarterly*, 3rd ser., XXIII (October, 1966), 513-48.

Welch, Joseph, *The List of the Queen's Scholars of . . . Westminster*. London, 1852.

Western, John Randell, *The English Militia in the Eighteenth Century*. London, 1965.

Wickwire, Franklin B., *British Subministers and Colonial America, 1763-1783*. Princeton, 1966.

———, "John Pownall and British Colonial Policy," *William and Mary Quarterly*, XX (1963), 543-54.

Wilkes, John W., *A Whig in Power; The Political Career of Henry Pelham*. Evanston, 1964.

Williams, Basil, *Carteret and Newcastle: A Contrast in Contemporaries*. Cambridge, Eng., 1943.

———, "The Duke of Newcastle and the Election of 1734," *English Historical Review*, XII (1897), 448-88.

———, "The Eclipse of the Yorkes," *Transactions* of the Royal Historical Society, 3rd ser., II (1908), 128-51.

Wolff, Mabel P., *The Colonial Agency of Pennsylvania, 1712-1757*. Philadelphia, 1933.

Index

Index

Index